BETWEEN WORD AND IMAGE

BETWEEN
WORD AND IMAGE

HEIDEGGER, KLEE, AND GADAMER
ON GESTURE AND GENESIS

DENNIS J. SCHMIDT

Indiana University Press
Bloomington and Indianapolis

This book is a publication of

Indiana University Press
601 North Morton Street
Bloomington, Indiana 47404-3797 USA

iupress.indiana.edu

Telephone orders   800-842-6796
Fax orders   812-855-7931

© 2013 by Dennis J. Schmidt

⊗ The paper used in this publication meets the minimum requirements of the
American National Standard for Information Sciences—Permanence of Paper for
Printed Library Materials, ANSI Z39.48-1992.

Manufactured in the United States of America

Library of Congress Cataloging-in-Publication Data

Schmidt, Dennis J.
    Between word and image : Heidegger, Klee, and Gadamer on gesture and
genesis / Dennis J. Schmidt.
        p. cm. — (Studies in Continental thought)
    Includes bibliographical references (p.   ) and index.
    ISBN 978-0-253-00618-9 (cloth : alk. paper) — ISBN 978-0-253-00620-2
(pbk. : alk. paper) — ISBN 978-0-253-00622-6 (electronic book) 1. Image
(Philosophy) 2. Aesthetics. 3. Thought and thinking. 4. Heidegger, Martin,
1889–1976. 5. Klee, Paul, 1879–1940. I. Title.
    BH301.I52S37   2013
    111'.85—dc23

                                                                2012022626

1 2 3 4 5   18 17 16 15 14 13

For
Zoe

Die Besinnung darauf, was die *Kunst* sei, ist ganz und entschieden nur aus der Frage nach dem *Sein* bestimmt.

—*Martin Heidegger, "Ursprung des Kunstwerkes"*
Zusatz of 1956

The manifestation of the wind of thought is not knowledge; it is the ability to tell right from wrong, beautiful from ugly. And this, at the rare moments when the stakes are on the table, may indeed prevent catastrophes, at least for the self.

—*Hannah Arendt,* The Life of the Mind: Thinking

The first enemy of the aesthetic was meaning.

—*Roberto Calasso,* The Marriage of
Cadmus and Harmony

CONTENTS

ACKNOWLEDGMENTS

My interest in the question of the relation of word and image grew out of two essays in my previous book, *Lyrical and Ethical Subjects*. Those essays—one on Cy Twombly's series of paintings *50 Days at Iliam*, the other on the question of writing in Plato's *Cratylus*—first led me to recognize the depth of this question. At that time, I did not recognize the full complexity of these issues, nor did I see the importance and originality of Paul Klee's contribution to them. The impulse for the new push that would lead to this book came from James Risser's invitation to present a lecture course on the hermeneutics of the image at the Collegium Phaenomenologicum in Città di Castello, Italy, in 2007. I am grateful to him and to all who attended those lectures for the intellectual stimulation they provided then and that continues still today. Other forums and audiences allowed me to address these questions in greater detail. Here I must especially thank Donatella di Cesare for her invitation to the Università di Roma, La Sapienza, where I was able to give two weeks of lectures on these themes. Other invitations—from Rodolphe Gasché to the University of Buffalo's "Just Theory" series, from Günter Figal to the Universität Freiburg's "Hermeneutische Symposium," from Jeffrey McCurry to give the Silverman Lectures at Duquesne University, and from Luc Van der Stockt to the Universiteit KU Leuven—provided much-needed criticism and support as I was bringing these investigations to a conclusion. I am always struck by how important such events can be in helping me understand myself better.

Conversations with individuals have reminded me in the happiest of ways that one is never alone when one thinks. Here, without detail, I need to thank the following friends: Maria Acosta, Andrew Benjamin, Robert Bernasconi, Walter Brogan, Miguel de Beistegui, Donatella di Cesare, Nicholas Davey, Paul Davies, Günter Figal, Bernard Freydberg, Rodolphe Gasché, Theodore George, Drew Hyland, David Krell, Jennifer Mensch, Michael Nass, James Risser, John Sallis, Charles Scott, Stephen Watson, and David Wood. My graduate students at Penn State have been a continual source of intellectual energy, and they continue to teach me more than I could ever teach them. Finally, I have come to realize that I will need to thank Hans-Georg Gadamer for the rest of my life. Even after his death, he somehow still remains a living conversation partner for me in a way that reminds me of the truth of the lines from Celan that Derrida cites: "Die Welt ist fort, ich muss Dich tragen." All of these people prove that Hölderlin was right when he said, "Denn keiner trägt das Leben allein."

This book would not have come to be without the help of Dee Mortensen at Indiana University Press and the careful copyediting of Julie Bush. I am grateful to Shannon Sullivan, head of the Philosophy Department, and to the deans of the College of Liberal Arts at Penn State University for funds to help cover the cost of permissions for the images reproduced here.

Among all of these conversations, the ongoing conversation with my wife, Jennifer Mensch, has been the most decisive and most instructive. She always manages to remind me that I could and should be clearer, more careful, and more rigorous. I have learned more from her than I have managed to tell her. That she always managed to take time away from finishing her own book to help me with mine has been to my great benefit. Her support, insights, and friendship mean the world to me. Our daughter, Zoe Mensch Schmidt, who took her first steps in Città di Castello during my final lecture on Klee, surprises me, renews my spirit, and reminds me every minute of the day what, in the end, really matters. She has made the world brighter than I could ever have imagined and continually lives up to her name, reminding me that creation always exceeds understanding. This book is dedicated to Zoe.

BETWEEN WORD AND IMAGE

THE GENESIS OF THE QUESTION

Four sets of questions gave birth and shape to this book.

The proximate and most specific of these questions was occasioned by the publication of a large portion of Heidegger's "Notes on Klee."[1] Those fragmentary notes, which Heidegger made during a visit in 1956 to an exhibition of Paul Klee's paintings, express a great excitement about Klee's work. It was an excitement that seemed unbridled and that would last for some years. So, for instance, three years after that first encounter with Klee's work, Heidegger wrote a letter to his friend Heinrich Petzet in which he emphasized the originality and radicality of Klee's work: "Something which we all have not yet even glimpsed has come forward in [Klee's works]."[2] And it is clear that Heidegger's enthusiasm for Klee had a great philosophical significance for him: he even spoke with friends of the need to revise or to write a "counterpart to" "The Origin of the Work of Art" in light of what he saw in Klee, and in 1960 he promised a seminar on Klee, Heraclitus, Augustine, and Chuang-tzu.[3] The impact upon Heidegger of discovering Klee's paintings and of reading his theoretical writings was great, and the consequences of this discovery were not simply to confirm Heidegger's own views but to change them. Indeed, Heidegger's acknowledgment of Klee's accomplishments constituted a reversal of his earlier sweeping condemnations of modern art as nothing more than the reflex of a technologically defined world. But it was not just Klee's painted works that gripped Heidegger; rather, Klee was a prolific writer, and his written texts were as esteemed by Heidegger as his painterly works. Just as Heidegger had found in Friedrich Hölderlin his poet, so too was it the case that during the years of his engagement with Klee he found his painter. Importantly, both Hölderlin and Klee were artists who were capable of theorizing the achievement of the work of art from out of the experience of that work. This capacity for theoretical reflection distinguishes most all of the artists to whom Heidegger turns in his discussion of the work of art and, as such, serves as a reminder not only that the work of art is worth attending to but also that there is a form of reflection that emerges out of the experience of the artist that is of genuine philosophical importance.[4]

Klee's work—both his painterly works and his theoretical works—has come to have a rather unique status among philosophers of the past half century.[5] Heidegger was not at all alone in finding something genuinely new for philosophy in Klee: Adorno, Benjamin, Deleuze, Foucault, Gadamer, Lyotard, Merleau-Ponty, and Sartre all single out Klee as marking something new and as making an advance on how we are to understand the world. The qualification that what each finds in Klee concerns something new *for the deepest concerns of philosophy* is important. The turn to Klee by these philosophers was not governed by a concern with "aesthetics"—an approach structured by categories thoroughly inadequate to understanding what is found in Klee—nor was it governed by the project of "criticism" or by a concern with cultural productions. Rather, all differences and disputes notwithstanding, this interest in Klee by these philosophers—all of whom were engaged in rethinking the very idea and possibilities of philosophy itself—was guided by the elemental tasks of philosophy: a concern with truth, with the nature of thinking, of nature, of being and becoming, of language, and of the image. Or, as Heidegger put it with reference not just to Klee but to art in general: "Reflection upon art is solely decided out of the question of *being*."[6] One finds an echo of this view in Klee when he says, "Art plays unknowingly with ultimate things and yet it reaches them,"[7] and, "[I am] perhaps a philosopher, without really wanting to be one."[8] What one soon discovers is that Klee's sense of being a philosopher and of the way the work of art enters the realm of "ultimate things" poses a very real challenge to traditional conceptions of philosophy. Not surprisingly then, it is those philosophers who call for philosophy to become different, who find its most cherished and long-standing assumptions in need of overcoming, who gravitate to Klee.

While Klee has been the subject of serious and extended philosophical reflection for several philosophers, it was reading the notes and other comments that Heidegger made during his study of Klee that, for me at least, crystallized the special problems that one confronts in a painter such as Klee and—more importantly—brought me to see and look more closely, with wider eyes than before, at the largest form of the riddle that one confronts in painting. Other painters and other philosophers might well lead to the same set of insights that one arrives at by thinking through Klee's work with Heidegger, but, for me, this combination, contingent though it may be, was an inspiration. Thus it is that Heidegger's "Notes on Klee" became the first impulse for this book, and the questions raised by those notes, as well as the issues one finds emerging with a special clarity in Klee, have combined to shape many of the concerns of this book.

––––––––––

The second set of issues that drive and give a direction to this book concern the question of the relation of word and image. The respective relation of words and images to thinking is among the inaugural concerns of philosophy—Plato makes it a central question of many dialogues, typically setting it up as a contest between the word and the image with respect to the possibility of truth—and so the issues raised here once again go directly to the heart of the project of philosophy as such. It is also a question with a long and involved history that finds its contemporary form in developments that begin with Kant and Lessing and that then move through Nietzsche into the present, where the question of the relation of word and image takes on a centrality in some traditions. Gadamer, for instance, takes the way words and images form texts as one of the first topics defining hermeneutic theory. For Gadamer, as for others, this question posed by the image understood as a text is a way of probing the limits of language and the need to challenge long-standing assumptions about the privilege of the word for thinking. Precisely this concern, this sense that the role of the image in thinking has yet to be appreciated, is the second motivation for me to write this book.

In light of the large sweep of this topic, it should be clear that I will not address its full extent or history. Nonetheless, one aspect of this question cannot be avoided and so must be made explicit at the outset and eventually addressed, namely, that as soon as one *speaks* of images, a complication sets to work insofar as one translates the image into the word. This translation, like every translation, is an interpretation and signals a shift, a move to something else, and so this shift needs to be understood. One cannot assume that this move from a text that is defined by and as an image to one defined by and as language does not lose what is unique to the image, what might resist such a translation, as soon as one speaks. The stakes of this problematic of word and image are far-reaching; indeed, one quickly finds oneself at the heart of the question of the very possibility of philosophy itself. The reason is simple: philosophy lives in and is oriented by the *logos*, by the word, but, insofar as one grants that the image does not let itself be translated into the word without resistance and remainder, the authority of the *logos* is immediately called into question. As is the case with the issues that emerge in taking up Klee's work, so too does this question of the relation of word and image serve to challenge the very idea of philosophy itself.

Taking up this topic of the relation of word and image, if done properly, if done self-consciously, can seem inhibiting. Nonetheless, for obvious reasons, one needs to address it—even if only in a preliminary way—with the appearance of the very first word regarding the image since it is the authority of the word that is called into question from the beginning. This hesitation before speaking, this awareness of the limits of the word, means that one is almost silenced from the outset. But it is precisely this very pregnant silence that truly opens the issues at stake and makes way for the attention —both the looking and the listening—requisite for addressing those issues.[9] Interrupting this silence, speaking too soon, one either loses the image from the outset, or one simply stutters. However, if one pauses and waits patiently with this expectant silence, the force of both the word and the image is gradually registered. And so, to be concerned with this relation of word and image is, from the outset, to respect this reticence, this reserve.

While the tradition of opposing word and image, of regarding them as in a competition, has been potent in the history of philosophy, recent work—in painting as well as in philosophy—has recognized that their relation is a complex one that is thoroughly entangled and so not at all settled as a matter of competition. Today it is the crossing of word and image into one another that is coming to be recognized. Adorno put the point well when he wrote: "In recent debates about painting the concept of *écriture,* inspired by works of Klee that seem to approach something like scratchy script, have become relevant. This is a case of modern art shedding light on the past: all works of art are writings, not only those that announce themselves as such. Works of art are hieroglyphs for which the code has been lost, and this loss is not accidental but constitutive of their essence as art works. Works of art are language only as writing."[10] On the whole, painters have been at the vanguard of exploring this crossing of word and image into one another. The reasons that painting can raise this question better will be discussed later, but they are indicative of a blindness proper to the word. Writing is word become image, and while philosophers have not made this mystery of the passage of word into image a topic of careful research, painters, especially in recent years, have indeed found it to be a key concern (one thinks, for instance, of Kiefer, Twombly, and Klee, among others).

The sense that the word has no hegemony with regard to truth and that a wider, larger sense of what "truth" means defines the third topic that led to the writing of this book and that shaped its concerns. Kant's third Critique opens this question and sets philosophy off in a new direction insofar as Kant argues that cognition that can be grasped by the concept is itself incapable of appreciating—let alone conceiving—what is disclosed in the experience that one deems beautiful. With Kant's third Critique, the horizons of knowing did not simply expand or contract along the same axis that had defined knowing over the centuries; rather, those horizons were fundamentally shifted, displaced, and dislocated such that knowing—and the notion of truth that had defined the perfection of knowledge—had to be seen in a different light and measured by different standards. Cognition and the ideals of knowledge that culminate in the sciences lost the singular authority that such cognition had long claimed for itself. Kant's insights in the *Critique of Judgment*—at least for one tradition that followed in his wake—meant that art, which was exiled from any claim upon truth from the beginnings of philosophy in Plato, now returned as a very real philosophical matter and as having a relation to truth that is not replicated elsewhere. After Kant, the talk of truth could not avoid a concern with the achievement of the work of art and the experience of the beautiful. Even if, like Hegel, one argued that art, from the standpoint of philosophy, was something past, something superseded for truth, one could not simply ignore the claim that art has a relation to truth. And yet, such a claim necessarily changes what truth means. Above all, it can no longer be said that truth belongs solely to the language of the concept and to what can be conceived according to the law of universality. The hegemony of the concept, which has defined the mother tongue of philosophy since its inception, was challenged by a different relation to language, one that does not find the summit of its possibilities in the ideality of the concept but that opens up upon a different idiom. Deleuze is right: "The philosopher is the friend of the concept."[11] But art has no real concern for, makes no submission to, the concept and so, as setting itself apart, always presents itself as a challenge to the authority of philosophy to speak the truth in concepts. Gadamer put the point well when he said that art "is not bound by concepts that are given, but points beyond the realm of the concept, and hence beyond the realm of the understanding."[12] Or, with a similar intent, one reads Adorno saying that art "articulates something that the language of meaning cannot articulate."[13]

The claim that art has an essential kinship with truth changes how we think about truth. Or at least it should change the way one understands truth. If not, then one ends up speaking like Nietzsche—stubbornly holding fast to a conceptual and cognitive sense of truth while simultaneously demonstrating the importance of art—when he says that "we have art lest we perish of the truth."[14] Rather than widen his understanding of truth, disengaging it from the concept, Nietzsche maintains the traditional conception of truth and so the exclusion of art from the domain of what can be called "true." Nonetheless, despite the persistence of this traditional conception of truth in Nietzsche and others, the struggle to reconcile art with the possibility of truth has only deepened its force and grip since Kant, so that by the time Heidegger wrote "The Origin of the Work of Art" in 1935 he could assign not simply a relation of art to truth but a *privileged* relation that is unique, original, and founding. After Heidegger, it would not be long until Gadamer would further this point in *Truth and Method* (1960) by taking art and aesthetic experience as the starting points for his analysis of the basic character of both experience and truth. In a similar fashion, Merleau-Ponty could argue that "art, especially painting" belongs to the "fabric of brute meaning"[15]—that is, that art touches upon the elemental character of the disclosure of a world. There are others who will carry forward this project—indeed one can, rightly I believe, argue that a commitment to this project of reevaluating the character of truth in the light of the challenge found in the work of art is the defining trait of what we call continental philosophy today. My own sense that this pursuit of a bond uniting truth and art is decisive for philosophy in the present age has consolidated and grown more confident over time. What has also become clearer is that to experience the world from out of this bond is to open oneself to the world in a new and more expansive sense. To credit the work of art with such an elemental disclosure, to bind it to the idea of truth, is to begin to understand the world differently. It is even to risk being changed by such experiences.

So it is that three sets of questions, concerns, themes, impulses, designated by names and notions paired—Heidegger/Klee, word/image, art/truth—became the original impulses for this project and came to drive the analyses and arguments that follow. They form the umbilicus around which other issues are taken up; they also mark the limitations of my remarks, which make no pretense to be either exhaustive or systematic in a strict sense. There are figures who by all rights could be the focus of my investigations here since their concerns are intimate with the concerns of those I do address and with my own aims. Benjamin, Merleau-Ponty, Adorno, Deleuze, Adorno, Nancy, and Sallis name just the most prominent and obvious of such options. All of these figures will, from time to time, enter the discussions that follow, but all could easily have been placed at the center of those discussions. In some sense, this simply means that the approach I have taken to the issues at hand is contingent insofar as it is rather arbitrarily restricted. I do not, however, believe that the results of this approach are contingent. Quite the contrary, I want to suggest that the way of approaching aesthetic experience and the work of art arrived at here has something compelling about it, something that does indeed need to be recognized insofar as one takes the appearance of the work of art in the world—and the appearance of beauty—to heart. The aim of this book is to unfold the most significant consequences of this appearance.

In order to pursue this aim, my intention in what follows is not to outline an aesthetics or a theory of the work of art. It is, in the end, a simple intention that governs the discussions here: to learn to see better what shows up in these quite strange works that we call art, works that have no purpose for being other than their own appearance in the world. My intention is also to understand something of what happens when we make the judgment that something is beautiful, especially when that something is something that a human being has brought into being. In many ways, these are grand ambitions, but in the end I have always returned to my simple and quite modest beginning with the fragmentary notes that Heidegger made upon viewing eighty-eight paintings by Klee. There is something said in Heidegger's efforts to articulate just what it was that he saw in Klee's work that bears saying and seeing again. Heidegger's notes on Klee bring the work of art and its contribution into sharper focus and begin a line of questioning that opens up in the work of Gadamer and others. My goal in what follows is to develop those insights and to give indications of the directions one might further press these issues.

Questions about the work of art and aesthetic experience have long been regarded as merely adventitious and so relegated to the margins of philosophical concerns; they have been judged not to carry the weight of other, more "substantive" issues that can be known with the clarity of the concept. Such a viewpoint is not only misguided, it is pernicious since it misses, right from the start, the questions that are most decisive for us and that drive most directly to the character of the beings that we are. Aristotle argued, rightly I believe, that the urge to make works of art is native to us, that it is *symphuton*—born with our nature. This impulse to bring into being that which has no reason for being other than appearance itself emerges straight from the heart of human being and is the manifestation of what is most enigmatic about such a being. Aristotle's argument that this impulse defines us is an argument that tends to be neglected until it resurfaces immediately after Kant's third Critique in Hölderlin, Schelling, Nietzsche, and Freud, among others. One finds in these figures the idea that there is a *Kunsttrieb* or a *Bildungstrieb* that is, for us, the most elemental of instincts. We are, as it were, born to make art, and this destiny is, as Hölderlin suggests, not an innocent matter but rather the most dangerous of occupations insofar as it operates at the heart of our being. Kant lets us understand why this is so when he notes that art must be recognized as the product of human freedom—that is, as emerging only from that abyss without a cause that is the deepest experience one has of oneself. This means that in this drive to art, we confront the very limits of the human; we are driven to our most extreme possibility. In such remarks, one is pointed to the enigma of the work of art and to the way this enigma defines us. This is why the questions put to us by the work of art are both ineluctable and of great consequence. They are not adventitious matters at all. This is the reason that works of art possess the capacity to grip us, to hold our attention, and to promise more than meets the eye. Such works stymie us; they can silence us. And, for all of these reasons, they also call for a most delicate form of reflection. Heidegger's encounter with Klee is an exemplary case of such reflection. In his rather obscure notes—at times only scribbles—one can see something of what can be found in Klee, and seeing this leads one back to the larger questions about the image in the work of art that have haunted philosophy since its inception. From this experience and understanding of the work of art, one is driven back to the origins of the very project of philosophy.

In order to pursue these issues that emerge in the work of art, I have chosen to address the painted image. This obviously represents a severe narrowing of the question posed by the work of art in general; after all, one should be cautious about speaking of works of art in general only on the basis of an investigation into one specific form that art can take.[16] While I do believe that there are grounds for some unity of the various forms that the work of art can take such that we can speak of art in general, the differences between these forms should not be effaced.[17] There is a complexity inherent in the notion of art that we erase in such effacement, a complexity that gives art its expansive nature. Nonetheless, I will risk some generalizations about the achievement of art in general on the basis of this inquiry into painting, even though these generalizations need to be considered with some suspicion. Likewise, I make no claim that the remarks that follow should be read as directed to the image as such, the image in general and in all of its modalities. Rather, my focus has been upon the image that calls attention to itself *as an image,* that is, to its image character. In other words, I have been concerned only with the image in the work of art. More precisely, I have been concerned only with the image that is born of some alchemy of our "drive for art" and freedom and that has been made by the human hand (as will be made clear eventually, the qualification "made by the human hand" is all-important to any understanding of painting). I hope that my reasons for this restriction become clearer in the course of this book, but for the moment this much can be said about the claim at the basis of this book: in the work of art, especially in the painted work, the image finds the summit of its possibilities, and—at the same time—it finds its closest proximity to the word since it is, quite literally, "hand writing." For the effort to think through the relation of word and image, painting, at least from the side of the image, offers the most promising approach.[18]

Against the expectations cultivated by centuries of marginalization of the work of art and "aesthetic" experience, I would argue that the stakes of these questions are high and involve basic decisions about how we understand the world. Philosophy began with, and was originally orientated by, questions that were defined by and pegged to precisely these sets of relations: of words and images, of philosophy and art, of truth and beauty. Plato's efforts to define philosophy—then a new form of speaking and thinking—were shaped by these concerns. But what is most important about the way Plato took up these issues and what has been most lost to our time is that Plato also recognized the high stakes in how one thinks about the work of art: his discussions of artistic practices are invariably set in a larger, typically ethical or political context within which their force and wider significance becomes more evident. It is this larger significance that has been lost over time. As art became a matter for aesthetics, as knowledge came increasingly to be measured according to the ideals of science, and as conceptuality achieved an unquestioned legitimacy, these questions lost their force and their elemental sense. One of the primary purposes of this book is to recover these questions and so to attempt to return philosophy to its roots.

This purpose arises out of the fourth question—in this case it is more of a conviction than a question—driving this book. In broadest outline, it is a question that asks about the ethical significance of the work of art for us. My sense is that engaging the work of art and aesthetic experience has the potential to change us and that the character of this change must be described as ethical. This is a difficult and rather risky claim to make and pursue, since it is so readily misunderstood (it can, for instance, veer easily into the bourgeois delusion that connoisseurship has a connection with ethical life and that those whom Kant ridiculed as "virtuosi of taste" have any claim upon "being attached to moral principle").[19] Although this conviction that the issue of ethical life is the real upshot of the questions of art and aesthetics is, for me personally, the deepest impulse of the investigations that follow, I will not pursue this topic as fully or forcefully as it deserves but will return to it only in the afterword in order to give some indications of how this promise might be explored. For now, let me simply refer to a notion that I believe points to this promise. It is found in a word used by Plutarch that Foucault highlights. It is a word that speaks of that which "possesses the quality of transforming an individual's mode of being: . . . *ethopoiein*."[20] This notion refers to the way in which *reflection upon* (a decisive qualification, especially for avoiding the misunderstandings just noted) art and aesthetic experience takes us to the deepest center of being human. It is a notion that implies what Rilke once suggested, namely, that the work of art always, when reflected upon properly, leads one ever so gently and in the slightest of ways to the realization that "you must change your life."[21] The deepest concern of this book is to call attention to this deep affinity, this real relation, between aesthetic experience and ethical life.

Those four questions shaped the project of this book. But there remain two questions that are insufficiently addressed here and haunt this book, marking its most severe limitations: the question of nature and the question of the possibility of art in our age. I believe that Kant is right when he argues that aesthetic experience necessarily opens up upon the riddle of the being of nature and that this riddle leads beyond the realm of aesthetic experience proper.[22] To assume that one can avoid the question of the being of nature in any full investigation of art and aesthetic experience is a mistake. This book commits that mistake insofar as it does not take up the question of nature, and this insufficiency with respect to this question in what follows needs to be acknowledged. The only defense that I can offer is that I would like to regard what I have done here simply as a prelude to that question. In the end, I hope to have prepared the way for asking the question of the being of nature in a better way.

The second question that I have inadequately addressed in this book is the one that asks if the work of art is still possible in our present historical juncture. It seems to me that, if one reflects on the idea of art today, one must ask if our age has lost the capacity for art. This is not a new question, and though the question seems directed to a specific time, it is not solely a question of this time. In some sense, Hölderlin asked it—"wozu Dichter in dürftiger Zeit?"—and Nietzsche struggled with it. Heidegger too spoke of the "Kunstlösigkeit" of our age. Perhaps the most famous expression of this despair about the possibility of art in the present age is Adorno's question whether art—he referred to poetry in particular—was still possible "after Auschwitz."[23] It is not difficult to see the reasons for such laments: from the grotesque barbarisms of our age to the quiet seductions of the consumer and technological world, ours is an age that is defined by a peculiar noise. We assault ourselves, we ravage our world, and we tacitly distract ourselves from the truth of our times. We are flooded with images, inundated with words, companioned with sounds. It does not require much reflection to see that in our times, it is increasingly difficult to be arrested by a work, to be silenced, to be brought to linger. If one takes the achievement of the work of art seriously, then one must ask if we can still measure up to it. To put the point bluntly: it seems somehow necessary to ask if ours is an age bereft of beauty.

I cannot begin to presume to propose an answer to this overwhelming question. I have, however, written this book out of the conviction that nothing less than the work of art will suffice "after Auschwitz," that works of art still hold the promise of helping us to better understand what we are capable of doing to ourselves and to others. Any reply to history and to our times needs to be drawn from the deepest center of who we are. To be sure, the crises and struggles of our times require immediate and direct action, but they also require something that is able to change us. My sense is that the experience summoned by the work of art has the potential to be precisely such an ethopoietic event. The most far-reaching aim of this book—one that it falls far short of reaching—is to contribute something, however minimal, to understanding the character of this potential.

CHAPTER 1

UNFOLDING THE QUESTION: AN EXCENTRIC HISTORY

As soon as one begins to speak about an image, one is entangled in complications. This is the case no matter how one approaches the image: critically, theoretically, appraisingly, admiringly, confusedly—it does not matter, since the problem is rooted in the difference between words and images. Philosophy is no exception and does not escape these complications. Quite the contrary, philosophy seems to have a special difficulty in confronting the image, since philosophy lives in and is oriented to and by the *logos,* by words, and since it tends to take the legitimacy of this orientation as self-evident. The authority of the logos defines the very idea of philosophy and, since it is invariably assumed that the logos cannot be grasped by an image, the superiority of the logos over the image also belongs to this definition of philosophy. The logos is understood, but never seen. Even if there is a sort of "seeing" involved in philosophy, this "look" to what we call the "idea" is not the same as the look to the image. Consequently, if one is self-conscious, if one is honest, then one must hesitate before this difference between the image and the word so that once one raises the question of the image from the perspective of philosophy, the peculiar presuppositions that govern and define the project of philosophy themselves come into question. The question of the image recoils back upon philosophy and its own presumptions. Once this happens, one learns that one needs to be careful about presuming that words and images translate into one another so that one can indeed speak of images and still do justice to them such that the nature of the image shines through the words. Despite this need for hesitation and self-reflection that should emerge right from the outset of any philosophical engagement with the question of the image, what is striking is just how easily the differences between words and images are effaced, how readily we are persuaded of the gifts of language and the power of language to articulate something true in what is said. This means that the first task of any effort to speak of images is to turn language back upon itself such that its own character begins to become a question. In order to begin, it is necessary to understand that the question of the image is not simply a question *for* philosophy but rather a question that goes straight to the heart of the very possibility and idea *of* philosophy. And yet, the "blindness" of language before itself remains its first and foremost trait: language is always poorest at speaking and articulating itself. This "blindness" of language, this poverty of its own nature, is what the encounter with the image can bring to light.

One of the most telling ways in which we can understand what this poverty of language means is found in the way that the word conceals within itself the enigma of the image. Insofar as it *can be written*—one might even argue that it *needs to be written*—the word exposes its own concealed iconographic nature. It is no accident that the question of *writing,* of *script,* is almost entirely absent from the history of philosophical reflections upon both word and image. Philosophy is a discourse wedded to the ideality of language, that is, to its capacity for abstraction and concept-formation. As such, it has an inherent tendency to suppress the iconographic element of the word in which the ideality of language is tethered to the concretion of the image. Hegel calls the kinship of the word and ideality upon which philosophy is founded the "divine nature" of language.[1] Plato, emphasizing the other side of this philosophical coin, calls writing "the corpse of a thought"[2] and so warns against the peculiar death that awaits thinking once it is translated into script. Of course, Plato's hesitations about writing and his rejection of painting as a way in which we learn something of the world both emerge out of this impulse to suppress the inscription of this iconographic potential of the word. The legacy of Plato is, in this case as in so many others, strong: though the history of philosophy is a history of written texts, there has been virtually no effort to confront the iconographic character of the language of those texts. But without writing, without that translation of the ideality of language into material form, even history as we know it would not be possible. Memory alone, memory without writing, could never yield history in the same sense and as the same mystery as that which emerges as a history forged in and by texts. Nonetheless, reflections on texts and on history have passed over this decisive event. This oversight, this poverty and blindness of language with respect to itself, is the first matter that needs to be engaged if one is to speak of the image. And so one soon learns that the problem of speaking the image begins with the first word and that it is the limit of the word that comes forward with ineluctable force and that needs to be recognized if there is to be a real philosophical engagement with the image.

This hesitation, a sort of stutter of language, a hesitation of reticence, should characterize the beginning of any philosophical reflection upon the image. As the self-concealing character of language emerges, as its own iconographic potential comes into view, the complications that belong to the effort to engage the image philosophically emerge as well. However, complications notwithstanding, the need to speak of images, to struggle toward the peculiar translation of such speech, is irrepressible: just as the word permits—or even needs—its own translation *into* an image, so too one might argue that the image harbors within itself the need for its own translation into the word. This drive to language, to be brought into speech, will belong to the image in the work of art as its own concealed nature. This is evident most acutely in the *intensification* of the image and of the word found in the artwork. Here one can begin—almost.

Until relatively recently, certainly until Lessing (1775), a sense of the essential translatability, or at least the basic and uncomplicated compatibility, of words and images has defined much of the philosophic history of attempts to come to terms with the image. This is an ancient assumption that one finds already in Simonides, the first literary critic of the Western world, when he said, "Painting is silent poetry, while poetry is painting that talks."[3] One finds similar remarks throughout the history of reflections on the arts. For instance, one finds in Horace the comment that "poetry is like painting; one work seizes your fancy if you stand close to it, another if you stand at a distance."[4] Or Augustine: "Though painting is without sounds, it would reproduce, nonetheless, the faces of the sorrowful, the groaning, and the weeping, as best it could."[5] In this long and dominant tradition, words and images, and so the summit of their possibilities that develop in the work of art found in poetry and painting, are understood as reflections of the same. On the basis of this presumed sameness, an assumption arose that speaking of images was not problematic from the start, and so in the history of philosophy, we find no real hesitation about speaking of the image in the work of art or about sitting in judgment of its value and meaning since the language of philosophy is but another, higher summit still of the possibilities of the word.

The oldest tradition that speaks from out of this assumption of the homogeneity of words and images is found in the genre of *ekphrasis*. The word *ekphrasis* referred to the manner in which images could be said to "speak" and hence enabled language to speak *of* images without a fundamental distortion.[6] It is a tradition in which a real fluency and an untroubled sense of the possibilities of translation were understood to define the effort to speak of images. It is also a tradition that has, in the end, invariably deferred to the word as possessing a greater capacity for and surer relation to meaning and intelligibility than one finds in the image. Sameness defines the relation of word and image here, but so does the superiority of the word with respect to its capacity to articulate what it presents.

The first example of *ekphrasis* is generally said to be Homer's description of Achilles' shield in book 18 of the *Iliad*. There is much that is odd about this passage, not least of all the fact that Homer, who was said to be blind, would be the one to inaugurate a tradition that would be so definitive for how we speak of the visual arts.[7] It is also unusual in that the shield described in this passage presents mostly benign images, images of life, even of a happy life. Normally, the shield one carried into battles never bore such peaceful images; rather, such shields were covered with threatening images, images of a Gorgon or some other terrifying figure intended to frighten those one was fighting. They were designed to show the enemy the threat that the shield protected: "behind this shield is hidden your death and the image approaching you is its arrival." However, the image that Homer describes on the shield of Achilles is a quite peculiar, even singular image—an image of the whole of life—of the heavens and earth, sun, and stars; of dances and wars; of pastoral life and city life; of marriage, death, and birth. These images do not serve as comments upon the war for which the shield is designated; quite the contrary, they refer to life more than to death, and in the fullness of that life, war, such as the one in which this shield appears, is but a small and fleeting moment. These images represent nothing but themselves. In fact, they do not represent anything at all, since these images are "alive"—they are the scene of life itself; they are not its representation. Finally, this "image" on Achilles' shield is also an image that never existed except in Homer's words. One might also say that it is quite simply the description of a painting that *cannot exist* as an image:

> And first Hephaestus makes a great and massive shield, blazoning
> well-wrought emblems all across its surface, raising a rim around
> it, glittering, triple-ply with a silver shield-strap run from edge to
> edge and five layers of metal to build the shield itself, and across
> its vast expanse with all his craft and cunning the god creates a
> world of gorgeous immortal work. There he made the earth and
> there the sky and the sea and the inexhaustible blazing sun and the
> moon rounding full and there the constellations, all that crown

the heavens, the Pleiades and the Hyades, Orion in all his power too and the Great Bear that mankind also calls the Wagon: she wheels on her axis always fixed, watching the Hunter, and she alone is denied a plunge in the Ocean's baths. And he forged on the shield two noble cities filled with mortal men. With weddings and wedding feasts in one and under glowing torches they brought forth the brides from the women's chambers, marching through the streets while choir on choir the wedding song rose high and the young men came dancing, whirling round in rings and among them flutes and harps kept up their stirring call—and the people massed, streaming into the marketplace where a quarrel had broken out and two men struggled over the blood-price for a kinsman just murdered.[8]

The reason that this "painting" *cannot exist* is that it is, in the words of Alexander Pope, the "complete *idea of painting,* and a sketch for what one may call *a universal picture.*"[9] In other words, it is a painting that is possible only as an idea and so possible only in words. What is spoken of in this "description" is so alive that it could be presented only as a living image, as an image that was itself alive. The description is not of the frozen moments but of movements, of events as they are happening. The shield does not simply represent its themes' dances, songs, and festivals, the course of seasons and the stars—things that are kinetic and, by their own definition, do not stand still; rather, this shield enacts and *is* what it "depicts." The image described as decorating Achilles' shield is eventful and not in the least a "representation." Homer describes this "painting" as an act full of life. Today one is tempted to think of it almost as a form of cinema *avant la lettre.*[10] Despite what Pope has shown to be its impossibility, the challenge of actually painting this image has excited the imagination of many artists from ancient times to the present who have tried to create such a painting (and of scholars who have sought to outline the dimensions of such a shield); nonetheless, there is a sense in which *any* particular image must fail. It is an image, drawn in words, that cannot be repeated in a painted image. It belongs essentially to the realm of images that only the ideality of words can summon. No painted image could ever realize it. The problem with realizing this image that Homer describes is twofold: any attempt to represent such a shield cannot present the *whole* of what is described (see figure 1), but any attempt to repeat the character of the *movement* of life that appears on the shield does so by sacrificing something of the detail that animates that description (see figure 2).[11]

Lessing discusses those Homeric words that create a painting in his *Laocoön*, which is one of the founding texts of modern aesthetics. It is also a text that begins to develop the differences between poetry and painting, between words and images, in a way that eventually opens up onto the twentieth century's question about the appropriateness of words that attempt to get images to "speak." Lessing is the first to make the argument that the arts each have their own nature and integrity, the basis of an approach to art in general. Simply by thematizing the assumption that words and images are essentially compatible, an assumption that for the most part was simply unexpressed until then, Lessing opens the door to even stronger challenges to that assumption.[12] However, even though he rejects the notion of a sameness between painting and poetry, Lessing still remains bound to the tradition that holds the view that words offer more to thinking than images can ever offer and so one form of art, poetry, has a superiority with respect to all of the others. The difference between words and images is recognized now, but there still is not parity between them. Lessing gives one key reason for this judgment when he says:

> Homer treats of two kinds of beings and actions, visible and invisible. This distinction cannot be made in painting, where everything is visible and visible in but one way. . . . For example, when the gods, who are divided as to the fate of the Trojans, finally come to blows, the entire battle is represented in the poem as being invisible. This invisibility gives the imagination free rein to enlarge the scene and envisage the persons and actions of the gods on a grander scale than the measure of ordinary man. But painting must adopt a visible scene. . . . Painting carries out this reduction. In it everything that in the poem raises the gods above godlike human creatures vanishes altogether. Size, strength, and swiftness—qualities which Homer always has in store for his gods in a higher and more extraordinary degree than that bestowed on his finest heroes—must in painting sink to the common level of humanity.[13]

Despite this privilege of poetry among the arts, Lessing grants painting a sufficient independence that the question of the capacity of the word to address the image is now raised as a real question and with a new seriousness. The problem of speaking about painting gained real traction at this point. Indeed, this newly sharpened question of the relation of word and image, of language and art, defined the most radical approach to the enigma of art yet: Kant's *Critique of Judgment*. Kant's discussion of the communicability of aesthetic experience and his need to speak of the "aesthetic idea" as defined by that which escapes language that is defined by its conceptual possibility are, in many ways, the consequences of a more acute sense of the problematic defined by the relation of word and image. In pointing to the aesthetic idea as that which does not adhere to the language and logic of the language of concepts, Kant begins to open up the question of the limits of language in the realm of art. This is the point at which philosophy's own reach and possibilities are called into question in a new and fundamental manner by virtue of an engagement with the work of art. Here the limits of language emerge with a new clarity and force in the task of communicating what is disclosed in the experience of the work of art.

And yet, even when the limits of language in the realm of aesthetic experience become a philosophical problem and even when the complexities of speaking about images are thematized, the privilege of the word over the image is typically maintained even by those who do indeed attempt to take seriously the possible incommensurability of word and image. Here one sees the philosophical commitment to the *logos* manifesting itself in a prejudice on behalf of language coupled with a quiet diminution of the image. Thus, Kant comments simply that "among all the arts poetry holds the highest rank."[14] In a similar fashion, Hegel argues that Spirit is not finished with its own aesthetic education (*Bildung*) until it is able to express itself in the poetic word. One sees this as well in Heidegger's insistence on the priority of poetry among the arts and in his claim that "thinkers are founders of that which never becomes visible in images."[15] One finds this view as well in Gadamer's claim that "being that can be understood is language."[16] In short, even when the limits of language come more clearly into view, the claim that there is a privilege in the word is a rather persistent one and so translates itself into the view that holds the art of language to be the highest form in which art happens. Nietzsche, who points to music as the most original source of the arts, is a rare exception. But, Nietzsche is aware that speaking of music is just as problematic as speaking of painting. That is why he laments of his own work on the arts that "it should have sung, not spoken."[17] For one who wants to *speak* about images, it is difficult to avoid the view that there is a peculiar privilege to the word that permits the word to gather the image into language. On the other hand, one can also despair of the capacity of words before the image and so come to believe that Leonardo da Vinci was right when he said that when the topic is an image, "one should avoid words, except when speaking with the blind." But the problem of speaking of images will remain for the simple reason that there is, in the end, what one must call a *need* to speak of images. It does not take much to come to understand that the proper response to the painted image is not to "simply" look (as if a look could ever be simple or "neutral") but to reply in words. The roots of this need of the image to come to word (and, by the same token, the need of the poetic word to generate images) require careful attention for they help point to just how one can think the relation of the word to the image. From the very first word, then, the question of the relation of word and image comes forward when one speaks of painting. One soon learns that this relation, and the questions that emerge out of it, is inextricably entangled in any effort to think through the character of the image: the question of language cannot be separated from the question of the image.

I will return to this point after one further preliminary discussion that helps to open the discussion of the image in painting.

————————

There is a tendency to underestimate what is really in question when we speak of images in painting. The tendency, of course, is to regard this discussion "merely" as a matter of aesthetics and to understand the concerns of "aesthetics" to be subordinate to the more "serious" concerns of philosophy. But to assume this is to fundamentally misplace the question of the image and its import. It is to miss the point of the question by confining it within the orbit defined by a concern with pleasure, beauty, feeling, and cultural critique and to judge these matters as of less significance than the questions of cognition and conceptual, rational knowledge. This prejudice, which so clearly defines the fields of philosophy today, needs to be overcome.

However, if one does take this opening of philosophy to such challenges to heart—in other words, if one genuinely appreciates the difficulties of the question one confronts when speaking of the image—then one begins to grasp the wide sweep and true import of what is at stake in a concern with the image in the work of art. One sees this above all in the way in which asking about the achievement of painting calls into question the authority of the word and, consequentially, the authority of philosophy itself. From its beginning, philosophy has rested upon a confidence in *logos*. It lives in the element of the word. John Sallis makes this point clear when he writes that "philosophy begins by reenacting the move beyond the image to and through speech. It sets out on its second sailing . . . by undergoing conversion from engagement with images to the assumption of *logoi*."[18]

More precisely, for almost all of its history, philosophy has understood itself as emerging out of the conceptualizing power of the word. So it is said that this power of language to gather and unite what is otherwise disparate constitutes the link binding language and truth. Hegel made this understanding explicit and in so doing demonstrated how one could argue that this link binding the conceptual capacity of the word to truth needs to be understood as absolute. At the same time, Hegel called attention to the most important consequence of this argument when he said that "what is called the unutterable is nothing other than the untrue, the irrational."[19] In other words, that which cannot be taken up into the word is untrue. In making this argument, Hegel simply makes explicit a prejudice, a presumption, constitutive of the philosophical project as such; namely, he develops the consequences of the essential philosophical orientation to the *logos*. This prejudice runs through the history of philosophy and continues even up to the present in which an attempt is made to call the project of philosophy itself into question. Even those who open the question of truth to the image and its achievement still exhibit a strong tendency to this orientation. Thus, with a different intent than Hegel, but similar reliance upon the word, Heidegger approvingly cites Stefan George's line "where word breaks off, no thing may be,"[20] and Gadamer asserts that "being that can be understood is language."[21] In short, the orientation toward the *logos* that has defined philosophizing since its inception naturally inserts itself even into the manner in which philosophy addresses the question of the relation of words and images.

But to take the image to heart *on its own terms* as it appears prior to any translation into speech and to treat this appearance as possessing an intelligibility of its own is to take seriously the prospect of an intelligibility that remains constitutionally *apart from* the conceptual language of philosophy. Obviously, the question of *how* one is to do this, how one can think intelligibility independently of the concept, is key. Here the notion of a "text" can be helpful since it is a notion that speaks of an intelligibility, of some understanding that is not necessarily wedded to the intelligibility defined by conceptuality. Insofar as images can constitute a text—that is, insofar as they can lay claim to being intelligible and understandable—one must take seriously the prospect that the word does not define the realm of the intelligible. Textuality is a way in which one can recognize and account for an intelligibility not restricted to linguistic and conceptual forms of intelligibility. There might well be a "language" of the image, but, if there is, it is a language that appears as the peculiar "writing" of painting, that is, in the form of the textuality proper to it. Such a language—if we insist on calling it that—is not, at least initially, a language we "speak." Indeed, strictly speaking it is not appropriate to speak of the "language" of the image at all. Adorno made a remark worth noting in this regard: paintings are "hieroglyphs for which the code has been lost."[22]

What needs to be borne in mind is that the question of the painted image only begins to be raised with any seriousness once the painting is approached as a sort of text. Among the best accounts of just what it is that constitutes a text is found in Gadamer's *Truth and Method,* where he speaks of *Verwandlung ins Gebilde.* The commonly accepted translation of that phrase is "transformation into structure," which is correct but misses the sense that although the word *Gebilde* can be translated as "structure," one also needs to hear how the word *Bild*—a word most commonly translated as "image"—helps define *Gebilde* so that a sense of "form" is emphasized.[23] *Gebilde* has several meanings: it is something created, a product, but it also refers to a geological formation, patterns in textiles, or the structure of a building. It is something with a recognizable pattern or structure that has been actively formed. Thus, to speak Greek for a moment, one might say that this "transformation" into "structure" is a process whereby the *energeia* that characterizes a *praxis* is transformed and consummated (*vollendet*) in the *ergon* of *poiesis.* In this process, actions complete themselves as the given world is taken up (*aufgehoben*) into a "work" in which the world appears anew. In other words, the process whereby something—anything really, an event, experience, object, act—is transformed into a structure is a process that changes everything: the "something" becomes a "work," and in becoming a work it finds a new presence. As Gadamer remarks, "Transformation into structure means that what existed previously exists no longer. . . . What no longer exists is the world in which we live as our own."[24] What is new in this transformation that defines a text—any text—is the coherence and the unity that emerges. The unity of the work that is the result of this "transformation into forms linked together [*Gebilde*]" is what lets the work be a text. The roots of the word "text"—*texere, textus* (and likely *techne*)—which refer to something woven (as is expressed in the related words "textile," "texture," and "tissue") emphasize how becoming a work is a matter of the coming together, the weaving together, of forms, of becoming a text. Plato makes a quite similar point when he says that for there to be *logos* (as a spoken language), there must be a *symploke,* that is, an "interweaving," of words.[25] One way this unity is able to be achieved is in the interrelatedness of words, but there are other ways such as those proper to tones, to movement, as well as those that belong to the nature of the image. Each of these ways of forming a text, each idiom, exhibits a coherence proper to its own nature.

There are two consequences of this transformation of the given into a work that should be noted before returning to the discussion of the special character of the form of intelligibility proper to the text that is constituted by the image. The first consequence concerns the relation of work and truth; the second concerns the relation of work and being. Gadamer describes this transformation as "a transformation into the true."[26] By this he means that this transformation discloses, the change that it introduces opens up something new, and the result of this disclosure is that understanding and intelligibility emerge as possibilities. Though it signals the arrival of a new condition, such "transformation into structure is not simply transposition into another world."[27] It is rather the unfolding of possibilities into relations that give structure, weave a text. In this sense, one can say that becoming a text is the setting into a work of the world. For Gadamer, the key to understanding how the operations of this transformation are to be understood, how this becoming a text happens, is found in play—the play of cats,[28] of children, of light, of music. The elemental features of play—a freedom not hampered by the rules it observes and the relationality, the reciprocity, of the to-and-fro that defines play (as one sees, for instance, in the way a cat plays with a ball)—are at the heart of work of "transformation." What happens in this coming into a structure is to be understood as the setting free into new relations of the given. Nietzsche's description of art as a "verklärenden Spiegel [transfiguring mirror]"[29] expresses a kindred sense of how one is to understand the work of the artwork: something new is brought into the world by virtue of the textuality, the coherence—however weak—of the text.

Gadamer specifies how this new situation, this new event, should be thought when he argues that "the concept of transformation should thus characterize the independent and superior mode of being of what we call structure [*Gebilde*]. From the perspective of this structure so-called reality is defined as the untransformed and art as the raising up [*Aufhebung*] of this reality into truth."[30] What is new is the arrival of truth in the world, namely, the disclosure of the given in its truth. It is important to note that truth here is not meant as any sort of copy of, or correspondence with, the real; it means rather that there is a recognition in which we not only "know something again" but "recognize *more* than is already familiar."[31] In other words, aspects of the familiar are taken up into the work and appear as elements in the text, which weaves together those familiar aspects in a new way such that the familiar becomes new even in being recognized. One sees the world differently and anew in the work; one sees it as if for the first time. The classical term for speaking of this experience of recognition that accompanies the artwork is *mimesis*. It is a notion that is traditionally interpreted as referring to something copied or imitated, which is then recognized as something familiar. However, Gadamer's sense of recognition differs fundamentally from this traditional understanding of *mimesis*. For him, the recognition that gives us such pleasure in the work of art is centered upon the appearance of what is new, not upon what we already know. For him, it is not a matter of the familiar being affirmed as familiar but of what was previously familiar being understood in a new way. That is what Gadamer means when he says that "with respect to the recognition of the true, the being of representation is more than the being of the thing represented; *Homer's Achilles is more than the original [sein Urbild]*."[32] In the work, the being of the given is recognized as what it is but in such a way that it is new and greater than the given.

The second consequence of the transformation of the given into a structure follows from this claim about the relation of work and truth. Since the work of art is something new and "more than the original," it is clear that "the relation of the image [*Bild*] to the original [*Urbild*] is fundamentally different than the relation defined as a copy [*Abbild*]. *It is no longer a one-sided relation.* That the image has its own reality means the reverse for the original, namely that it comes to presentation in the representation. . . . Through this presentation it experiences an *increase in being [Zuwachs an Sein]*. The content of the image is defined ontologically as the emanation of the original."[33] In the image, in the painting, we encounter not a copy but an "event of being [*Seinsvorgang*]."[34] The work of art does not repeat the world; it enlarges it as it illuminates it. One should be careful in how one understands the character of this "increase" in being. It is obviously not a quantitative increase; rather, it refers more to what one might call an *intensification* of being, a coming forward or a "radiation" of being, that occurs in the world being brought into a "structure." This increase is not a matter of "more" of the same, "more" of what is already given. It is rather the alteration of the given into something different, something new. For the purposes of addressing the question of the image, what most needs to be said is that in being regarded as a text, the intelligibility, the truth, of painting is able to emerge, and when this intelligibility does emerge, one understands that it cannot be accounted for as a cognition of the given but must be thought as a recognition that is, in the end, a disclosure of the familiar as new. One comes to see that the intelligibility of the painting is not a cognitive matter but demands an attentiveness to how the world is changed in becoming the text that the painting is.

In light of these consequences of this becoming a work, this becoming a text, one can understand why I suggested that it is only once we come to understand the image as a text that we begin to take the question of painting seriously. One sees as well even more clearly the extent and depth of the stakes of asking about images in the work of art. When properly understood, the questions one asks are not able to be domesticated by being regarded as a matter of "aesthetics," a lesser form of cognition, or as only a matter of pleasure and nothing more. Instead, the work of art needs to be understood as a "knowing," a way in which truth happens, that cannot be measured by the standards of knowledge proper to the sciences. Gadamer's hermeneutics starts with this demand, and it is no accident that he formulates the very idea of a hermeneutics and his conception of human experience by taking the experience of the artwork as his starting point. This privileging of the experience of art as an entrée for, and exemplary of, the analysis of experience in general is the reason hermeneutics takes the task of understanding the work of art as its primary concern. Even more: such a hermeneutic approach to the work of art recognizes that the relation of art and world is not one-sided—as if art, especially the image, simply mimed the world—rather, it recognizes that art *changes and alters* the world, which it increases as it enters. The stakes of the question of the image, of reflections upon painting, touch upon the heart of experience and the character of a world. They are far from being able to be contained by what has long been defined as the realm of aesthetics.

Before I can turn to a discussion of the image from a hermeneutic point of view, some comments about the history of such reflections upon images in philosophy are necessary. Many of the assumptions that we take for granted when discussing paintings are not givens but the outcomes of a history, and calling attention to this will be helpful in the effort to refine and clarify what is at issue in such images. To that end, there are three moments in that history I want to mark and briefly comment upon: the ancient Greek account and judgment concerning painting; the recuperation of the image that begins with Kant and moves up through Nietzsche; and the contemporary situation of reflections upon painting. Once I come to this third stage, I will, at last, be able to begin to formulate the question regarding painting as I want to address it.

Pliny says that "the art of painting set itself apart" in the middle of the fifth century BCE; in other words, painting was no longer regarded as in the service of something else—such as ritual or as decoration—rather, it came to be regarded as an autonomous process and product.[35] Significantly, that period—a time that began some fifty years before Plato's birth and continued into the middle of his life—was also the period in which reflections on painting began in earnest. Prior to this historical moment, painting was regarded, if at all, as an element or aspect of something else—for instance, religious service, architecture, or storytelling. But painting underwent a revolution in those years, and as a result of that revolution, painting called attention to itself and won attention for itself, not for its service to something else. This revolution was, by and large, a revolution in techniques. For instance, the invention of new techniques—such as foreshortening, perspective, gradation of colors—allowed painters to transform a flat surface into a surface that gave the illusion of three dimensions. One other innovation of this time is especially significant: the autonomy of painting was also signaled by the new movement to paint on portable surfaces, such as wood, so that the painting was not simply regarded as a decorative element of architecture but could be moved and displayed in different places, thereby separating its own identity from its setting.

Because of this portability of paintings, collecting paintings now became possible and, in the first form of reproduction of paintings, copying important works also won a new popularity. These innovations did not simply change the techniques of producing paintings; rather, they fundamentally changed how paintings were regarded. From this point forward, paintings called attention to themselves *as* paintings. Despite all of these changes, the themes of these paintings did not change much at all—they were typically celebrations of victories or mythological scenes from the stories of poets—so in some sense, such paintings continued to serve a narrative or other function.[36] Just as paintings began to win an identity of their own and to be separated from what else was being served—a story, a building—so too were painters beginning to be recognized and identified. In this way too, the uniqueness and "auratic" quality of paintings began to be clarified.

Polygnotus was among the most celebrated of these revolutionary painters. Frequently mentioned by philosophers, Polygnotus seems to have had some sort of relation with Simonides, who would be among the first to theorize the relation between words and images.[37] Unfortunately, nothing of Polygnotus's work has survived (though there are a few vase paintings attributed to him or to his school). His most famous works were large-scale paintings and murals displayed at Delphi and in the entrance hall to the Acropolis. However, while we do not have examples of these works, we do have lengthy descriptions—in words, of course—by Pausanius that were written some seven hundred years after the paintings were made (second century AD).[38] Those descriptions are remarkably detailed, at least regarding the subjects of the paintings (not the colors), and so reconstructions of them have been attempted. One of the notable features of Polygnotus's paintings of human figures was the manner in which he depicted faces with mouths open and as expressive of emotion. He was so significant a figure that philosophers spoke of Polygnotus—indeed, he is almost the only painter mentioned by philosophers of this period. Plato refers to him twice, but only to invoke his name as a well-known painter, never to speak about his paintings.[39] Aristotle praises Polygnotus's work, calling him an "ethical painter,"[40] and in the *Poetics* he sets up Polygnotus as a sort of exemplar for the tragedian: after having singled out Polygnotus as "one who depicted people as better than they are,"[41] Aristotle says that "since tragedy is a representation of people better than ourselves we must copy the good portrait painters [*eikonographous*] who while rendering the distinctive form and making a likeness, yet paint people better than they are."[42] Polygnotus is the only one named as such a painter who can serve as something of a model for the tragedian in this regard. His painting "improves"—ethically speaking—the character of those whose portraits he paints.[43] But, by and large, the transformation in how painting is regarded during this period is not expressed in remarks made about any particular painter or work. We never find any extended comments about individual paintings; rather, what one does find in writings about painting at this time is a real recognition that the philosophical status of painting as an activity and a way of commenting upon the world has been recognized and that painting is now understood as philosophically significant. The most notable change in how painting is treated is that during this period, painting *as such* came to be taken as claiming a relation to the real; it claimed, one might say, to be a sort of transcription of reality. Painting came to be regarded, by some at least, as another language of the real. In the case of painting, that "language" is the language of the image, while in the case of philosophy or poetry, it is the language defined by the word that forms a commentary upon the real. Importantly, those who held this view typically held as well that there is no difference between the language of painting and the language of words. Simonides expressed this view regarding the sameness of words and images compactly when he said "ho logos ton pragmaton eikon estin"—the word is a picture of things.[44] This argument that words and images are fully commensurate and so reduplicate one another is an argument that would maintain real traction throughout the history of philosophy. Of course, typically unspoken but just as entrenched in philosophy's history is that assumption that when there is a difference between words and images, it is the word that has the superior claim.

It is this new claim that painting "speaks" of the real that Plato so forcefully denounces, arguing that painting does not present us with the truth of what is real but that it is only an illusion that can, perhaps, conceal its illusory character and thereby convince us of its truth. According to Plato, painters who create in this way—that is, those who present us with images that claim some relation to the real—in truth present us only with "phantasmata ouk onta," phantasms, not reality.[45] This does not mean that Plato is criticizing only paintings that are "realistic." The problem with painting is not that it can actually deceive in the manner of a trompe l'oeil; rather, the problem with painting for Plato is found in the nature of the relation of the painting to the original. Since the painting is regarded as a copy, a representation, of something else, in order to judge the "truth" of the painting, one must look away from it to the original that is its source. From this point of view, the relation between the image and the original is a one-sided one in which the image is simply understood as a derivation of something else. If the image can be said to be meaningful, then it will be so only by virtue of something else, something that it is not. At best, the image can be said to have a secondary relation to the real, but even if such a claim is granted, the image finds its relation to the real only by pointing away from itself, by being a sign of some sort.

Plato's treatment of the image is far more complex, subtle, and sophisticated than I can indicate here. Discussions of images—painted and otherwise —run through many, if not most, of the dialogues, and, as is typically the case with Plato, these discussions are not at all grasped by the wooden Platonism that followed in Plato's wake. However, my intent is not to take up the analysis of images in Plato; it is rather to mark a historical moment that has been decisive and enduring for the treatment of the image in the Western philosophical tradition. In this first, defining moment of philosophical reflections upon the image, a certain reception of Plato has been crucial. In this view, there are essentially two characteristics of the image that define every image—again, painted or otherwise. One finds both of these characteristics well expressed in Plato's *Sophist* when the larger concern is to develop a new context for the determination of the sophist. This new context concerns the sophist as "eidolopoiike" ("image-maker" or better: "portraitist").[46] I will not rehearse this important conversation about images, but I do want to recall the two points made in that conversation that have had an enduring legacy. The first point is that the image both is and is not the original that it is "like" so that, as Theatetus says, "non-being seems to have become entangled with being and it is very much out of place [atopon]."[47] This involvement with non-being that constitutes the very nature of the image, of any image whatsoever, will render every image problematic. Every image will have something "unreal" about it, and this "unreality" will infect even that which it in reality "is." The second point is that the image (eidolon) must always be measured in a relation to that which is imaged (on) so that the image is always understood as derivative. The image itself is not original; the image as image is not worthy of interrogation; only the reference that the image makes to something else matters. Heidegger comments on these points by saying that

> Plato is not here interested in the being of the image as such or in the phenomenon of image-ness [Bildlichkeit]; nor does he have the means to unpack these structural relations. . . . For Plato it is much more a matter of showing that the image-object [Bildobjekt], . . . that is the representing object, is indeed present, but that as this present object is not that which it shows itself to be as an image. For Plato everything comes down to this difference: that the image . . . is not itself what it purports to be. What interests him about the being of the image is the relation of the being of the image as object to that which is imaged.[48]

At the moment painting began to be noticed and considered as painting so that an examination of the image became necessary, that same examination led to the concealing of the image as image. In the end, the image itself never becomes a question.

Thus, the first (Greek) moment in the history of the philosophical conception of the image results in an obscuring of the image as image. The being of the image is passed over insofar as it is regarded only from the perspective of its relation to the original, and insofar as the image is discussed at all it is said that an unreality belongs to its being. Just prior to Plato, the word apate (deception, trickery) was introduced to describe what happens in painting insofar as the painting hides its own unreality. Plato likens this logic of the image to what the sophist does: it needs to conceal its own nature; it works by virtue of a deception. This concealment of the image as image, this one-sided relation from out of which the image is regarded, and this sense that painting is a copy that, at best, can deceive, would be the legacy of the first Western reflections upon art. The consequences of this retreat of the image as image are great and have been decisive for many of the decisions found in philosophy's history. For instance, a conception of the nature of thinking emerges out of this decision: thinking has no room for images; it is strictly the province of the *logos*. But for my concerns, the consequence of this Greek legacy that is most significant is that painting is never taken as a text, as what Gadamer has described as *Gebilde* or what Plato called *symploke*, but is ultimately regarded only as a trick. Put in other words, painting does not have its own intelligibility; it is able to be understood only by turning away from the painting and turning to something else.

This withdrawal of the image from the realm of intelligibility and being is the first stage in the evolution of the philosophical conception of the image. This withdrawal marks the inception of the question of the image. But there is one other legacy of the Greek approach to painting at this moment of inception that needs to be noted, namely, that the critical vocabulary for discussing works of art tended to be developed without regard to the specific character of the form or genre of art. So for instance, Aristotle developed his vocabulary for considering artworks almost exclusively through an analysis of tragic theater (even more specifically, through an analysis of Sophoclean tragedy). Plato considered a wider variety of arts—including painting—but in the end tended to develop his own framework for discussing the work of art with reference to poetry (here, more specifically, it is Homeric poetry). What this means with regard to the discussion of painting in particular is that key terms—for instance, *mimesis* or even *eidolon*—have evolved out of an analysis that is not always appropriate to the specific task of speaking about painting. Coupled with the withdrawal—or better: suppression—of the character of the image itself, this conflation of the language used to discuss works of art only serves to further drive the question of the image away from the concerns of philosophy.

———

While the first pivotal moment in the history of philosophical reflections on painting and the image marks the covering over of the question of the image as image and the denigration of the achievement of painting, the second pivotal moment in that history marks the return of the image as a problem in which the specific complexity of images is addressed as well as the recovery of painting as a valuable human achievement. Kant initiates this new moment in two ways. First, by no longer regarding the relation of image and world as one-sided—as if the image could be understood only as a copy of the given—Kant begins to understand that the image is an appearance in its own right and that it can no longer be understood simply as a copy of something else. Second, by disclosing the real originality of the work of art as well as the relation of art and truth that is a consequence of this originality, Kant opens the way for a consideration of painting not as a trick of perception but as a text with a claim to truth. The recovery of the image as a question takes place primarily in the schematism of the *Critique of Pure Reason;* the newfound disclosure of the importance of the work of art takes place in the *Critique of Judgment.* A few comments about how this new impulse is introduced in each case will be helpful.

Jean-Luc Nancy makes Kant's significance for the opening of the question of the image clear when he writes: "The Kantian imagination is indeed the first modern figure . . . of a faculty of images that is not representative . . . but presentative . . . constitutive or productive of its object . . . and thus, in the end, a purveyor of knowledge. . . . It is a knowledge through the image, for the imagination is what presents all things—the object and the subject, the triangle and ultimate ends, the imaginable and the unimaginable."[49] In other words, the image not only has some claim to intelligibility but is now recognized as *constitutive* of intelligibility as such. The image belongs to the dynamic at the roots of experience, at the possibility of experience, that defines the character of knowledge that is possible on the basis of such experience. In the first Critique, Kant's efforts are directed toward an analysis of the sort of experience in which objects can be known according to the categories of the intellect and thus yields scientific knowledge. In the third Critique, his concern is with the sort of experience that yields reflective judgments, that is, a "knowing," an "understanding," that is not able to be determined by concepts. The most important point, though, is that Kant's argument identifies the image as productive and not merely as reproductive—whatever the experience is, whatever sort of "knowing" it yields. The schematism, which Kant describes as "a concealed art in the depths of the human soul, an art the true movement of which nature will hardly ever . . . let us see," is that through which "images first become possible."[50] A thorough discussion of the operations of the schematism, a discussion that ultimately leads to the relation of time and the image,[51] goes beyond my concerns here. Furthermore, there is some sense in which Kant's explicit treatment of the image in the schematism does not recognize the full significance of Kant's own recuperation of the image from the suppressed status it was accorded in the Greek philosophical beginnings. In the matter of the image, Kant is in this case (as in so much else) a bad interpreter of Kant. In light of this, I do not intend to speak of the schematism; however, I do want to comment upon how Heidegger turns the image into a question through some of his interpretations of the schematism since Heidegger's reading of Kant on this matter uncovers the full force of the Kantian recovery of the image for philosophy. The key to Heidegger's reading of this point is found in the way that he finds in Kant a sense of the image that is not developed from out of a one-sided relation with the world, a relation in which the image can appear only as a copy. Rather, Heidegger's concern is to demonstrate how the image is itself originally productive of appearance, not merely reproductive.

In a lecture course of 1925–26, in which he discusses the place of the image in the Kantian schematism, Heidegger says that "here a concept of image emerges which is different than the concept of image as copy [*Abbild*], but that is still connected to that concept."[52] Heidegger makes this comment after having just discussed a rather strange example of an image that seems only to be a copy, a reproduction of something else: a photograph of a death mask. Curiously, Heidegger completely passes over what is so strange about the image he has chosen, namely, that he is speaking of a photograph of a death mask. Nothing of the utter strangeness of this choice of an image—that he is talking of a photograph, not directly of the death mask, and that he is speaking of an image of death, of what has no image, and that this image itself takes the form of a mask, a copy of the face—is mentioned. Instead, he simply takes this as an instance of an image that is the copy (the photograph) of a likeness (the death mask). He speaks of the same example in *Kant and the Problem of Metaphysics* as well:

> It is possible to produce a copy (a photograph) again from such a likeness, of a death mask for example. The copy can only directly copy the likeness and thus reveal the "image" (the immediate look of the deceased himself). The photograph of the death mask, as copy of a likeness, is itself an image—but this is only because it gives the "image" of the dead person, shows how the dead person appears, or rather how it appeared. According to the meaning of the expression "image" hitherto delimited, making sensible means on the one hand the manner of immediate, empirical intuiting, but on the other hand it also means the manner of immediate contemplation of a likeness in which the look of a being presents itself.

Now the photograph, however, can also show how something like a death mask appears in general. In turn, the death mask can show in general how something like the face of a dead human being appears. But an individual corpse itself can also show this. And similarly, the mask itself can also show how a death mask in general appears, just as the photograph shows not only how what is photographed, but also how a photograph, in general, appears.

But what do these "looks" (images in the broadest sense) of this corpse, this mask, this photograph, etc., now show? Which "appearance" (eidos, idea) do they now give? What do they now make sensible? In the one that applies to many, they show how something appears "in general." This unity applicable to several, however, is what representation represents in the manner of the concepts. These looks must now serve the making-sensible of concepts.

This making-sensible can now no longer mean: to get an immediate look, intuition from a concept, for the concept, as the represented universal, cannot be represented in a repraesentatio singularis, which the intuition certainly is. For that reason, however, the concept is also essentially not capable of having a likeness taken.

Now what in general is meant by the making-sensible of a concept? What pertains to it? With this making-intuitable, how is the look of what is empirically, accessibly at hand or visualized—that is to say, the look of its possible likenesses—shared?[53]

In the lecture course of 1925–26, Heidegger specifies that he is referring to a photograph of the death mask of Pascal (see figure 3).[54] The choice of an image of a dead face, of a corpse, as an image is, of course, no accident and echoes the central role that death plays in *Being and Time* (which Heidegger was writing during this period). Nonetheless, a photograph, moreover a photograph of a death mask, is an odd choice of an image to enlist in an effort to clarify the role of the image in the Kantian schematism, and it is made all the more peculiar as a choice since Heidegger makes no connection between what is imaged here and his treatment of death or of the corpse in *Being and Time*.[55] Here the concern is solely with the image-character of this photograph of the death mask. More precisely, there are two points in particular that Heidegger emphasizes: first, that there is a peculiar oscillation that defines such images insofar as they can indeed be understood as presenting something "in general" and, at the same time, can be understood as a representation of what is singular and unique (this is what "a" death mask looks like; this is what Pascal's "unique" death mask looks like); second, that the concept, as defined by its relation to generality, cannot be adjusted to this oscillation of the image between universality and uniqueness since the concept cannot be represented as a singularity, as simultaneously universal and unique. Thus "the concept is essentially not capable of having a likeness taken"[56]—it remains too tethered to the universal, to what is generalizable, but never at the same time a singularity.

But while such an interpretation of the image as an oscillation and as a doublet of the universal and the unique does help elucidate a sense of the Kantian schematism (which has as its task the synthesis of intuition and intellect), there is more that should be said about the image than Heidegger does in this case. Above all, something needs to be said about the peculiar character of this special image of an image, namely, that it is a death mask. More precisely, what needs to be discussed is the way that the image in general resembles the corpse.[57] Both the image and the corpse are and are not what they appear to be; likewise, both call attention to an absence. The corpse is, in one sense, *only* a likeness—in some sense it *is* its own image. A pure ambiguity, the corpse is the likeness of that which has withdrawn and can no longer appear as itself. One might almost say that the corpse is as close to pure likeness, pure image, as one can find. But Heidegger does not speak directly of the corpse *as* a corpse; rather, he speaks of the death *mask,* more precisely, of a photograph of such a mask, thus setting the question of this peculiar image in a complex context that makes this image all the more haunting. Just as he does not comment on the peculiarities of the corpse, of the image of the dead, so too he does not comment upon the peculiarity of masks. The mask too both is and is not what it presents to us. Even more: the mask looks back at us from empty eyes with an uncanny gaze of one who is eyeless. Günter Figal puts this point well when he says that in the mask, "the open, the empty place, has become the eye itself."[58] One encounters a look that is no longer a look; no one looks back from out of the empty eye sockets, and yet one still recognizes the face. In its empty eyes that stare out of it, the mask can be distinguished from the portrait bust, and this uncanny difference, in the end, does make a telling difference. But simply taken as images, the mask and the bust are notable for their sameness: both remain silent—no words come from the mouths shown—and yet both silently seek to be something identifiable and singular; in other words, both are portraits and so bear an inseparable relation to their subject. The true character of the portrait, like that of the mirror image, is not to be found in any sense that it is a copy; it is rather found in recognizing that it remains inseparable from what is presented.[59] So, the image of the death mask to which Heidegger refers in his discussion of the way the image is recovered by Kant is a peculiar sort of image, one that ties itself quite powerfully to the world while, at the same time, announcing a sort of distance from the very same world that it summons.

Heidegger does not comment on the quality of the death mask as *mask* and on the peculiar sort of image it presents. But, even more surprising is that he also never comments upon the fact that this is a *death* mask, in other words, that it is the image of a face that is—even in the moment of its imaging—no longer a face. Nor does he comment upon the fact that the photograph seems to place us at one further remove from what is being shown. He does say, however, that while this photo of the death mask can be regarded in many ways—for instance, as an illustration of death masks in general and of a death mask that is singular insofar as it is Pascal's unique death mask—it is, in the end, inescapably a singular image. Like a portrait that is inseparably tied to its subject.[60] Like the image in a mirror.

What is important to see here is that, despite its singular bond with the being of Pascal, the death mask as an image cannot be grasped simply as a copy of that singular being—if for no other reason than that the original has already withdrawn. The death mask is rather *a pure resemblance of that which has withdrawn;* it is as if it were a resemblance without original. Or better: the image in this case is the real trace and residue of the original since the image is not able to be differentiated from the original, just as the image we see in a mirror is not that of the mirror but of the one reflected.[61] Heidegger argues that this presencing of the original in the image, this non-differentiation with a difference, is what defines the image in the work of art.[62] Such images lie "between" the conception of the image as "copy" and as "illustration (or schematization) of a concept."[63] One sees again that the image *as* image needs to be understood as an ambiguous figure, one that is more appropriately characterized as a "between" than as a replication of something else: it bears a relation to something other than itself, but that relation does not define or exhaust its own nature. Some images, such as the death mask, amplify this rather ambiguous characteristic of all images. Plato recognized something like this when he noted that the image partakes both of being and non-being at the same time. This doubled, ambiguous nature of the image is at the root of its strangeness. The image of the dead, the death mask, is only the intensification of this truth of all images. One might rightly say that *the strangeness of the peculiar resemblance of the death mask (and of the corpse) is the same strangeness that we find in the image in the work of art.*

This link between the dead and the image is among the first ways in which the image was discussed, and so in recovering this sense that in the dead we learn something of the most original being of the image, we return the idea of the image to its ancient Greek roots. The Greek notion of *eidolon,* which was the name given to the shades of the dead, was a sort of effigy of one who had withdrawn from life. It was the word that described the way in which the dead remained for us in memory. The *eidolon* was the strange presence in which one who must remain at a distance can still, in some sense, be present. Once we come to understand that this insurmountable distance proper to how we can "see" the dead equally defines what it is that we "see" in the image, we need to come to understand as well how it is that the image sets us in a relation with that same distance. Being set into relation with this strange mix of intimate presence and insurmountable distance, the image oscillates between a sense of the familiar and the mysterious—in this oscillation in which the image is grasped *as* image and not simply as a copy, the strangeness of the image begins to become evident.[64]

While Kant's treatment of the image in the schematism does not go this far in exposing the strangeness proper to the image as such, his analysis of the image in the schematism does begin the process of opening up the image and recovering it as a philosophical question. By demonstrating the productive character of the image and by showing its doubled nature—as simultaneously something singular and something in general—Kant brings the question of the image back into philosophy from its Greek suppression. After Kant, the image can no longer be discounted as simply the copy of something else; instead, it now needs to be taken as posing a serious and original question for philosophy.

Kant develops this point in the schematism that is found in the analysis of experience in general that he undertakes in his first Critique. But in his third Critique, he makes yet another argument that further entrenches the image as a philosophical question and defines how the image is taken up as a question henceforth. Kant does this insofar as he demonstrates that the work of art is an original locus of truth. Doing this, Kant defines the second moment in the recovery of the question of the image as above all a question of the appearance of the image in the work of art, especially in painting. Since for Kant the work of art is always understood as the *beautiful* work—art (*Kunst*) always means fine art (*schöne Kunst*)—the question of the image becomes preeminently the question of the beautiful image. More precisely, for reasons that have to do with the relation of the work of art to freedom, it becomes a question of the image that is *produced* and summons the peculiar pleasure of beauty; in other words, the question of the image becomes wedded to the question of the *work*.[65] There are three arguments that Kant develops in the third Critique that are important for understanding the impact of his contributions to the question of the image: first, the analysis of the *beautiful* and its resistance to concepts; second, the disclosure of a form of presentation other than the schematism, namely, the *symbolic hypotyposis;* and third, the rooting of the production of art in *freedom.*

When analyzing the character of the judgment that something is beautiful, Kant lays out a number of elements that define the beautiful, but he stresses two hallmarks of beauty above all: first, that the beautiful is always a *singular* judgment, a judgment about a "this," and second, that the beautiful is that which *cannot be brought under a concept.*[66] This inability to conceptualize the beautiful—the fact that it is always a matter of a "this" and never able to be set into a rule—is what drives Kant to speak of a new form of presentation (*hypotyposis*), one that is not defined by the logic of the schematism. He describes this other form of presentation, this other root of possible experience, as a "symbolic" hypotyposis. It is a form of presentation that opens a space of appearance that is different from the space of schematized experience that culminates in the concept.[67] Just as the beautiful presentation does not yield a concept, so too is it the case that the beautiful presentation cannot be grasped or thought by a form of thinking that is guided by conceptual reason. A different form of thinking, one not animated by concepts, is demanded if such beautiful presentations are to be thought. Likewise, if we are to attempt to understand the operations of the mind that produces such works, that is, the mind of the artist, then we must not assume that the rational idea can give an account of those operations. This means that the thought processes of the artist cannot be understood with reference to the thought processes determined by rational cognition. Consequently, a different sort of "transfer" of the mind is at work, one that he describes with reference to the "aesthetic idea." Kant defines the aesthetic idea as "a presentation of the imagination which prompts much thought, but to which no determinate thought whatsoever, i.e. no *concept,* can be adequate, so that no language can express it completely and allow us to grasp it."[68] In short, to think the beautiful —either with respect to its coming into being in the form of the artwork or to its presentation in the experience of one who judges—one needs to think differently than one thinks when one cognizes experience according to the rules of conceptual reason. Beautiful presentations summon thinking to open itself up to that which cannot appear within the horizon of scientizable experience. Simply put, to grasp the beauty of a work of art requires that we approach it not as we would an object of analysis but in a manner that enables the unexpoundable character of the presentation to appear. The beautiful also challenges language as well as the character of thinking since it claims to present that which "no language can express." This challenge to language, to the *logos,* is at the heart of Kant's analysis of aesthetic experience. He defines such experience as simultaneously carrying within itself the need to communicate, to speak—a need born of the *sensus communis* characterizing aesthetic experience—and the equal yet opposed need to recognize the failure of words that attempt to speak of such experience. In the end, this antinomy of language proper to aesthetic experience leads to the conclusion that speech about the work of art needs to be a different sort of speaking, one not governed by the syntax and logic of the concept but rather elastic and sufficiently agile to speak of that which appears according to a different form of presentation and appearance. In the encounter with the work of art, thinking and speaking alike need to take a different form. That is why after Kant, philosophy needs to take a new form.

One other point from the third *Critique* leaves footprints that guide the discussion of the image and the work of art and thus needs to be noted; namely, that when giving an account of the production of works of art, of our way of bringing such beautiful presentations into being, Kant argues that "by right, we should not call anything art except that which is a production through freedom."[69] This is what distinguishes the beehive as a production —one that we might even find beautiful—from the work of art such as the architecture of a house. Saying this, understanding art as the practice of freedom in the world reaffirms Kant's analysis of the role of the image in experience, namely, that it is not the product of a reproductive capacity but of a productive one. This, in turn, means recognizing that works of art cannot be grasped as what they are by thinking of them as copies; rather, one needs to approach such works as something like an objectification of freedom in the world and thus as an expression of what most defines us. The drive to produce works of art emerges out of what is elemental to us. It is not simply an expression of individual or private concerns or experiences; rather, it is the appearance of what is most "human."

This point will have a powerful legacy. The notion of a *Bildungstrieb* (formative drive) such as one finds in Hegel, Schelling, and Hölderlin is a direct descendant of this Kantian claim, as is Nietzsche's notion of a *Kunsttrieb* (artistic drive).[70] Both of those notions only deepen and strengthen the sense that art, the drive to form, is elemental for us. One might say that the human being is "born for art."[71] From this point of view, the elementality of art and the originality of such works become evident so that the work of art now needs to be understood as an archaic presentation, as the appearance of something primal and not simply as a copy or derivation of something else. The image itself *as image* is now regarded as worthy of serious philosophical reflection. Not surprisingly, archaic art such as primitive cave paintings (see figure 4) have now become a matter of interest for one who would reflect upon what one finds in painting.[72] This is the reason Merleau-Ponty can claim that "in some sense, the first painting had already arrived at the farthest reach that the future will have."[73] Likewise, forms of the archaic that are repeated in each life—the drawings of children and doodles (see figure 5)—take on a new interest. Freud makes an explicit link between such forms of the archaic impulse to make art and more developed works of art.[74] Klee makes the same link when he says that "there are primitive beginnings in art, such as one usually finds in ethnographic collections or at home in one's nursery. Do not laugh reader! Children also have artistic ability."[75] In this drive to make images, something raw and untouched by conscious life and the laws of cognition but something that is nonetheless central to our own natures appears. In short, the need to make images is a need that defines us.

Nietzsche is the one who presses this drive to make art to the deepest point, and when he links this drive to art with the productive character of images, he unites the two aspects of the reawakening of the question of painting that began with Kant. Nietzsche makes this point quite clear when he notes that when the mind is alone and by itself, when it has shut out the external world and so is engaged only with its ownmost nature, that is, when we sleep, we make images—we dream. The most intimate conversation of the soul with itself, the dream, takes place in images.[76] In order to illustrate this point and to draw attention to the way that painting needs to be understood as the developed form of the dream, this peculiar conversation that no language can reach, Nietzsche gives an example of what he takes to be a painting that "represents . . . the primitive process of the . . . artist."[77] To this end, he refers to Raphael's *Transfiguration* (figure 6), saying that "from this shining appearance [*Schein*] there arises . . . a new visionary world which is like vision, but which those who are captured by first appearances are not able to see."[78]

In other words, here we find a "symbolic painting" that presents an image of what we normally overlook, an image of the primordial appearing, the "shining," at the root of all experience. One might say that this painting is an image that exposes something of the emergence of images.

Nietzsche says of this painting that "what shines here is the shining of the reflection of the eternal contradiction, of the father of things,"[79] and in his further remarks on this painting Nietzsche problematizes the question he had already raised about the insufficiency of words before the image. The discussion of *Transfiguration* is not detailed; nonetheless, this instance of *ekphrasis* forms the beginning, in some sense at least, of Nietzsche's first book and so serves as something of an opening to his thought. Given the Christian nature of the content of this painting, it is clear that content is not what draws Nietzsche to it but rather the character of the image itself. With Nietzsche, painting becomes more a matter of how the painting "appears" or "shines" (*sein Schein*) than what it "copies." The "content" of the painting, the objects it "depicts," are not the real achievement of the painting. That achievement rather is found in the way something more original, something primordial, shines out of the painting.

Nietzsche marks the end of the second pivotal stage in the history of philosophical reflections upon images that Kant inaugurates. Nietzsche's conception of art as the will to power and thus as the expression of the most elemental drive of life is the direct descendant of Kant's claim that art is the expression of the freedom that defines us. Likewise, Nietzsche's reference to the "shining" of the image should be understood as the culmination of the move of art away from the language of the concept, the orbit of the idea. Art now no longer sits within the horizon of what philosophy can claim as its own. Thus, Nietzsche can say that "we have art lest we perish of the truth."[80]

But there are two other developments during this period that need to be noted as having left a lasting mark upon philosophical discussions of the image. Both of these developments stand out as contradicting other developments of this period between Kant and Nietzsche. This means that one needs to understand the legacy of this second stage as conflicted and ultimately unsettled. First, directly contradicting the claim on behalf of the originality and truth of art that we find in Kant and Nietzsche, Hegel claims that art is a "thing of the past," that from the point of view of truth, art is simply passé. Hegel's argument is, in the end, rather simple: art is not finished or completed but, from the standpoint of truth, remains undeveloped and unfinished—hence passé. The standpoint of truth is the standpoint of the concept, of philosophy. Hegel's claim had its appeal, and thanks to the force of his argument, the relation of art and truth will remain an open question. Heidegger affirms this point and says that "the decision about Hegel's claim is not yet made; behind this statement we find Western thought since the Greeks."[81] It is important that Heidegger's assertion that "behind this statement we find Western thought since the Greeks" be given its full weight. From its inception, philosophy has wedded itself to the *logos,* so the challenge that art poses to philosophy is—as Plato well knew—a fundamental one.

The second development during this period between Kant and Nietzsche is the retreat of beauty as the signature of the work of art. For Kant and German Idealism, beauty is the hallmark of the artwork: art means fine art (*schöne Kunst*). However, their treatment of the work of art and the new expanse of the significance of art along with the development of new forms and techniques of art served to open the possibilities of what would qualify as art to such an extent that the restriction that art must be beautiful would be lifted.[82] Art would be defined as the expression of a drive, as the product of the will, and not by the judgment of taste that may determine it as beautiful. This diminishment of the role of beauty in the determination of art proceeded so far that Nietzsche deemed beauty "insufficient" for any decision about aesthetic experience. By the turn of the twentieth century, the very notion of beauty seems to have lost all relevance for any reflection about art. So, when Heidegger writes "The Origin of the Work of Art," it is not surprising that he does not speak of the beautiful at all. He presses this matter even further in *Besinnung* and suggests that insofar as beauty remains the fundamental determination of art, art itself will remain metaphysically determined.[83] But, as was the case with the question of the relation of art and truth, the question of the beautiful, once seemingly answered, would ultimately come to be understood as an open question about which a decision has not been made. And so one finds Gadamer arguing for the "relevance of the beautiful." By making this argument, Gadamer separates himself from Heidegger and makes the notion of beauty, long unquestioned as the signature of the work of art and then subsequently abandoned as a question at all, a question once again.[84] The tenacity of a sense of the beautiful will not easily be set aside.

So the second stage of the philosophical concern with the image would be the period of its recuperation. More precisely: it would be the period in which the radical character of truly asking about the image, of letting the authority of the *logos* be called into question, would be made evident. It is no accident that the recovery of the question of the image largely coincides with the announcement of the "end of philosophy"—at least the end of philosophy as we have largely known it hitherto. The hegemony of the concept, of the *logos,* needs to be opened and challenged if what one finds in the image is to appear in its full force. But the legacy of this second stage in this history is not a settled one. Quite the contrary, it never seems to complete or decide its own most pressing questions, and when the next stage of questions and understanding launches itself, it will confront a rather conflicted inheritance on matters such as the relation of art and truth and the relevance of the beautiful to art. But it will also inherit a clear sense of the elemental importance both of the work of art as well as of the effort to ask about the image and its role in experience and thinking.

––––––––

The third stage of the problematic confronting philosophical reflections upon painting began sometime around the year 1889—it was this year that signaled a turning point in the evolution of modernity and in the development of painting. Coincidentally, that was the year of Heidegger's birth (also of Cocteau, Chaplin, Collingwood, Marcel, Wittgenstein, and Hitler). It was the year the Eiffel Tower, that great metaphor of modernity as a technological achievement, was built. The Eiffel Tower would be the master image of the promises of modernity with its technological paradise to come. Built by an engineer, not an architect, it would signal the triumph of technology in a realm once reserved for art. But the optimism that seemed to be inaugurated in 1889 was not an easy one, nor was it without its self-consciously darker side. That would also be the year that van Gogh painted *Starry Night* and a self-portrait that had an intensity seldom matched before. That centenary year of the French Revolution was also the year Nietzsche had his breakdown in Turin. After 1889, the situation in which philosophy found itself and the state of painting would be profoundly different from the situation that had defined either of the two previous stages in the history of philosophical reflections upon painting. Images, such as the image of the Eiffel Tower, seemed to be guided by something new and different, and, like that tower, they often seemed to be visible signs of the future. Even more: new ways of seeing seemed to be opening up thanks to such achievements of technology. When the Eiffel Tower opened in 1889, nearly a million people ascended it and from it were able to see Paris in a new way: as a series of rooftops that were simply forms and patterns. It was the geometry of Paris that one saw, its cubes and the jumble of fragments layered over one another. No one had seen the world quite like this before.[85]

The first moment of the history of the philosophical conception of the image was determined largely by a conjunction of two historical factors,

namely, the birth of philosophy and a profound transformation in the possibilities of painting (above all, its newly found autonomy as an art form).
The second stage of that history was driven primarily by theoretical developments in philosophy (above all, by Kant), and although painting itself
was evolving it was, unlike the first stage, not in a period of real revolution
in its own nature. The third stage of this history, however, was shaped
largely by political and cultural forces and, as in the first stage, by revolutionary developments in painting, some of which were driven by technological developments apart from painting (for example, the development
of photography and of film).[86] This, I would argue, is the stage in which we
find ourselves in the present, and it is out of this situation that the issues
I want to address in the following chapters emerge and get addressed. As
with the previous stages, the conditions of our present will likely come to
be understood only slowly.

Political forces—indeed, often naked and brute (and brutal) force
itself—shaped the situation of art as well as of one who would speak of
paintings during the early phase of this history. While 1889 would announce
a somewhat complex optimism regarding the future, that optimism, and
the place that technology had in constructing it, would not last long. World
War I would be the first truly mechanized war and would be the most
brutal war in Western history up to that time. It would scar the consciousness of the age and strip it of the faith in a benevolent technology. The
machines would be used to kill the comrades, family, friends, and children
of those who had invented them. The new images of modernity now were
defined more by shattered bodies than by towering works of engineering.
Gottfried Benn, a doctor who served on the front and a poet of this new
consciousness of shattered lives, presents vivid and disturbing images of
bodies damaged seemingly beyond the imagination.[87] Painting too, especially its new forms, would no longer be able to be discussed without at
least some awareness of its place in a political universe. Painting was finally
drawn into the political sphere as it struggled to render visible what had
never been seen before. It does not seem surprising that this is the moment
in which beauty seemed to lose its claim to reality once and for all.

A decisive point in this development, and the end of the beginning
of this third historical moment, happened in 1937 when the Nazis set up
an exhibition of paintings titled *Entartete Kunst*. This phrase is taken from
Nietzsche, who used it to characterize works of art that were defined by
the wish to be "beautiful."[88] For Nietzsche, works of art that were governed
by the ideal of beauty were more akin to kitsch than the real possibilities of

art that emerged as an expression of the will to power. Such art was "degenerate art," art that was stepping back, nostalgically, to a time in which the possibilities of art were not fully grasped. It was art that still hewed closely to the aims of beauty and the hope of truth, and in doing this it fell short of the great achievement of art that outstrips both beauty and truth. Though the Nazis appropriated this term from Nietzsche, they enlisted it to quite different ends (indeed, in one respect at least they enlisted it to directly antithetical ends).[89] Nazi "theorists" purportedly used this term to describe art that was "un-German" and lacking in beauty, but the real goal of their use of "degenerate art" was far sharper and far more pernicious even than the nationalism that was borne by the notion of that which is "un-German." The real aim was twofold and unabashedly circular: to dehumanize entire groups of peoples by linking them to an art that was morally bankrupt, and to expose the art of the avant-garde as morally bankrupt by linking it to peoples lacking humanity. The sweep of what would be deemed "degenerate" was enormous, and the intention was far greater than the eventual destruction of contemporary art movements. National Socialism was deeply interested in aesthetic issues. There are many reasons that can help account for this, but whatever account is given, from Speer to Riefenstahl, the Nazis enlisted art to propaganda purposes and as a means, often even subtle, of cultivating the "values" of that movement.[90] Indeed, across the street from the first exhibition of *Degenerate Art*, the Nazis set up another counter-exhibition, titled *Große Deutsche Kunstausstellung* (Great German Art Exhibition) in which ideals of National Socialist art were displayed. Those works were highly sentimentalized and idealized treatments of neoclassical and popular themes. They were displayed as reflecting "good German" "moral values," above all "beauty without sensuality."[91] The works, which were presented as the self-representation of the National Socialist world, were pure kitsch. Very few people attended that exhibition.

In contrast, the exhibition of *Degenerate Art* was among the best-attended exhibitions of all time at that point. The exhibition gathered some 650 paintings—many quite significant works—that were examples of what Nazis found "wrong" with modern art.[92] Among the artists represented in the *Degenerate Art* exhibition were Beckmann, Chagall, Ernst, Kandinsky, Klee, Kokoscha, Marc, Modersohn-Becker, Nolde, and Picasso—to name only some of the most prominent artists. In short, it was a collection of truly important and innovative art. In a twist of historical fate, this exhibition would serve as one of the first sweeping events defining modern art. However, the intention of the exhibition was not to give definition and clarity to a new art movement but to debase and destroy such art and to use those works to help debase and destroy entire classes of people. Drawing upon a pseudo-scientific book that was first published in 1928, *Kunst und Rasse* (Art and Race) by Paul Schultze-Naumburg, this exhibition attempted to show simultaneously that modern art was the product of a diseased mind—by linking it with diseased bodies and mental illness—and that diseased bodies and impaired minds were moral distortions (by linking them with modern art).[93] The developments of painting that came in response to the violence of the early years of the twentieth century were taken as evidence of the decline of the modern age, and they were equally seen as evidence of the racist claims of National Socialism. Schultze-Naumburg's book was well represented in the exhibition and was very influential in the peculiarly warped style of the exhibition (juxtaposing works of modern art with photographs of physical deformities and "racial characteristics").

The installation of the exhibition was a performance of its point: many of the works were displayed with their frames removed; frequently, the paintings were deliberately hung askew; questions would be posed next to paintings asking if this was the work of an artist, a madman, or a child. The politicization, racialization, and sexualization of art that was the intent of this exhibition served to define "modern art" as a break not simply with traditional forms of art but also with "traditional"—in this case: National Socialist state-authorized—values. Strangely though, by linking modern art and its break with representation to madness, deformity, and the decline of Western culture, this exhibition would make it difficult to avoid the genuinely revolutionary aspects of modern painting and the way in which that revolution signaled something greater than what was seen on the canvas. In its effort to break modern art off of history and set it aside, this exhibit had shown—against its own intentions—just how truly original, innovative, and challenging such art was. My intention in referring to this exhibition as marking the end of the third stage of the philosophical history of reflections upon painting is certainly not at all to credit the Nazi curators with any real philosophical or aesthetic judgment or ability. The Schultze-Naumburg book that formulated the "theory" driving this exhibition and the sensibility of its curators illustrate the crude character of the Nazi attitude toward art and the way in which the Nazis enlisted even works of art to repressive and violent ends. Rather, I mention this exhibition in order to point out that by this time, the very real revolution that had taken place in the arts at the turn of the century was finally becoming evident. It was becoming clear that the work of art, especially modern art, was a genuine response to the transformations in history and that in this response something new was being exposed. The exhibition *Degenerate Art* was intended to discredit such art and to shut down the new space such art was beginning to open up. In the long run it had, in many respects, just the opposite outcome.

Looking back on this period (though without any reference to the *Degenerate Art* exhibition), Gadamer describes the revolutionary character of modern, non-objective art by saying that "we are faced with a genuine revolution in modern art that began shortly before the First World War. We see the simultaneous emergence of so-called atonal music—an idea that seems as paradoxical as that of non-objective painting. At the same time we also see—in Proust and Joyce, for example—the disappearance of the naïve, omniscient narrator who observes events hidden to others and lends them epic expression. In lyric poetry we hear a new voice that interrupts and inhibits the familiar flow of melodic language and eventually turns to experimentation with quite new formal principles."[94] Elsewhere, Gadamer speaks of the "enormous gap between the traditional form and content of Western art and the ideals of contemporary artists."[95] In a similar fashion, Klee writes in his diary that "the currents of yesterday's tradition are really becoming lost in the sand. . . . A great moment has arrived, and I hail those who are working toward the impending reformation."[96] A self-consciousness of the rupture marked in such works equally defines those works. For one who would reflect upon such images, this self-consciousness along with the politicization and even the threat posed by such images necessarily shape the context for those reflections. Something new emerges in modern art, and it poses a very real challenge to many long-standing assumptions. The task of philosophy in the present age is to come to terms with this challenge and to pursue this opening. It is a context out of which we still think about painting today.

A renewed sense of the originality and truth of images was inaugurated in the second stage of this somewhat excentric history of philosophical concern with images. In that stage, which begins with Kant and moves through Hegel to Nietzsche, there also emerges a sense of the insufficiency and of the inappropriateness of some of the most long-standing aesthetic categories and assumptions by which such images were interpreted. Among these categories and assumptions that need to be overcome, two stand out above all: that the image needs to be understood essentially as a copy, as a representation, and that the only true signature of the work of art is beauty. Thus, at the very same moment that the worth of painting as an original philosophical concern was consolidated in Kant and Hegel, the philosophical assumptions and the traditional frameworks for interpreting painting collapsed. By the time Nietzsche takes up the questions posed by art, this collapse seems complete.[97] To add to the disorientation of this situation, it is precisely at this juncture that painting underwent revolutionary transformations, above all with respect to representation and to objects. Non-objective, non-representational, abstract painting completely changed the questions raised by painting. By the time Klee takes up the topic of modern art in his celebrated lecture of 1924, and by the time Heidegger writes "The Origin of the Work of Art" in 1935, finding an orientation to modern painting required starting out from ways of thinking that were as new, revolutionary, and radical as was exhibited by such works of art. It is in this context that one needs to understand the damage wrought by such distortions and pernicious manipulations of modern art that one finds in an exhibit such as *Degenerate Art*. The intention of that exhibit was to shut down the opening to new questions and new perspectives opened up in modern works of art and indeed in the work of art generally. In the case of that exhibition this was done in order to preserve a closed and violent space, a space from which a delusion about "moral values" could be imposed. But there is a less obvious and crude way in which this closure of the new happens. I will return to this point in the afterword.

What becomes evident from this excentric history that was inaugurated by ancient Greek philosophical reflections upon the relation of word and image is that it is only now, after this long history, that we arrive at that Greek beginning with the sort of understanding and perspective that lets us be ready to take up the questions posed there—long ago—in a new way. The current situation in which we address painting today permits us to ask again the same questions Plato posed about speech and writing, painting and thinking, the nature of the image, and the authority of the *logos*. We should not be too confident in this situation since we are just at its beginning, and the beginning will be long. But it is clear that if we are to address these questions anew, then we need, if nothing else, a new vocabulary for speaking of painting, one that is not tethered to the notion that such images need to be understood as representations and as copies. Of course, this does not mean that we can simply jettison old aesthetic concepts as if they were simple fictions or errors; rather, it means that we need to understand the radicality of the challenge to philosophy and to speaking that is confronted in painting. This challenge has always been present, but modern art is able to make its character evident in the most striking of ways—and so, we begin there.

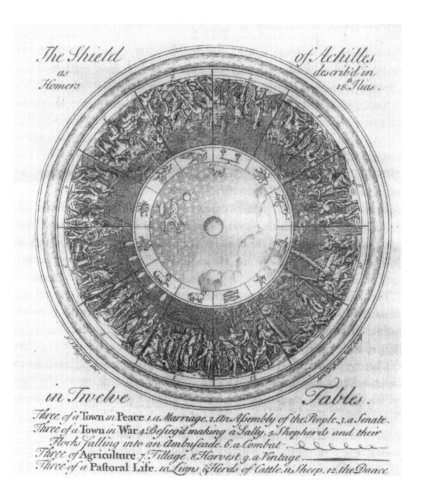

The Shield of Achilles as Homers described in 18.th Ilias.

in Twelve Tables.

Three of a Town in Peace. 1. a Marriage. 2. an Assembly of the People. 3. a Senate.
Three of a Town in War. 4. Besieg'd making a Sally. 5. Shepherds and their
Flocks falling into an Ambuscade. 6. a Combat.
Three of Agriculture. 7. Tillage. 8. Harvest. 9. a Vintage.
Three of a Pastoral Life. 10. Lions & Herds of Cattle. 11. Sheep. 12. the Dance.

FIGURE 1. Achilles' shield from Alexander Pope's translation of Homer's *Iliad*

FIGURE 2. Cy Twombly, *Fifty Days at Iliam, Shield of Achilles*, 1978

FIGURE 3. Pascal death mask

FIGURE 4. Cave painting (Lascaux)

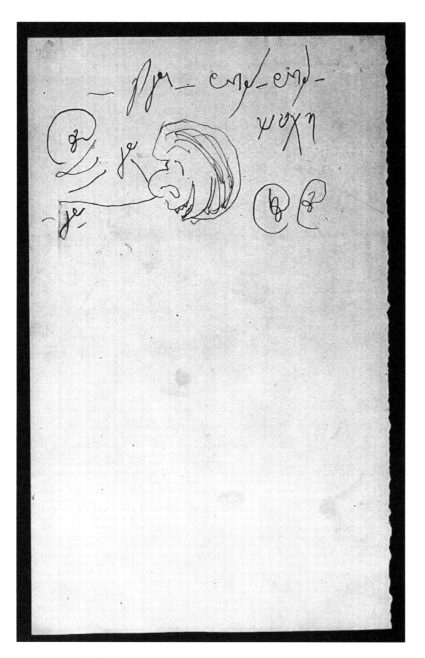

FIGURE 5. Freud doodle

FIGURE 6. Raphael, *Transfiguration*, 1516–20. Scala / Art Resource, N.Y.

FIGURE 7. Franz Marc, *Deer in the Forest*, 1913. *The Phillips Collection, Washington, D.C.*

FIGURE 8. Paul Klee, *Tod und Feuer* (Death and fire), 1940. Oil and colored paste on burlap, original frame 46.7×44.6 cm. *Zentrum Paul Klee, Bern*

FIGURE 9. Paul Klee, *Sichtbar machen* (Make visible), 1926. Pen on paper on cardboard, 11×30.3 cm. *Zentrum Paul Klee, Bern, Livia Klee Donation*

FIGURE 10. Paul Klee, *Mural from the Temple of Longing*, 1922. Oil transfer drawing and watercolor on primed gauze on cardboard, 26.7×37.5 cm. © *The Metropolitan Museum of Art / Art Resource, N.Y.*

FIGURE 11. Paul Klee, *Der Gott des nördlichen Waldes* (God of the northern forest), 1922. Oil and pen on canvas on cardboard, 53.5×41.4 cm. *Zentrum Paul Klee, Bern*

FIGURE 12. Paul Klee, *Kleine Felsenstadt* (Small town among the rocks), 1932. Oil on canvas, original frame 44.5×56.5 cm. *Zentrum Paul Klee, Bern*

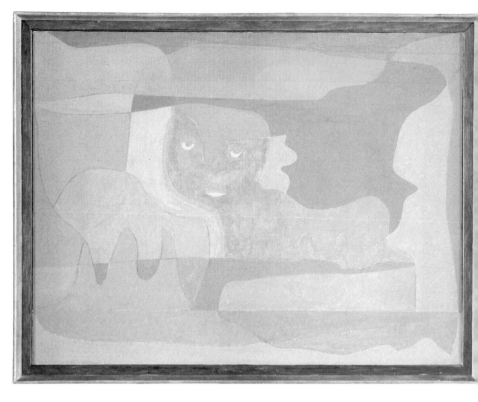

FIGURE 13. Paul Klee, *Ruhende Sphinx* (Sphinx resting), 1934. Oil on primed canvas, original frame 90.5×120.5 cm. *Zentrum Paul Klee, Bern*

FIGURE 14. Paul Klee, *Harmonischer Kampf* (Harmonized struggle), 1937. Pastel on cotton on colored paste on burlap, original frame 57×86 cm. *Zentrum Paul Klee, Bern*

FIGURE 15. Paul Klee, *Gesicht einer Gegend* (Face of a region), 1938. Colored paste on paper on cardboard, 40.6×66.7 cm. *Zentrum Paul Klee, Bern*

FIGURE 16. Paul Klee, *Heilige aus einem Fenster* (Saint from a window), 1940. Watercolor, red chalk, and chalk on paper on cardboard, 29.2×20.8 cm. *Zentrum Paul Klee, Bern*

FIGURE 17. Paul Klee, *Hoher Wächter* (Superior guard), 1940. Wax paint on canvas, original frame 70×50 cm. *Zentrum Paul Klee, Bern*

FIGURE 18. Paul Klee, *ein Tor* (A gate), 1939, 911. Tempera on primed paper, 31.8×14 cm. *Fondation Beyeler, Riehen/Basel*

FIGURE 19. Hon'ami Kōetsu, *Calligraphy of a Poem,* Edo Period (1615–1868), early seventeenth century. Gold, silver, and ink on paper, mounted as a hanging scroll, 7½×6¾ in. (19×17.1 cm), mounted 33¾×11¾ in. (85.7×29.8 cm). *Philadelphia Museum of Art*

FIGURE 20. Werner Scholz, *Antigone*, 1949–50. © *Museum Folkwang, Essen, Germany.*
Despite intensive research, the copyright holder could not be completely identified. Further
information can be obtained from the Museum Folkwang in Essen, Germany.

FIGURE 21. Julius Bissier, *Fische* (Fishes). © *2011 Artists Rights Society (ARS), New York /* *VG Bild-Kunst, Bonn*

HEIDEGGER AND KLEE:
AN ATTEMPT AT A NEW BEGINNING

Has the challenge of modern art, the new that it exposes, been addressed philosophically? To what extent have those who today work out of the tradition defined as moving from Kant to Nietzsche through Hegel—a tradition that, for the lack of a better word, we call "continental"—managed to take up the questions about art and the image, the questions about painting, posed by that tradition? To what extent has the hermeneutic situation of the present genuinely opened up the question of the relation of word and image in a way that allows the presumed authority of the *logos* to be interrogated? There are three promises, three outstanding questions, that define the legacy of this tradition and that need to be posed today if the question of the image and the challenge of the work of art is to be pursued.

First, does the work of art open up a path of thinking outside of the empire of the metaphysical assumptions that have defined philosophy since its inception? Since Plato, philosophical considerations of the work of art have tended either to regard such works as exiled from thinking or to credit them but only by subordinating their achievement to the authority of philosophy. To ask, as one today must ask, if art marks out a prospect for thinking apart from philosophy as it has long been defined is to risk opening thinking to fundamentally new possibilities that are not defined by philosophy as it has been. So, one would need to ask, What might philosophy become if it took its start and impulse from the experience that art opens?

Second, if this experience is to be appreciated, then some cherished philosophical prejudices will need to be overturned. More precisely, since the framework and language that have long defined philosophical approaches to the work of art have been defined by assumptions that conceal the image and denigrate the achievement of the artwork, a new approach and a new vocabulary for thinking and speaking of the work of art are needed. For instance, one must ask how it is that language can let painting show itself without demanding only that it "speak." A translation between word and image will always be necessary, but it is no longer possible to be unselfconscious about the shifts and alterations introduced by such translation, in short by moving the image into the domain of the *logos*.

Third, art underwent its own revolution that began just at the end of the tradition that ends with Nietzsche. This means that if the work of art is to be taken seriously, if the challenge to philosophy that comes from the image as image is to be confronted, then the new forms of painting— abstractions that present images without objects—that now define how art opens the world need to be addressed from the outset. But if that is to happen, then one needs to ask how far one can bridge the gap between traditional forms and modern forms of painting. To what extent has modern art opened something fundamentally new, something that escapes even what art of the past had brought forward? Or is it the case that such novel forms of painting represent another evolution in the same possibilities of painting that we have always confronted?

—————

The first significant effort to take up the questions posed by this tradition and to move forward to a new philosophical beginning by addressing the originality of the work of art is Heidegger's "The Origin of the Work of Art." Completed in 1935 (two years before the *Entartete Kunst* exhibition), "The Origin of the Work of Art" went through three drafts (1933–34) and was not published until 1950 (in *Holzwege*). It was a text that Heidegger criticized very soon after he delivered it as a series of lectures, and yet it was also a text that he drew upon constructively throughout his career. "The Origin of the Work of Art" was the first significant, but certainly not the last, step in a long series of essays, lectures, and seminars devoted to exploring the possibility of thinking art anew and of beginning philosophy anew on the basis of this possibility.[1] I do not intend to take up this text in all of its complexity. I do, however, want to highlight some of its key points and then turn to Heidegger's own criticisms of it in order to ask about its limitations with regard to the task of thinking painting at this historical juncture. Heidegger is clearly attempting to address the questions and to push forward the possibilities with regard to the achievements of the work of art that have been opened up by the continental tradition of reflections upon the work of art. His intent is clearly to take seriously the full and most radical implications of the work of art. The question, however, is how far he has succeeded in doing this and how far he has recognized the transformations in art—especially painting—at this historical moment.

The project of destroying traditional philosophical categories for speaking of artworks is among the primary intentions of "The Origin of the Work of Art." The opening section of the text that quickly dispenses with notions like substance and accident, sensation, and formed matter makes this abundantly clear. Every inherited framework for speaking of the work of art is exposed as a distortion of the work. Heidegger's argument is that rather than opening up the being of the work, these notions foreclose it from the start. But Heidegger's purpose is not simply to destroy traditional aesthetic categories; his effort in this text is equally to forge a new vocabulary proper to art: notions like work, world and earth, struggle, clearing, rift, and endowing all need to be understood as efforts to resituate the language that speaks of art. In light of these opening criticisms of traditional philosophical categories, there should be little doubt that Heidegger understands the project of this text as being something completely apart from what has long been called aesthetics or art theory. The link between art and truth, which is characterized as a fundamental event when Heidegger says that art is an "essential manner in which truth happens,"[2] highlights the point that Heidegger sees as his task in "The Origin of the Work of Art," namely to demonstrate how the work of art can serve as an element in the new beginning that philosophizing must find if it is to respond to the deepest needs of our times. In short, it is immediately evident that "The Origin of the Work of Art" explicitly addresses the first two questions that I have identified as confronting one who would take up the challenge of art to philosophy at this stage in the history of those questions. But what of the third question, which refers to the new challenges posed by *modern* art? If Heidegger does respond to the contemporary revolutions in art—especially in painting—then it is in a far less obvious manner, if indeed there is any response at all. The one feature of his text that does make at least a reference to modern painting is, of course, his mention of van Gogh's painting of the peasant shoes. However, there is no clear consideration of the way in which van Gogh's work stands at the beginning of the transformations in painting that will serve to separate it from traditional forms of painting. In other words, Heidegger does not seem ready to address the specific challenges of modern art that are put to philosophy, above all to the question of the relation of word and image.[3] One explanation for this is that Heidegger is generally not as interested in painting as he is in poetry. Immediately after the publication of "The Origin of the Work of Art," Heidegger found himself beginning a preoccupation with Hölderlin's work that would last for several years; painting seems secondary to Heidegger's concerns with art. Nonetheless, van Gogh, who as much as anyone marks the entry into modern painting, is not an insignificant figure for Heidegger generally, and Heidegger's obvious and real interest in van Gogh antedates the references to van Gogh in "The Origin of the Work of Art."

Heidegger's relation to van Gogh is marked by a strong identification with van Gogh.[4] This relation began early in his career, but with very few exceptions no trace of it seems to remain after the time of "The Origin of the Work of Art."[5] From Heidegger's letters to Löwith and Jaspers as well as Gadamer's recollections, we know that Heidegger "read" van Gogh's letters "too much" during the First World War but that he still had not yet seen an original work of van Gogh's as of 1922.[6] Indeed, Heidegger did not see an original painting by van Gogh until he visited Amsterdam in 1930. When he writes of van Gogh's painting in "The Origin of the Work of Art," Heidegger is very likely looking at a postcard reproduction of a painting he had never seen.[7] There is a strange sense that the painting itself is not so terribly important. Indeed, in light of this and other ways in which Heidegger's discussions of painting seem to rapidly become abstractions, one ultimately begins to suspect that Heidegger's first attraction to van Gogh was primarily through van Gogh's letters to his brother, Theo, that is, through words rather than images.[8] Indeed, Gadamer tells us that Heidegger copied passages out of those letters and kept them on his desk. This view is reinforced by the fact that the first reference to van Gogh in Heidegger's lecture courses (1923) was to van Gogh's letters, not to his paintings. That reference is to a letter from October 15, 1879, in which Vincent writes to his brother that he would rather "die a natural death than go to the university"; of this, and of the struggle of van Gogh to paint, Heidegger said that "he worked, tore paintings from out of his body and went insane in this confrontation with existence."[9] It is one of the indications that Heidegger's identification with van Gogh concerns the non- or even anti-academic character of van Gogh's attitude to the world. Van Gogh's letters to his brother give voice to a feeling for life that runs deeper than anything that can be given voice in traditional philosophy or academic argument. One finds in those letters a sort of existential authenticity that is expressed by the non-academic and tortured relation to the world that van Gogh himself documents. Heidegger so deeply related to those letters that when he had his house built in Freiburg (1928), he had a citation from the Bible that he very well might have found among van Gogh's letters placed above the entry door: "Behüte dein Herz mit allem Fleiss; denn daraus geht das Leben [protect your heart with great diligence for all truth passes through it]."[10] In the end, one begins to suspect that Heidegger's relation to van Gogh was as much, if not more, based on literary grounds as painterly ones. In light of this, it is not so surprising that Heidegger's remarks about the van Gogh painting of the peasant shoes in "The Origin of the Work of Art" tell a story that one cannot easily see in the painting itself.[11] Nonetheless, even if it does not seem primarily to be his paintings that attracted Heidegger, van Gogh would stand as the chief representative of painting—and not just modern painting—for Heidegger in "The Origin of the Work of Art."

One other painter whom Heidegger seemed to admire during the early years and to whom he turned at a decisive moment in a lecture course is Franz Marc. The course in question took place in 1926, when Heidegger was hard at work on *Being and Time*. The reference to Marc surfaces in the context of a discussion of the notion of truth as it is understood in light of the problematic of time. In that lecture, after a discussion of the Kantian schematism, Heidegger refers to Marc's painting *Deer in the Forest* (see figure 7) in order to give an illustration of what he means by a "hermeneutic concept," which is a concept unlike the ordinary conception of a concept since it is defined not by its universality or stability but by its agility. Such a "hermeneutic concept" is a concept that is sufficiently subtle and supple to be the concept proper to truth. After saying that the presentation of the image in art opens a realm of presentation that is defined neither as a copy (*Abbild*) nor as the schematization of a concept in the Kantian sense,[12] Heidegger says:

> The photograph of a dog and the image of a dog in a zoologi-
> cal handbook and a painting of "the dog" in each case present
> something different and in a different way. The deer in the forest,
> which, for instance, Franz Marc has painted, are not these deer in
> a particular forest, but rather "the deer in the forest." . . . In artistic
> presentation a concept is presented which, in this case, presents an
> understanding of something existing; more precisely, it presents
> an understanding of a being and of its being in the world as a being
> with me in my environment; namely, the being-in-the-forest of the
> deer and the way and manner in which its being-in-the-forest is
> presented. This concept of the deer and this concept of its being
> we call a hermeneutical concept in contrast to a pure concept of
> the thing.[13]

Gadamer often recounted the dramatic way in which Heidegger spoke of this painting: Heidegger would imitate a deer in the forest and how it noticed the presence of another animal by smell, sniffing the air, lifting its head suddenly, and becoming very still. This was one of the ways in which he spoke of what the word *Wesen* meant: as a presence that is noticed before it is able to be known. Heidegger's point does not concern the deer directly; rather, it is the painting of the deer that, as Heidegger suggests, "presents an understanding of something" that is at issue here. What is significant is that the painting is not guided by the "pure concept" but rather by the "hermeneutical concept," that is, by a concept that is situated and that does not lift what is to be understood out of its situation. But this turn to Marc, like the turn to van Gogh in "The Origin of the Work of Art," never presses the point of what it is about the painting that permits such a hermeneutic concept to emerge, nor does it seem to be responsive to the specifically modern character of those works and to the special challenges posed by paintings in which the object is beginning to disappear. In other words, while Heidegger does turn to painting in order to break out of traditional philosophical orders, he does not seem to fully recognize the full force of the revolutionary character of painting in the present age.

The years immediately following "The Origin of the Work of Art" were a time in which Heidegger increasingly came to see a connection between the question of technology and the task of thinking the work of art: both needed to be thought from out of their roots in the Greek notion of *techne*. "Making" and "production" became key concepts in Heidegger's further reflections upon the work of art. Paintings seem to drop out of the picture for Heidegger; references to artworks became almost exclusively references to poetry, and these references were almost always to the poetry of Hölderlin. This was also the period in which Greek tragedy tended to become increasingly important (though it too would typically be mediated by Hölderlin), and with the notion of tragedy the idea that the task of art is to expose and present an ineluctable agony—the agon of existence itself—took hold. One should not be blind to the political circumstances surrounding—and at times even saturating—Heidegger's thought at this time.[14] Though Heidegger, since "The Origin of the Work of Art," linked the achievement of art to the founding of a political world, he stayed far away from all such discussions that concerned the National Socialist manipulation of the aesthetic sphere. In fact, it was during this period that Heidegger developed a sense both of the failure of art in the historical present and of the limitations of his own efforts to grasp the achievement of art in "The Origin of the Work of Art." Thus, we read the obvious self-critique in the fragmentary text "Die Überwindung der Metaphysik" (1938–39), where Heidegger says, "That is why the attempt to rescue art by means of a more original interpretation of the work of art is misguided."[15] Heidegger's sense that the present is a time in which art is "lacking" and in need of "rescue" is clear, but the sense one found in "The Origin of the Work of Art" that philosophical reflection was capable of such a recue mission has quickly evaporated and been replaced by a real despair about the possibility of art in the present age.

This does not mean that Heidegger believed it necessary to completely jettison the analysis of the artwork that he developed in "The Origin of the Work of Art." Quite the contrary: one of the convictions that was central to his approach to art in that text would only be reinforced in subsequent years. More precisely, Heidegger would reaffirm and continue to emphasize the links between art and history, as well as that between the history of art and the history of metaphysics. Thus, in *Beiträge* he writes: "The question of the origin of the work of art does not seek a timelessly valid definition of the essence of the artwork, which could serve as the guiding thread of a retrospective account of the history of art."[16] If there is to be a determination of the character and achievement of the artwork, then it will need to be thought in relation to a genuine sense of history. Furthermore, this history, properly understood, is essentially the same history that is at stake in the determination of the nature of philosophy itself: "That which holds true for 'metaphysics' in general also holds true for reflections on the 'origin of the work of art'; a reflection which prepares a decision that is historical and transitional."[17] The condition and future of philosophy cannot be fully thought independently of the work of art. Hegel makes a similar claim about the importance of history in taking up the challenge art poses to philosophy, but he focuses the movement of this history more on the material character of the work and the relation of this materiality to the form of the work; in other words, he operates within the form-matter distinction that Heidegger so severely criticizes.[18] For instance, marble (and sculpture) especially suited the Greek world and its sense of form incarnate, while painting was more appropriate to the Christian world and its more abstracted sense of form. The difference in each case depended upon what it was that needed to be expressed (the world of animals and plants, the real presence of the divine, the transcendence of the divine, and so on). Each stage of Spirit's appearance in the artwork reflects as well how Spirit is "preoccupied with its [sensuous] other";[19] in other words, at each stage of its history, art measures itself (and is to be measured) according to the highest stage of Spirit in that moment. And, of course, for Hegel that highest stage will be defined by philosophy. The "pastness" of art emerges once Spirit becomes preoccupied essentially with itself, that is, once philosophy comes to realize that philosophy itself is its own highest theme. Once this happens, it no longer has any need to find itself in its "sensuous other" but is able to operate in the plane of Spirit *as* Spirit. That, for Hegel, is the point at which philosophy ceases to mirror the character of the art of its times. That is the point at which philosophy comes into its own sphere, and it is, for the same reasons, the point at which art—as well as its history—is no longer able to match the history and achievement of philosophy. Until that point—which according to Hegel is first attained in Hegel's own thought—the history of art and of philosophy are, in some sense, doublets on one another.

In his 1942 lecture course on Hölderlin's "Der Ister," Heidegger once again emphasizes this interwoven kinship of art, history, and philosophy, and he returns to the topic of the image in order to criticize metaphysical conceptions of the image. This time he refers specifically to the allegorical, symbolic, and metaphorical approaches to images, all of which he contends rest upon the metaphysical distinction between sense and meaning, sense and the non-sensible, form and matter—a distinction that, as phenomenology has long since demonstrated, is no longer tenable. Heidegger argues that only once we learn to see images independently of this distinction, only once we think the sensible freed of its subordination to the supersensible, will images cease being regarded metaphysically.[20] But Heidegger's chief concern in this lecture course is to reaffirm the significance of history for addressing the image in the work of art and to once again draw a line between that history and the history of metaphysics so that the overcoming of one can be seen of a piece with the overcoming of the other; that is why he notes that "the essence of art stands and falls with the essence and the truth of metaphysics."[21] He makes this link clearer and gives it some substance when he says that the

> transformations in the essence of metaphysics correspond to transformations in the essence of art found in the sensible image. That is why, for example, Greek vase painting, the murals of Pompeii, the frescoes of the cathedral on Reichenau from the Ottonian period, the paintings of Giotto, a painting of Dürer, and an image from C. D. Friedrich are not only different in their style, but also the style itself comes from different metaphysical essences. What is called reality in Dürer's picture of "Columbine" is defined differently than the reality of a medieval fresco; more precisely, both works of art bring the real in different senses of reality into the appearance of an image.[22]

In some sense, such a claim is neither original nor terribly controversial. That one can speak of a zeitgeist or a worldview (two notions of which Heidegger was invariably critical) that embraces most every form of human creativity is almost a platitude. There is indeed some sense in which Heidegger's remark in this instance, which he does not significantly amplify, does not go far beyond such a commonplace. But his point does aim well beyond that commonplace. One sees this, for instance, in his remark that "nonetheless, the manner in which art penetrates the being-in-the-world of historical human being, illuminates and positions human being with respect to itself and with respect to the world—in other words, the manner in which art is art—receives its law and fittingness from the way in which the world as a whole is opened to human being." He continues by noting that "since Plato, the law and fittingness of the openness of the world, and the assignment of human being in the world, is determined by that which one has called 'metaphysics.'"[23] In order to explain this, Heidegger notes that metaphysics has been defined by a division of all that "is" into two realms: *aistheton* and *noeton,* the realm of sense and the realm of supersensible intelligibility. He then turns to these examples of painting that he lists as a way of showing how the transformations in the history of metaphysics—now understood as the transformations in the history of this division—are mirrored in the transformations in the history of art. What one sees are different forms, different manners, in which the world of sense is presented by the world of intelligibility that is defined by art.

Heidegger has a number of intentions in this brief passage (sandwiched between interpretations of Hölderlin's poetry, which shape many of his larger concerns in this text), one of which is to show why and how it is that throughout the history of metaphysics, philosophy is seen as "higher" than art when measured with respect to truth, and another of which is to show that Nietzsche's inversion of that judgment still operates within the same economy of a division between sense and intelligibility. His argument, however, is that it is precisely this division itself that is in need of overcoming. The turn to Hölderlin that follows pursues this overcoming in that poetry. What is curious about this remark is not that Heidegger finds something of a duplication operating between the history of metaphysics and the history of painting, nor that he finds Hölderlin's poetry to be a resource for overcoming the limitations constitutive of the very project of a metaphysically determined thinking, but that he does not carry his remarks about art through to the present age. Nothing is said to suggest any kinship between the end of metaphysics and the revolution in painting that had been taking place for almost fifty years by this point (Heidegger made this comment in 1942). Nothing is said of the disappearance of the object, the non-representational character, of modern painting. In fact, the only thing that is said of art at this moment in history is simply that ours is a time of "artlessness." The specific question of modern art and of the challenge it makes to philosophy is not asked. In the end, one wonders if this question *can* be asked in the context developed in "The Origin of the Work of Art."

The central—indeed the exemplary—artwork in that text, the discussion of which serves to open many of the key notions for the discussion of art in general, is the work of architecture, namely, a Greek temple. While van Gogh's painting of the peasant shoes does play a significant role in Heidegger's analysis of art in "The Origin of the Work of Art"—indeed, it serves as the most important opening of the question of the work of art—its role is ultimately trumped by the work of architecture, specifically, Greek architecture of the time of the pre-Socratics. When he introduces the architectural work, he does so by saying that he has "deliberately" chosen a work that "cannot be counted as representational art . . . [and that] does not copy [*abbilden*] anything."[24] Once again, one is struck by the absence of any mention here of non-representational modern art and also by the reference instead to an exemplary artwork that is no longer possible in the fullest sense; one could not build such a temple in such a fashion except as something that would border on kitsch. Heidegger suggests that what must be said of this temple—which, significantly, is now a ruin and hence in some sense no longer a temple—is that it gathers (a term that he strangely uses in the present tense) a people into their historical situation and lets *physis* be seen. Heidegger puts it this way: "The temple work joins together and gathers around itself the unity of those paths and relations in which birth and death, disaster and blessing, victory and disgrace, endurance and decline acquire the form and the course of the destiny of human being. The ruling expanse of these open relations is the world of this historical people."[25] Heidegger is well aware that the Greek world to which this temple belonged and the stage of philosophizing that it mirrors are both past (of course, this is a complicated notion that does not simply mean "forgotten" or "insignificant" or even "gone"). He is also clear that the new beginning—which, he argues, thinking needs to find today—does not entail a sort of replication of the first, Greek, beginning. The temples of today, if such are to be built, will not be mimes of this temple of the sixth century BCE.[26] The peculiarity is not that Heidegger turns to a work of architecture here—there is, of course, room for a fruitful analysis of architecture in this context—but that Heidegger's example is anachronistic and thus makes a statement not just about the character of the work discussed but equally about the absence of works of such a character. And yet, Heidegger does not address the anachronism of his own key illustration, nor does he ask what might be said of art of the present age.

Heidegger describes the ancient Greek temple as setting history in motion, as giving it a "jolt" and galvanizing possibilities, as gathering a people and a place into possibilities. This "power" of the artwork is decisive in the movement of history and in a very real sense "defines" the achievement of the work of art far more than any sense of the pleasure we might take in the beauty of such works. But the real question posed by Heidegger's anachronistic exemplar of the ancient architectural work of art is whether or not a painter such as van Gogh still possesses the power of setting such relations into motion. Does the painting that hangs in the museum still preserve the founding power to gather a people together in the modern age? Can the painted work still gather a people into its appointed historical destiny? Can art still open the relations that found the life of a people?[27] Such are the questions that one needs to ask in light of the analysis found in "The Origin of the Work of Art."

––––––––––

Heidegger did not ask these questions—to the extent that he asked them at all—until after the war. In the end, it would be almost two decades after the publication of "The Origin of the Work of Art" before he even broached these issues that had their roots in that essay of 1935. Instead, during the two decades after the composition of "The Origin of the Work of Art," Heidegger's first impulse regarding modern art was to see it as an instance of the technologization of the world and as belonging, in some sense, to the *Gestell*. For instance, he explicitly says this as late as 1956 in *Der Satz vom Grund* when he situates "non-objective" and "abstract" art within the world construct of technology and science, thereby subordinating the question of art to the question of technology.[28] In short, the radical character and the power of the work of art is fully tamped down whenever the topic of art is defined by modern art. In its first formulation, Heidegger's encounter with art was intended to develop fundamental words for thinking in our times. So, in "The Origin of the Work of Art," one sees clearly that the real achievements of art are profound and reach into the movement of history itself—at least insofar as art is defined by the sort of art one can understand from out of the exemplary case of the Greek temple.

However, for the two decades following that text, the achievement of art—at least insofar as it was measured with respect to modern art, above all to modern painting—not only lacked such radical power but actually needed to be understood as an instance of the powers that constrict the world in the present age. Far from being a site of liberation from the closing down of history, Heidegger tended to regard modern art as yet another instance of the dominance of technology as a force of driving the closure of the space of appearance. The exception to this, of course, was not found in painting, especially not in modern painting, but in Hölderlin's poetry, which sets a standard and opens possibilities that reach far into a different future.

This judgment about modern painting—that it ultimately needs to be judged as an instance of modern technicity—would, for many years and for the most part, be Heidegger's final word about abstract painting. Occasionally, he acknowledged his own limitations with respect to such works and so confessed, as he did to the art historian Erhart Kästner, that "I cannot make any judgment about your interpretation of modern art because I lack the necessary experience."[29] With one significant exception, these are the poles—either damning it as the simple reflex of modern technicity or conceding his own ignorance with respect to it—that define Heidegger's relation to modern painting after "The Origin of the Work of Art." But the one exception to these alternatives marks an engagement with modern painting that has a profound impact upon Heidegger, and it opens questions and possibilities that Heidegger never satisfactorily answers, never closes. When Heidegger finally does honestly engage the challenge of modern art in the form of non-representational painting, he does so almost exclusively with reference to the work of Paul Klee.[30]

It is difficult to know precisely when Heidegger began to take notice of Klee's work. No record of any remarks by Heidegger about Klee can be found before 1956 (since much of Heidegger's work is still not available to us, there always remains a chance that something will surface); nonetheless, one would have expected some familiarity at least. Klee was closely associated with Franz Marc, whom Heidegger admired, and Klee's affiliation with the Bauhaus must have caught Heidegger's attention, even it was a negative attention.[31] What we do know is that in 1956 Heidegger visited Basel where he saw the Beyeler Foundation's exhibition of eighty-eight recently purchased Klee paintings. The impact of these paintings upon Heidegger was immense and seemed not only to overturn his negative views regarding modern art but also to alter, if not genuinely shift, his understanding of what was at stake in the work of art in general. He was so struck by what he saw in them that he would write of those paintings to Heinrich Petzet (almost two years later) that "something which we all have not yet even glimpsed has come forward in them."[32] Heidegger would also begin to speak with friends about his plans to write a "pendant" to "The Origin of the Work of Art" that would start out from what he believed he had found in Klee's work.[33] In short, Heidegger saw in Klee's work possibilities for thinking the achievement of art that outstripped the reach of that achievement as it was outlined in "The Origin of the Work of Art."

A qualification is necessary from the outset here: when asking what it is that Heidegger found in Klee's paintings, it is important to recognize that Heidegger did not regard Klee simply as representing an outstanding case of modern art but rather as a true exception to such art. In other words, Heidegger's criticisms of modern, abstract painting still remain largely in place even as he discovers Klee's work. Klee is the exception—an almost singular exception in the West—for Heidegger (the qualification "in the West" is important here). It does need to be said that Klee is not quite the sole exception since there are other cases that also seem to qualify as exceptions to the desolate condition of modern painting: besides van Gogh and Cézanne, one might also include here Modersohn-Becker, Braque, and Chillida, all of whom are mentioned at some point approvingly but, with the exception of Chillida, none of whom receives any extended attention or genuinely philosophical attention.[34] But in the end, it is Klee who opens the question of painting for Heidegger anew and, in the process, opens a window to something other than the "artlessness" that Heidegger has long deemed to be the character of modern art. While Hölderlin might be said to give indications of the future of poetry, Klee seems to be the one who can give indications of the future of painting. In both cases, the significance of that future reaches far beyond anything constricted by the notion of aesthetics. Both reach into the future of a community and the possibilities of thinking the world that are liberated from the calcifications of metaphysics. Both, in other words, open realms of great promise.

But this discovery of Klee in 1956 had a brief life: it arrived with great suddenness and no clear anticipation, and it vanished with the same suddenness and absence of any preliminary signs of that departure. So, despite this initial excited sense that there indeed is a painterly opening upon the future, a mere four years after that sudden enthusiasm, Heidegger wrote a letter (to Krämer-Badoni) on April 25, 1960, that repeats his previous rejection of modern art: "You write that I have 'overlooked the epoch of abstract art [in "Origin of the Work of Art"].' Expressed more cautiously:

abstract art never gets explicated. Why not? Because in my opinion there is nothing thoughtful to say about it so long as the *essence* of technicity—i.e. the essence of truth (language as information) that emerges with technicity—is not sufficiently clarified."[35] In other words, there is an obstacle defining our historical moment that prevents any genuine engagement with painting. That obstacle is the still-unthought essence of technicity, the essence of production in the present age. To think that essence, one needs to begin by thinking the destitution, the abandonment, of being in the historical present. While the encounter with the work of art belongs to the effort to think this essence of production, Heidegger's contention is that modern art is unable to offer this opening simply because it has been caught up, unthinkingly, in the distortions of modern technicity.[36]

And yet, for a brief period Heidegger seemed to find such an opening in the work of Klee, in whom there is "something which we all have not yet even glimpsed." It is worth noting that Heidegger was not alone in this judgment. Foucault, for example, says that "in relation to our century, Klee represents what Velásquez had been able to represent in relation to his."[37] Others too singled out Klee's work as privileged for the task of thinking painting today: Gadamer, Benjamin, Merleau-Ponty, Deleuze, Adorno, and Bloch, to name only the most prominent among them. In light of this, it is fair to say that "ascertaining Klee's influence on these thinkers is not only a historical matter but also a philosophically significant task. Indeed, the sequence of these philosophers' interpretations of Klee reads like the descent of twentieth-century philosophy itself."[38] Heidegger's comments on Klee, most of which are found in the so-called "Notizen zu Klee," are often fragmentary and lack a clear context. In the scant texts in which he mentions Klee, Heidegger gives what seem to be rather oblique and often obscure hints as to what it is that he finds in Klee that is so exceptional.[39] While Heidegger's texts on Klee do not provide sufficient detail or clarity to presume that one could offer a detailed or systematic interpretation of his encounter with Klee, they are sufficient to point the way to issues and questions that stimulated Heidegger so much and were the source of such excitement. To do this, and then to pursue the possibilities that Heidegger so abruptly abandons, is the intention of this book.

To follow this intention, it is helpful to return to the problematic that opens this book: how is one to speak of such images without presuming that language will not distort as well as disclose what those images are "about"? There is one way in which Klee was clearly exceptional as a painter and that helps one who would speak of his painting, namely, Klee was someone with very real literary tendencies and gifts, and, for several reasons, Klee's writings will be the best way of entering Klee's work as Heidegger understands it. Klee was a prolific and uncommonly articulate writer. His attention to language and his inventiveness and almost poetic gifts as a writer show up in many ways: his lectures on art and about his own paintings; his notebooks, diaries, and letters; and even in the self-consciously significant role that titles play in his paintings. Uncommonly sensitive to the problem of speaking of images, Klee was also uncommonly dedicated to the task of doing just that, appropriately, thoughtfully, and in a way that deepens, rather than departs from, what is to be seen. So, while we lack substantial texts from Heidegger that might help us understand how we might best see and understand Klee's paintings, we do, nonetheless, have a large number of texts by Klee himself that can present something of his self-understanding. Heidegger too read these texts of Klee, and he let what he saw in the paintings be guided in a very real sense by those texts.

———————

Most of Klee's writings would not be published until after his death (1940) and after the war (1945). The years between Klee's death and the publication of most of his writings—the years of the Holocaust, of the atomic bomb, of Dresden, and of slaughter and destruction on a scale never before seen or even imagined—would profoundly change the world and demand a new self-understanding of our being in the world. Art would be changed as well, and because Klee's work sits on one side of this historical divide, his work is regarded as belonging to the "classical" modern, that is, to art that had not yet confronted the unimaginable that happened and the radical turning point in history that still has no single name but that seems to find its apotheosis in the name "Auschwitz."[40] So, most of Klee's writings would first be distributed in a world almost unrecognizable to the world in which they were composed (curiously, Heidegger's "The Origin of the Work of Art" had the same fate: composed finally in 1935, it would not be published until 1950). The one important exception to this is Klee's text "Schöpferische Konfession [Creative Confession]," which was published in the quite prominent series of texts titled *Tribune der Kunst und Zeit* (1920). The first sentence of that essay is well known and has been cited often: "Art does not repeat the visible, rather it renders visible."[41] Composed fifteen years before Heidegger would complete "The Origin of the Work of Art," Klee's text anticipates the central assumption driving Heidegger's essay; namely, it is a declaration that art, properly understood, cannot be thought as being a copy of something existing but needs to be thought as an origin, as calling into being something hitherto unseen. "Creative Confession" was one of the few major essays published during Klee's lifetime. One written text that would eventually be recognized as one of Klee's most significant texts, "On Modern Art," was not published until after the war (1945), even though it was first presented in 1924 as a lecture commemorating the opening of an exhibition of modern art in Jena. That essay, together with "Creative Confession," must count among the first and most important statements about the nature of painting understood by a painter who was speaking from and to the point of view of modern art. Not surprisingly, Heidegger's reading of these two texts, which he undertook in 1956, seems to have been quite careful and thorough (he even went so far as to compile his own index), and he would use those texts as interpretive guidelines for his own efforts in approaching Klee's paintings.[42] But it should be remembered that in this case, unlike the case of van Gogh, it was the paintings themselves, paintings that were once classified by the Nazis as "degenerate art," not the literary works, that would send Heidegger back to Klee's essays. In the end, it is the paintings, not Klee's written texts, that are at the center of Heidegger's concerns and to which the texts are to return us. Even after Heidegger finally came to appreciate Klee's written texts, he would never come to regard them as measuring up to the achievement of the paintings. He would never fully accept or adopt Klee's own vocabulary for speaking of painting, and he would never turn to an extended study of Klee's more detailed pedagogical texts. Nonetheless, one best comes to understand what Heidegger saw in Klee's paintings by first understanding something of what he found in Klee's own articulated self-understanding.

Klee's lecture "On Modern Art" begins by speaking about the limitations he faces by the fact of having to *speak* of painting at all, above all to speak of, and even in front of, his own paintings. In short, he begins by remarking upon the classical philosophical problem of the relation of word and image. He ends the lecture by calling attention to the relation of painting to the movement of life. It soon becomes clear that Klee's lecture, which is dedicated to asking what it is that we are to see in his paintings, stands as a real counter, a real reply, to the long history of the philosophical dismissal of painting. He begins:

> If, in such proximity to my works, which really should speak
> their own independent language, I still seek words, then I feel a

little bit anxious about whether there are sufficient reasons to do this and about whether I will do it in the right way.

For, as much as I feel certain that—as a painter—I possess the means of moving others in the direction that I am driven, I am just as certain that I feel that the word is not given to me to point out those paths.[43]

This comment is not a platitude that says simply that paintings should speak for themselves. Klee never hesitated to search for words proper to images. Quite the contrary, he had an uncommon literary sense, even a sense of the *need* or the *summons* of the image for the word despite every acknowledged antagonism between them. His awareness of the problematic —and yet necessary—relation between words and images is acute and is a decisive concern of both his writings *and* his paintings. His pictorial works often present this enigma of the relation of the word and the image in a painterly manner. In such instances, one sees that there is for Klee a sort of double life of the word and the image; each crosses into the other even while remaining itself.

So, for instance, in the image of the painting *Tod und Feuer* (Death and fire), the word *Tod* is spelled out (figure 8). Likewise, in *Sichtbar machen* (Make visible), the eyes of the person are simply the repetition of the same letter *S* that is found in the title, which is itself a part of the painting (figure 9).[44] The examples of words that enter into the painting as a very real element of that painting are numerous. One soon comes to realize that the opening words of this lecture in 1924 call attention to a very real question about the relation of words and images driving Klee's work. One can also argue, rightly I believe, that Klee's reflections on this question go far beyond what one typically finds on this matter in the history of philosophy.

In his diaries, Klee writes of his desire "to be able to reconcile opposites! To express the great manifold in a single word!"[45] The urge to bring images and word into some sort of reconciliation drove Klee. He wrote (both poetry and prose), gave lectures, taught, and took the titles of his works so seriously that he referred to the giving of a title as the "baptism of the work." One cannot account for Klee's hesitations about speaking of his paintings by suggesting that, as a painter, he was simply more "at home" with images than with words. Not only was Klee fully at home in both words and images, but his great goal was to find a way to reconcile them. However, being at home in both forms, Klee was also fully aware of the difference between words and images that makes such a reconciliation ultimately impossible. He explains what this difference is later in his lecture, when he makes more precise the difficulty of speaking of paintings by call-ing attention to the "different dimensions" of each. When he does this, he calls attention—against all expectation—to the "deficiency of the temporal character of language" with respect to painting. He writes:

> It is not easy to find one's way in a whole that is composed of parts which belong to different dimensions. And nature is just such a whole, as is its transformed copy [*Abbild*] art.
>
> It is difficult to survey such a totality—whether it is nature or art—and it is even more difficult to help another find such a comprehensive view.
>
> This is due to the temporally distinct methods, which are the only ones available to us, for conveying a clear spatial image [*Gebilde*] in such a form of representation [*Vorstellung*]. The reason for this is the deficiency of the temporal character of language.
>
> With such a means we lack the ability to discuss a multi-dimensional simultaneity in a synthetic manner. Despite all of these deficiencies we must concern ourselves with the parts in their detail. . . .
>
> That which the so-called spatial arts have long achieved, that which even the temporal art of music has achieved with its resounding precision in polyphony, this phenomenon of a simul-taneous multi-dimensionality which helps drama reach its climax, is something that we unfortunately cannot find in the realm of linguistic didactical expression.
>
> Contact with these dimensions must, *in this case,* take place externally, after the fact.[46]

In short, the complexity of the image, which emerges out of its "multi-dimensional simultaneity," outstrips the capacities of language that are wedded to a sequential consequentiality. In making this comparison between words and images, Klee echoes Lessing, who spoke of the same compression of painting and the same extension of the narrative as well. Lessing, like Klee, sees in this the heart of the irreconcilable issues that bind words and images. But Lessing, unlike Klee, finds in this same difference the "advantage" of language. Lessing is clear: "And what are these advan-tages? The liberty to extend his description over that which preceded and that which followed the single moment represented in the painting; and the power of showing not only what the artist shows, but also that which the artist must leave to the imagination."[47] In other words, Lessing—and in this he is quite representative of a long-standing philosophical prejudice regarding painting—understands painting as riveted to, and thus limited by, the moment, whereas language stresses itself across time. Klee's remarks take this traditional understanding of the roots of the distinction between word and image—the temporal difference between them—and turn the evaluation of that distinction on its head. His emphasis on the temporality of the work points to one of the keys of his own understanding of painting, namely, that the painting needs to be seen as a movement, not at all as static, not frozen in the moment.[48] Klee understands the painting as the product of a dynamic activity, and, insofar as it succeeds, the painting remains a dynamic work. Many of Klee's own paintings (for instance, figure 10) make an effort to present this movement of the painting by means of arrows and other directions for movements. There are many ways in which Klee's paintings exhibit this dynamic quality. In his lecture, he refers to what he calls the simultaneity of forms or the "multi-dimensionality" of painting, which is found in layering, overlapping forms, depth, perspective, and other manners. This palimpsest-like character of Klee's work is not to be explained simply as a spatial overwriting of images; rather, it is one way in which a painting simultaneously presents a happening of events that are different, and this overwriting of images is, at bottom, a temporal matter. There are other ways in which this movement at the heart of painting is presented in Klee's work. But this movement, whether or not it is explicitly depicted as such, belongs to the essence of all painting for Klee. It belongs in the relations between colors, shapes, and lines, as well as in the manner in which the painting comes to be. To see the painting is to see the movement of life that courses through it.

Further developing this point, Klee alludes to a kinship between the "spatial art" of painting and the "temporal art" of music. Understanding this inherent proximity uniting music and painting moves to the heart of Klee's understanding of painting and to how it is that we are to see his paintings as a matter of movement. It is not insignificant that he was a quite accomplished musician (a violinist) and was always surrounded by musicians (his father was a music teacher, his mother a trained singer, his wife a pianist). His lecture notes from the Bauhaus, in which Klee "scores" his thoughts on painterly composition, even bear traces of this deep relation to music, and a great many of his paintings have explicitly musical themes. This bond between painting and music for Klee is fundamental and calls to mind Nietzsche's remark that music gives birth to painting by giving off "sparks of images."[49] Klee would, I believe, agree but would also add that painting, in a like fashion, must be understood as giving birth to music. But it is not the subject matter or the titles of Klee's paintings that serve as the real link between painting and music for him. It is rather in the form that this temporal link is most deeply expressed.[50]

Klee often spoke and wrote of "polyphonic painting" as a way of clarifying the simultaneity that can define painting. In a 1917 diary entry, he writes that "simple movement seems banal to us. The element of time [as sequence] must be eliminated. Yesterday and tomorrow as simultaneous. In music, polyphony helped to some extent to satisfy this need. . . . Polyphonic painting is superior to music in that in it the time element becomes a spatial element. The notion of simultaneity stands out even more richly."[51] In his lecture "On Modern Art," Klee gives two reasons for this liveliness of painting, this relation to time that outstrips even that of music (which is, of course, nothing but time made loud). The first reason has already been noted: the simultaneity of forms or what Klee calls the "multi-dimensionality" of painting, which is found in layering, overlapping forms, depth, perspective, and other manners. This palimpsest-like character of modern, abstract painting is not to be explained simply as a spatial overwriting of images; rather, it is one way in which a painting simultaneously presents a happening of events that are different. The second account that he gives of this temporality of painting is more complicated and goes to the core of what he says in his lecture. To make this clear, Klee's text itself needs to be cited in more detail and to be given a more extended commentary.

At the outset of that lecture, Klee compares the artist and the tree:

I want to compare this many-rooted and many-branched order [of the things of nature and of life] to the root work of the tree.

The sap flows to the artist from the root, flowing through him and through his eye.

In this sense, he stands in the place of the trunk.

Pressured and moved by the power of this flow, he leads his vision further on, into the work.

Just as the crown of the tree unfolds itself temporally and spatially, becoming visible on all sides, so too with the work.

It would never occur to anyone to demand that the crown of the tree should grow in the image of its root. Everyone understands that there cannot be an exact mirroring relation between above and below. It is clear that the different functions of different elemental realms must produce lively divergences.

. . . In the work of art, which has been compared to the crown of the tree, there is a necessary deformation by virtue of entering into the specific dimensions of the pictorial. For in this we find the rebirth of nature.[52]

Art is thus no longer understood as copying nature; rather, if there is a sense in which art "copies" or "repeats" nature, then it is in this parallel between the coming-to-be of the painting and the life of nature as it is witnessed in the growth of the tree that is rooted in the earth and reaches toward the heavens. The movement of life that pulses through the tree is the same movement that defines the successful work of art. Both movements bring into being something new. Both give birth to a world. From this point of view, in which we see that what painting repeats is the movement of life at the heart of nature, we can come to understand why it is that art is not the reproduction of nature but its rebirth. This movement, out of which the natural world itself emerges and comes to be, that drives the growth of the tree and plant, is what the artist needs to repeat and further. As such, art furthers life. Klee argues further that more than simply not being a "copy" of natural "realities," when painting takes nature up there is a "necessary deformation" attending this rebirth. Such a deformation of "realities" is not at all a failing or failure of art. Quite the contrary, it is the consequence of the vital energy that defines art, just as the crown of the tree is the outgrowth of the vital energy sent forth by the roots of the tree. The real failing of art, if one is to speak of that, is lodged in the effort to wed oneself to the "realities" of nature and to insist upon their "reproduction" or "representation" rather than to let this deformation take place. But this deformation is not, in the end, of great significance, since the artist knows that the finished "forms of appearance" and such "realities" in nature do not come close to the heart of nature itself. That heart is first found once one approaches nature's "formative powers":

> First, he does not attach any compelling significance to natural forms of appearance as do many realist critics. The artist does not feel so closely tied to these realities because he does not see these finished forms as the essence of the creative processes of nature. Rather, the artist places more worth upon the formative powers, than the resulting forms.
>
> The artist is, perhaps unintentionally, a philosopher. And while, like the optimists, he does not hold this world to be the best of all possible worlds, and while he will also not say that this

world around us is too bad to be taken as an example, he will nonetheless say:

in its present shape, this is not the only possible world of all worlds.

In this way, the artist surveys with a penetrating gaze the things which nature parades, formed, before his eyes.

The deeper he looks, the easier it is for him to extend his view from today to yesterday. In this way, he is all the more deeply imprinted by the essential image of creation as genesis, rather than by the images of the finished products of nature.

. . . There, where the central organ of all movement—temporal and spatial alike—whether it is called the brain or the heart of creation, activates all functions—who would not want to dwell there as an artist?

In the womb of nature, in the archaic ground of creation, where the secret key to all lies kept safe.

. . . But our pounding heart drives us down from above, deep down to the archaic.

That which grows up from these drives, whatever it is called—be it dream, idea, phantasy—is only to be taken with complete seriousness if it is united in a form with the proper means of making images [passenden Bildnerischen Mitteln restlos zur Gestaltung verbindet].

Then those curiosities become realities, they become the realities of art which enlarge life as it typically seems.

Because the realities of art not only more or less give back (with some feeling) what is seen;

they also make secret visions visible.[53]

If one wants to say that the painter "copies" or "repeats" nature, then it is the power of nature to create, to bring into being, the life of nature—not any of the particular results of that life—that is "repeated." This distance from a concern with objects and with the visible, this preferred proximity to the *life* of nature, can, perhaps, help us understand Klee's diary entry of 1920 that reads: "On this side, I am ungraspable. For I live just as well with the dead as with the unborn. Somewhat *closer to the heart of creation* than is usual, and yet by far not close enough."[54] This passage crystallized what Heidegger found in Klee; it became so central for his understanding of Klee that he copied it and kept it on his desk. As Merleau-Ponty would say, the painting is "the blueprint of a genesis of things."[55] It is not a reproduction of the finished products of that process of genesis. Modern art is closer to its own heart, to this "genesis of things," insofar as it has let go of the lure of representation and has recognized that this process of genesis emerges more clearly in abstraction. For Klee, the object is something of a distraction in the artwork. The given "reality" at any particular moment is contingent and can (and will) look different at another time. The essence of the painting cannot be found in what is represented since the finished forms of nature, objects, are not what drive the artist. What drives the artist is not found on the visible surfaces that characterize the finished forms, the objects, of appearance. Gripping though these surfaces may be, fascinating for vision that does not see far, objects are, in the end, a distraction from the deepest and most intense vision that guides the painter: "This being so, the artist should be forgiven if he regards the present stage of the appearing world as accidentally fixed temporally and spatially. He regards it altogether inadequate in comparison with the depth of his vision and the intensity of what he feels."[56] Or, as the opening sentence of "Creative Confession" puts it, "Art does not repeat the visible, rather it renders visible"—what it makes visible is the life of nature: *genesis itself.*

There is one more point that Klee makes in his lecture "On Modern Art" that needs to be noted. It is a remark in which Klee acknowledges that this creative life, this effort to draw close to genesis itself, is not a life lived in isolation or apart from history. The passage reads:

> I said "with the proper creative means." For in this the decision whether images or something different will be born. Here too is the decision about the kind of images.
> Our tumultuous times have brought out much confusion and chaos—if we are not too close to these times to be deceived.
> . . . Sometimes I dream of a work of such a great expanse, ranging through the entire realm of the elemental, the objective, the substantial, and the stylistic.
> This will surely remain a dream, but it is good, from time to time, to keep in mind this vague notion.
> Nothing can be rushed. It must grow, it should grow up of itself, and if the time for such a work ever comes, all the better!
> We still need to search for it.
> We have found parts, but not the whole.
> We do not yet have this final power, for:
> no people carries us [uns trägt kein Volk].

But we seek a people, we began over there, in the Bauhaus.
We began there with a community to which we each gave what
we had.

We cannot do more.[57]

This final remark about the relation of the artist to a community comes
as something of a surprise since nothing said hitherto would seem to pre-
pare for it. The reference to the Bauhaus, which the Nazis would take over
(removing Klee's right to teach and sending him into exile in Switzerland),
is fairly clear: a community of like minds to share ideas, especially when
such minds are working outside of inherited forms and traditions, is something one can appreciate. In the end, one does not give birth to the new
in full isolation, but *as an artist* one seeks a community. One must do this,
even if such a community does not exist as yet. But the remark about the
need the artist has to be borne[58] by a people is rather puzzling: "no people
carries us." Klee seems to be suggesting that there is a necessary social and
political role of the artist. The creation of new forms, the making visible
of what has not yet been seen, the conduit to the "heart of creation" serve
to give birth to new possibilities. This seems to be the role of the artist,
but it is the task of a people to carry this creative opening within itself. The
generative character of the work of art opens the world, enlarges it, and
brings forward possibilities that shape who we are and can be; it shapes the
ground of a community. Despite this grand claim on behalf of art, Klee
ends with the sad sense that in our times, such an opening is not the case.
This concluding remark is not far from Heidegger's claim in "The Origin
of the Work of Art" that art founds and gathers a people into its historical
destiny. Klee's sense that art brings possibilities into the world is akin to
Heidegger's argument that art initiates a "shock" in history and that it is, in
the end, best understood as an origin. And this too: the despair one hears
in Klee—"no people carries us"—is not far from Heidegger, who laments
the "artlessness" of our times and wonders if art can still happen in the age
of the culture industry.

––––––––––

Let me return to Heidegger and take up his remarks on Klee from
1956. In the notes that he made during his visits to Basel to see the Klee
exhibition, Heidegger comments upon—and even sketched—ten works by
Klee (see figure 8 and figures 11–17).[59]

Heidegger saw these paintings without yet having read Klee's written works, and so his relation to Klee at this point was solely defined by

the paintings themselves, not by any theoretical concerns that Heidegger would later find to be articulated by Klee. Heidegger's notes are very fragmentary; at times, they even seem to be quite disconnected, so the hermeneutic problem of attempting to find a point of view in the notes is especially difficult. Nonetheless, one can detect themes and concerns that are to be expected in light of his work in the years following "The Origin of the Work of Art." For example, one finds a concern with the limitations of the image metaphysically conceived as a copy; in other words, the idea that representation can ever lead us to understand the image in the work of art is simply discounted. And yet, at the same time one finds the reaffirmation of Heidegger's earlier conviction that modern non-representational art remains metaphysical, that is, that the non-objective character of much of modern art is really only the negation of the object, not the disappearance of the object in favor of the appearance of something else. To regard the object as simply "negated" is to suggest that modern art is still tied to the object—even if only as that which needs to be annihilated. But one even finds hints of a criticism directed at "The Origin of the Work of Art" in Heidegger's notes. So, for instance, one finds the remark: "work—*ergon; energeia*—metaphysics? Does the look to the work-character suffice? Can there still be works? Or, is art destined for something else?" The implication of course is that one of the key notions for thinking through the character of art unfolded in "The Origin of the Work of Art" is perhaps insufficient for this task. Perhaps art is destined to be something other than a "work." Amid all of these criticisms—of representation, of modern art, of Heidegger's own approach to the work of art—there is one exception noted: Klee. In his works, something else, "something which we all have not yet even glimpsed," appears. That is why Heidegger writes: "transformation of art? The sign of that—!Klee." The question of course is what does—or should—one see in Klee's work?[60]

Heidegger's notes emphasize—as does Klee himself in his lecture— the need to move away from a focus upon the object in the painting, as if the reproduction of what is given were the task of painting. That is why Heidegger writes, "The less the object is indicated—the more appearing; the whole world comes along." Of course, given Heidegger's condemnation of modern art in general as simply presenting the "negation" of the object and not its genuine disappearance, it is clear that the fading of the object in Klee needs to be seen as something new and not simply as the negation of what is. Other notes give some clarity about this disappearance of the object and, all importantly, of the subsequent visibility of something "not yet even glimpsed." Thus, one reads the following: "not images, rather conditions" and "no longer mere *eidos*," and with reference to *Heilige aus einem Fenster* (see figure 16), Heidegger comments: "When one does away with [*auslöscht*] the image-character—what is *'seen.'* What ones 'sees' is 'production' [*Hervorbringen*]." The "transformation in art" that one finds in Klee's work is "a transformation of 'positing' [*Setzens*] into a different bringing forth [*Her-vor-bringen*]." So the image itself as an *eidos* of sorts, as representing something else and as something "posited" by the artist, is "transformed" in Klee's work into another way in which something is brought forth. It is no longer the case that something is "posited" in the painting, something placed in it as representative of something else. Rather than a positing, one sees in Klee's work a different bringing forth, a different letting be seen, namely one that lets the bringing forth itself appear. This different bringing forth, this different production that one can see here, is, perhaps, what Klee called "the genesis of things." In other words, one sees this genesis itself, not the "end result" of that process of genesis, not the objects of the world.

Two further notes by Heidegger seem to reinforce this view: "That which *Cézanne* prepares for and begins in *Klee*: production [*Hervorbringen*]!" and "Decisive: the freedom of the motion of infinite 'genesis.'" Both of these remarks emphasize that what Heidegger sees in Klee's work—something that is anticipated by Cézanne as well—is *movement, the movement of life itself.* Painting here is seen to be a matter of becoming, of infinite genesis, of birth. It is a *free* motion without reference to cause, without concern for a "why," and without letting this motion come to rest in a finished form, that is, in an object that has been represented. It is not the object as such that is presented but the coming into being of a world, the presentation itself, that is presented. The similarity of these notes that Heidegger made while viewing Klee's paintings in the quite private setting in Basel with Klee's own comments about the temporal character of the painting is striking, especially given that Heidegger had yet to read Klee's own comments.

In his notes, Heidegger concedes that the framework of "The Origin of the Work of Art," which, he says, thinks from out of works of art of the past, cannot account for this productive element that is to be seen in Klee's work. Consequently, rather than turning to "The Origin of the Work of Art" to think through what appears as this free motion, this genesis, in these paintings, Heidegger turns instead to his own later notion of *Ereignis:* "No longer should future art be handed over to the setting up of world and the production of earth, as was thematized in the work of art essay: rather, the bringing forth of relations from out of the happening of the fugue [*Erbringen des Verhältnisses aus Ereignis der Fuge*]." By thinking the artwork from out of his own notion of *Ereignis*, Heidegger is able to say that "in this 'production' objects do not need to disappear, but as such [as objects] they step back into a world that is to be thought from out of the *Ereignis*." This reinforces Heidegger's long-standing contention that abstract art need not be understood as escaping the metaphysical character of representational painting. It is not the mere absence of the object that lets the movement of genesis be seen. The object does not "need" to disappear; in fact, the object is not at all the issue; it is, in some sense, simply a possible distraction. So, in the end one must say that it is possible, indeed just as possible for representational painting as for abstraction, to render this genesis visible. This is so much the case that one must say that it is the sense of this emergence, of the painting as a giving birth, that has always defined the height of painting's achievement. This emergence out of that which grants relations, out of *Ereignis*, this production that Klee himself refers to as a relation to *genesis*, is, for Heidegger, what renders Klee's work beautiful—one should add, it is this that defines the character of beauty in all painting: "Where does the height and the depth of being [*Seyns (das Ereignis der Fuge)*] hide itself for Klee? *The beautiful—Ereignis und Erblickung.*" This means of course that beauty is not, as Kant argued, a matter of the harmony of the faculties, nor is it a matter of the representation or the reproduction of objects: "The less the object is indicated—*the more appearing;* the whole world comes along" (emphasis added). Rather, beauty is a matter of this "appearing," this "more appearing," "more shining." The phrase that Heidegger uses here, the "um so erscheinender," is key and should be heard in the Greek sense of *phanesthei*. There is an intensification named here. It is not a matter of suggesting that what is presented shows something of the "essence" of what is seen, but rather this intensification is rooted in the way there is *life* that is seen—life in the sense of movement, genesis, becoming, birth, even, it will need to be said, of death.

Heidegger had made a similar remark in connection with his discussion of production in "The Question Concerning Technology." The context of that remark, which is found in the analysis of techne and technology, is not an accident but is rather indicative of what is at stake in asking about all showing and appearance—including that which is proper to the work of art—in the present historical moment. Heidegger had long insisted that the still-unthought essence of technicity is what hindered the possibility of the work of art in our age, but now, with the help of his comments on Klee, one can see now that the colonization of the sense of production in the age of technological domination is what obstructs the work of art as itself a quite different form of production. In "The Question Concerning Technology," Heidegger does not pursue the confrontation of art and technology in the present historical moment. Rather, he simply alludes to what will need to be pursued if this confrontation is to happen, saying that art "brings the true into the splendor of what Plato in the *Phaedrus* calls *to ekphanestaton,* that which shines forth most purely."[61] Beauty then is the intensification of the coming into being of the world. This is what is missing in the age of the *Gestell* and of *Machenschaft*—an age in which the stamp of reproduction and multiplication have assumed the place where coming into being can happen. This coming into being one finds in the work of art is, in some sense, to be understood as a sort of birth, and it is precisely this birth of the new, this movement into and of life, that is obstructed in the present age.

The sense of "newness" that belongs to great art, the sense that it has never been seen before no matter how often it is seen or how old the painting is, is one indication of this relation of the painting to birth. Merleau-Ponty makes a similar point when he says, "The painter's vision should no longer be regarded from the *outside,* only as a 'physical-optical' relation with the world. The world is no longer in front of him through representation; rather, it is the painter who is born in things by virtue of a sort of concentration and coming to itself of the visible. In the end, the painting does not relate to anything empirical unless it is first 'autofigurative.' It is only the spectacle of something by being a 'spectacle of nothing,' by breaking the 'skin of things' to show how things become things, how the world becomes world."[62] What Heidegger found in Klee was precisely this painting of genesis, this presentation of birth into a world. One finds a love and sense of this articulated in Klee's theoretical work as well, especially in his lecture "On Modern Art," which Heidegger eventually read and admired. This is what Heidegger sees in Klee, and while he finds hints of this in a few other painters, it will be Klee's work that most embodies this sense of birth and genesis. One can argue—rightly I believe—that this sense of genesis can be seen throughout the history of painting. It is certainly not entirely nor solely the province of Klee's work, nor would Heidegger suggest that it was. But, for Heidegger at least, it was Klee who opened his eyes to this possibility that defines the image in the work of art.

Seeing the painting not as a reproduction of the given but as the trace of production itself, as the bringing forth of relations, as repeating something of a birth into the world, is no small matter. Nor, given our habits of seeing, is it easy to see the coming into a form rather than focusing upon the finished form itself.[63] Heidegger argued that there is an essential connection between Western conceptions of the image—as a sort of *eidos*—and metaphysics: we have not yet truly seen what painting can show because we have been looking in the wrong ways. To paint apart from such images that are concerned with reproducing the world is to begin to set art on a new, non-metaphysical path. It is even to move art away from what it has always been for Western culture. That, for Heidegger, is what one can see in Klee's work: "not images—rather states [*Zustände*]. No more mere *eidos*, and nothing present, no object." While Heidegger does not say it, I think that he might be quite comfortable with the claim that Klee is a painter of what the Greeks called *physis*. Our sense of nature as a realm of given objects (open to measurement and calculation among other relations we might have with them) does not at all say what *physis* named for the Greeks. *Physis* was typically used as a word to correspond to transitional moments that were fundamental.[64] While this sense of *physis* as an event, as generative, is so strong that by the time Aristotle conceptualized the sense of this word, he would do so by speaking of it in terms of its relation with *genesis*, it would lose this meaning after Aristotle, becoming, by the modern age, the word "nature" understood as a realm of determinate objects.[65] Even as the meaning of this word changes over time and through translations, some echo of its original Greek sense will never quite be obliterated. Thus, the Roman word *natura* with its root sense still attached to the meaning of "birth" and "natality" (*natio*). To say that Klee is a painter of *physis* is to say that he recovers the original ancient Greek sense of that word: *physis* is thus a matter of the archaic, beginnings, and sources. But it is equally a matter of death, endings, and disappearances—of the full movement of life into and out of being.

While Heidegger, like Klee himself, emphasized the productive and generative character of Klee's work, that emphasis should not eclipse the equally significant countermovement to the productive character of *physis* that also defines the movement of *physis:* the movement of disappearance, decay, and death, of the passage into darkness as well as into light.[66] In this regard, it is worth noting that Heidegger was especially taken by a number of Klee's paintings that have suffering, loss, or a sort of melancholy as their theme (which, given Klee's general playfulness, is not always what one first sees in Klee). In other words, the darker side of the movement that operates in Klee's work did not go unnoticed by Heidegger. We know from Petzet, not from Heidegger's own notes, how deeply affected Heidegger was by three paintings in this regard: *Patientin* (Woman patient), *Gezeichneter* (Marked man), and *ein Tor* (A gate) (figure 18).

Patientin was completed in 1933—a time of great despair and of a profound sense of loss and departure for Klee.[67] Petzet describes Heidegger's encounter with that work as follows: "In front of the picture 'Woman Patient' . . . a picture that seems to reach with its deepest roots into the most extreme recesses of agony, Heidegger remained looking for a long time and eventually said that our mutual friend Nagel (a doctor) must see this work for 'a doctor can learn more here than from out of a medical textbook.'"[68] In a similar fashion, Heidegger was especially drawn to the first painting that Klee completed after he learned of his fatal illness and the suffering that lay ahead—*Gezeichneter* (1935).[69] It is a work full of resignation and sadness. About the third painting, *ein Tor* (1939), Heidegger remarked that "that is the gate through which we all must pass sometime—death."[70] Klee's late work, still marked by the sense of genesis and birth that Klee had early on identified as the hallmark of painting's greatness, is increasingly stamped by a sense of loss and death. This does not signal a change of sensibility; rather, it signals the growing awareness that death belongs to the movement of *physis* just as much as does birth. These are the transitions that define our relation to the world and that define the movement of life that is *physis*. Here the painting comes to be understood as a matter of becoming, and here the representational character of the work becomes insignificant for the presentation of *physis*.

While Heidegger's comments can begin to open up the challenge of art from outside the orbit of metaphysical assumptions, and while they might even help clarify what one should see in Klee's work, questions nonetheless remain. Above all, how, if at all, do these comments, especially the claim that the painting is at its heart the presentation of the movement of life, bear upon the ancient question of the relation of words and images that has long intervened in any question of painting? Does seeing something like genesis, like *physis*, at work in painting have any impact upon how one is to understand the wider significance of the work of art?

———

One finds hints as to how Heidegger might answer such questions in a seminar titled "Die Kunst und das Denken" that Heidegger held together with the Japanese Zen master and philosopher Hoseki Shin'ichi Hisamatsu on May 18, 1958—two years after Heidegger's first encounter with Klee's work. In that seminar, Heidegger speaks of the way in which he finds in Klee a breaking away from Western presumptions and habits of seeing. It is a discussion in which Heidegger speaks of how the very notion of art that shapes the Western standpoint inhibits any effort to think the experience of art. The questions of earlier years are taken up once again here: To what extent can art free itself from metaphysical assumptions? How is one to understand painting without reference to representation and objects? What, if any, future does art have in the present age? Heidegger opens the discussion by saying:

> We want to make an effort to come to terms with some essential traits of art by starting from our European standpoint. The question whether or not art still has a place in our times is a pressing question.
>
> [But the discussion immediately switches to East Asian art and so Heidegger asks Hisamatsu—]
>
> Is it an *image* that is seen in an artwork in Japan?
>
> [To which Hisamatsu replies by speaking of a Japanese word for art that was used before the Japanese conception of art was influenced by the West—]
>
> That is 'Gei-do': the way of art. 'Do' is 'Tao' in Chinese; it does not only mean way as method. It has a deeper inner relation to life, to our essence. Thus art plays a decisive role in life itself.
>
> [Heidegger contrasts this with European art, which—]
>
> in its essence is signaled by the character of *presentation* [*Darstellung*]. Presentation, *eidos*, making visible. The artwork, the structure of the image [*Gebilde*] brings into an image, makes visible. In the East Asian world on the other hand representation is an obstacle, that which is bound into an image [*Bildhafte*], the image itself that makes visible is an obstruction. . . . In East Asian art, nothing objectified that has an effect upon the viewer is set forth. At the same time, the image is not a symbol, not an image laden with meaning [*Sinnbild*]. . . .
>
> [To which Hisamatsu adds—]
>
> Indeed, the essence of the line that is drawn does not lie in the symbol-character, but in movement. . . . The artwork is not an object behind which a meaning or a sense might be found; it is rather an immediate effect [*Wirken*]—movement.[71]

Both Heidegger and Hisamatsu make a point of saying that Western abstract art fails to open this possibility of art because it remains too bound to forms insofar as it is defined by the obliteration of form. In other words, both contend—as Heidegger had long insisted—that Western abstract painting is still not painting that emerges from out of a different experience of the world; rather, it emerges simply out of the negation of the world as it has long been understood and, as such, remains tethered to that world, even if only as its negation. Hisamatsu puts the point this way: "Abstract painting: the essence of its abstraction lies in the fact that the painter pursues the annihilation of that which has a form. This movement over and beyond forms is still bound to the form precisely because it seeks something over and beyond it. Zen painting, on the other hand, moves in precisely the opposite direction. It is concerned with bringing the formless self to us."[72] Heidegger makes a similar point: "In East Asian art nothing of an object that acts upon the observer is brought forward. The image is not a symbol, not an image with meaning; rather, in painting I perform the movement to the self."[73] Zen painting is not at all attached to a form or structure but is centered on letting this movement come forward. Western art, with its insistence upon the importance of what is represented, misses this sense that the real significance of art is found in the movement it inaugurates. Focusing upon the object is, in the end, simply a distraction and even an obstacle to what it is that art can bring forward. But while the criticisms of Western art are rather sweeping, Heidegger makes a point of once again exempting Klee from this charge and thus of suggesting that something new appears in Klee's work. Something, one might say, that is non-Western emerges from within the Western tradition in the figure of Klee.[74]

What is most striking about this seminar protocol is the similarity of the language used to describe Klee's works in the notes of 1956 and the language used to characterize Zen art in this seminar of 1958. The same themes are emphasized: the disappearance of the object, the distraction of representation, the effort to see a movement in painting, the sense that painting touches upon what is original in the sense of originating, of birth. The protocol of the seminar discussion does not press the issues as far as one might like, but it does open the way to a conversation about the very definition of art, the relation of art and culture, as well as about the future of art in our times. In passing, the question is posed about the different realms in which one might find an art form proper to Zen. Flower arranging and the tea ceremony are mentioned as examples; calligraphy too is a possible form and one that could open up difficult questions regarding the work of art and how we are to understand the image. Calligraphy is singled out again when, the day after the seminar, Hisamatsu says to Heidegger that Klee's work "somehow has something of Japanese calligraphy about it"[75] (see, for example, figure 20).

Had this question of writing been pursued, a productive opening to the question of the relation of word and image could have been found since among the great mysteries of language is the fact that it *lets itself be written.* There is an iconographic potential in the word, and the realization of that potential in script is the transformation of the word into a wholly new form. Zen calligraphy is one possible way of thinking through the ancient question that appears when we recognize that writing is language placed into an image, just as paintings, if they can be said to be a language of sorts, are a language only as written. Plato saw something of this when he has Socrates say to Phaedrus: "Writing, Phaedrus, has this strange power, quite like painting in fact; for the creatures in paintings stand there like living beings, yet if you ask them anything they maintain a solemn silence. It is the same with written words. You might imagine they speak as if they were actually thinking about something, but if you want to find out about what they are saying and question them, they keep on giving the one and same message eternally."[76] In Zen calligraphy, one finds another, perhaps quite different way of approaching this question. Plato criticizes both writing—"the corpse of a thought"—and painting for the silence that each maintains before a question. But in saying this, another aspect of the sameness of writing and painting is overlooked. What is the same in painting and writing is not found in the character of what is represented, nor is it lodged in a putative silence before a question. Rather, their sameness rests in the way each gives evidence of the "free movement"[77] of life. This, according to Hisamatsu, is what one finds in Eastern paintings that is so submerged, and even lacking, in Western painting. But in Klee, one finds a promising opening to this topic.

————————

This opening, like the other openings that are promised by the engagement with Klee, is never fully taken up and developed by Heidegger. The day after the seminar in which the opening to something not defined by Western metaphysics is announced, Hisamatsu left Freiburg and Heidegger presented him with a book of Klee watercolors and sketches. Hisamatsu presented Heidegger with an image of the temple where the tea ceremony was first practiced.[78] Heidegger largely ignored Klee after this seminar—at least in his written works. At the outset of the lecture "Time and Being" (1962), he mentions Klee's *Tod und Feuer* and *Heilige aus einem Fenster,* but only to invoke these as examples of what one cannot immediately expect to understand. They are presented as illustrations of what needs interpretation.[79] It is not just Klee but the very question of painting itself that disappears from Heidegger's reflections. When he writes "Die Kunst und der Raum" in 1969, none of the language of the "Notizen zu Klee" is to be found, and the theme is sculpture and its relation to place; painting is no longer a defining question. In light of the enthusiasm and insights of Heidegger's earlier encounter with Klee, this is both surprising and disappointing. But there is a reason that painting—indeed the very idea of art and its promise—drops away for Heidegger. Clearly, such a reason would need to be far-reaching in order to turn Heidegger away from the prospects that he found so promising in the work of art. And yet one does find in Heidegger a real turn away from the promises he found in Klee. With increasing frequency, Heidegger would come to regard our historical moment as one in which the possibilities of a production such as one might find in Klee are extinguished.

This sense that ours is an age in which vital possibilities are foreclosed was not new for Heidegger; rather, what was new was the sense of a foreclosure of possibilities now needed to triumph over an opening that Heidegger found, however briefly, in Klee and that promised to break through the closure of our times. The optimism ignited with his encounter with Klee, the sense that the West might still be able to break out of the grip of historical forces that served to calcify the free movement of life, is a rare interruption in an otherwise quite bleak view of our historical present. Already in 1938, Heidegger would judge the work of art in our times to be so captured by the framework of metaphysics that the attempt to think it from out of its "originality"— as was done in "The Origin of the Work of Art"—must be called "misleading."[80] This was said only three years after the completion of the lectures on "The Origin of the Work of Art." He would even denounce the forms of artworks in the present age as "the ordering of the system [Anlage] of making [Machsamkeit] all things. . . . Art, in its essential sameness with technicity and history, takes over the ordering of beings, the being of which has been determined in advance as machination [Machenschaft]. . . . In this we see the fulfillment of the metaphysical essence of art."[81] The logic of the making that defines machination had seeped into and saturated even the promise of the free making that had long defined the work of art.

So Heidegger's discovery of Klee in 1956, and his sense that in Klee a bridge to non-Western art and its possibilities had been found signaled a change in the exceedingly bleak view of 1938. He saw in Klee another possibility of exercising our productive forces, of understanding how we might find ourselves in the world, and so the promise of seeing the world differently. That is what makes it so surprising when the bleaker view of art returns just a few years later, so that this hope seemed, once again, closed off. This is what one finds expressed in 1961, when Heidegger wrote that "in the time of the culture industry, art is increasingly used up as an option in the modern industrial society. At the same time, the question today remains whether or not art can be destined to a confrontation with the technical world, to take up what is closest to modern technicity and to lead it."[82] A few years later, he would write: "We *no longer* have an *essential* relation to art. We do *not yet* have an *essential* relation to technicity."[83] The question of art is, once again, displaced by the question of technology. Ours is then the time of "artlessness," a time in which art cannot appear in a manner that lives up to its promises. Hegel spoke of the pastness of art, but he never spoke of technology, nor did he speak of technicity as a challenge to art, and in this sense his claim about the pastness of art is not the same question that, according to Heidegger, we face about art today. In contrast to Heidegger's sense of the failure of art to live up to the needs of the times, Hegel's sense of the "pastness" of art is not a sense of despair about the possibilities of the future. Quite the contrary, it is rather an expression of great optimism that history has delivered up even better forms of grasping ourselves and our world in our times than the forms one finds as defining the possibilities of art. Heidegger, on the other hand, suggests that this question about art and this suspicion that ours is an age of artlessness are *the* questions of our times precisely because, unlike Hegel, Heidegger holds to the conviction that something appears in the work of art that cannot appear in other ways—it cannot be overtaken by better forms of thinking ourselves and our world. For Heidegger, then, to say that art is passé—or at least to say that it is absent today—means history has lost the place for art to appear at all. If that is true, then it is a fundamental loss. It signals a loss of the sources that nourish us.

It is important to recognize that, for Heidegger, this decision that art is closed off to us today as a possibility is not simply the judgment that a significant form of cultural life or personal, even human, expression has been lost. Heidegger's despair about the possibility of art at this historical juncture is rooted in far-reaching concerns: "The reflection upon what *art* might be is thoroughly determined and decided only from out of the question of *being*."[84] The despair about art is, at the same time, a despair about that which defines us and which lets us make *sense* of our world and ourselves. Although Heidegger will resist the urge to designate an "essence" of art that is jeopardized today, his remarks on Klee, as well as his 1956 "Addendum" to "The Origin of the Work of Art" (composed in the same year as the "Notes on Klee"), single out the notion of *Hervorbringen* (bringing forth or production) as the key to what is at stake in reflections upon art in our times. Precisely this possibility of production that defines the work of art, that is set free in art, is what is lost in the present age of technical productivity, the age of the *Gestell*.

There is an unspoken assumption that Heidegger makes when he arrives at this decision about the absence of art in our age, namely, that history can extinguish a form of production that is so fundamental, so basic, that it lives—in Klee's words—"close to the heart of creation." The assumption behind Heidegger's assessment of this historical moment is that the evolution of our ways of making and bringing beings into the world has closed off the most vital of those forms of making. This assumption, if we accept it, is sweeping and devastating. It begins with the recognition that somehow, in the midst of all the processes that define the productive life of nature, there is given as well an open space in which we too bring things into being. The web of nature as causal is not so tightly bound that we cannot enter it and indeed even alter it. Among the things we bring to appearance are works of art, works that, as Kant so rightly noted, emerge out of nothing but the abyss of freedom. Other things we bring into being emerge out of a need or purpose, such as the need to sustain ourselves: we grow food, make gardens, reserve water sources, build houses. Others have other, more complex impulses: we build ships to explore space and the sea; we look for ways to ever accelerate forms of communication, to reproduce sound and images, to improve our health and our lives. In short, we live in the world productively and do so in many different ways. We have long known that our productions can work against the life of nature, that our productions are capable of disrupting the fine balance defining nature's own processes. Dams can alter the course of rivers; digging for oil can destroy air, sea, land, and animals; toxins can enter the food chain. But Heidegger's primary philosophical worry is not that we will destroy the economy of nature; his primary concern with the present age is not simply that we are destroying the environment, ourselves, and the fine balance of nature. It is rather that our own doings, our own productions, might be capable of foreclosing the open character of that space for our own productive efforts—even if, by some miracle, our productions did not destroy the economy of nature, even if we did indeed improve rather than damage our world, we would still close off something necessary for the movement of life. More precisely, the worry is that our own productions might foreclose the open space that is not defined by purpose, intention, need, or even reason. In short, what is at risk today are those efforts that are not defined by utility or need but that are defined only by freedom and that illuminate something of ourselves and our world. What is being closed off is the *space* of appearance into which we may make an entry. It is the space of *production* that is closed down in our times. Heidegger argues that the space of production is being constricted insofar as it is increasingly restricted to the horizon of what can be calculated, manipulated, and ordered. While Heidegger does not diminish the importance and stakes of how technology can threaten the economy of nature, it is the economy of production that is his concern and that he finds most in need of attention today.

We belong to the relations and processes of nature, but we have never been held captive by them. But we find ourselves in a sort of double jeopardy today: not only do our actions threaten the relations that define nature itself, but we also threaten to colonize and close off the free space preserved for us in nature. In other words, the threat is that we will hold ourselves captive to the framework of our own machinations, namely, that we will submit the standards of production only to those productions we believe we can control and manipulate. The danger is that only one form of production —that which we believe we can compose and control—will remain possible for us. Clearly, the extinction of productive forms is possible—letter writing provides a clear illustration of such an extinction in our time, powerfully marked by the practice of writing email. The closure of this form in which we produce ourselves has happened quietly, without fanfare or compulsion. A tacit collusion has led to the disappearance of this form of shared language. Nothing forbids letter writing; indeed, for the most part, we have participated in this extinction without hesitation. New forms of communication have emerged—governed by speed and brevity—and it is rather clear that as these new forms come to dominate how we write to one another, few of the coming generation will ever have any relation to the idea of a letter. Even today, insofar as it is still practiced, letter writing has become a boutique form. Obviously, changing a form of production does not only entail a loss, nor should it be the case that a nostalgia for the past sets the standards by which we attempt to understand and judge the present. However, what we do need to understand is that our forms of producing ourselves and of bringing beings into the world shape the possibilities that we hand down to ourselves. As a thought is reduced to a tweet, as the narcissism of the blog comes to govern how we express ourselves, we too risk being reduced. Heidegger's worry is that art, which he has labored to show is the most living and nourishing of our ways of bringing forth into the world, is at risk in our times. And so, in the after-word to "The Origin of the Work of Art" he asks, "Is art still an essential and necessary manner in which the truth that is decisive for our historical existence happens, or is art no longer this?"[85] Is the reduction of the space of free production so restricted, so governed by the logics of what can be calculated, abbreviated, or accelerated, that we are destined to reduce our world and ourselves to the point at which the very possibility of such production is itself extinguished?

Heidegger has not made this decision about the present state of the claim of art upon truth. From his point of view, this decision can, of necessity, only remain as a question at this time, and as a consequence he oscillated between some sense of the possibility of art and, more commonly, a profound sense of its exhaustion. In the end, the sense of the exhaustion of the present age tends to win out, and so even when he found moments of hope, such as he found in his encounter with Klee, that hope would invariably be shadowed by a sense that the shape of our world displaces the possibilities of art. This shadow was so persistent for Heidegger that, in the end, his efforts to pursue the sense of art seem destined to be preempted by a sense that productive life in our times has been colonized in the Gestell. That is why, when he spoke at the Academy of Arts and Sciences in Athens in 1967, Heidegger asked a series of questions that interrupted his previously announced efforts to speak of art in the present age: "How do things stand with art in the industrial society, one whose world is beginning to become a cybernetic world? Will statements about art become a type of information in and for this world? Will the modes of bringing forth of art be defined by how they suffice for the process character and perpetual consumption of the rules of industry? If this is so, can the work still remain a work?"[86] Furthermore, "within the present world which is determined by technicity, is art essential, necessary, and therefore possible?"[87] These are questions that Heidegger would never fully or finally answer but that he understood as defining the basic character of our times.

Heidegger understood ours as a time of transformation (Wandel). It is a time of crisis in the strict sense of that word, namely, the time of a breaking point, a time that cannot endure without a change in its own character. At one point, Heidegger held on to the hope that the "transformation of art" that he saw blossom in Klee (and others eventually: Chillida, Modersohn-

Becker, for instance) would open onto a future that was more alive. But that hope dimmed, and insofar as it remains it does so only as a question that is inseparable from the question of technology: "Art corresponds [*entspricht*] to *physis* and at the same time it is not an afterimage or a copy of what is already present. *Physis* and *techne* belong together in a mysterious way. But both the element within which *physis* and *techne* belong as well as the realm into which art must take itself in order to become that which, as art, remain hidden."[88] This sense that art needs to be traced back to its roots in *techne* is a long-standing conviction on Heidegger's part. What is new is the sense that the open space that has long defined the relation of *physis* and *techne* has been shut down. When Heidegger turned to a serious examination of the work of art in "The Origin of the Work of Art," his argument was that art opened up the possibilities of truth anew and that the effort to find the proper idiom of truth, and to engage history, the world, and the earth in a productive manner found an answer in the being and the achievement of the work of art. Art was that which lived near the sources of life and of its free movement. Heidegger's encounter with Klee did more than renew that argument. In Klee he saw something even more than he had seen before, and Heidegger came to understand the stakes of the question of art with still more clarity. But, in the end, what he saw was insufficient to offer a reply to what he also saw as the force of the *Gestell*.

For Heidegger, then, the task of thinking the relation of word and image as idioms of truth, a problematic that arose in the context of thinking the character of the work of art, gives way to the question of the very possibility of art in the modern technological world. In the end, Heidegger seems to come to the view that the word will degenerate into the mere bearer of information and that the image will be merely the means of manipulation. The hope that art could open up history to new and productive possibilities yields to the fear that the liberating possibilities of production have been supplanted by forces that eventually close off the movement of life.

CHAPTER 3

ON WORD, IMAGE, AND GESTURE: ANOTHER ATTEMPT AT A BEGINNING

Three texts published in 1960, the same year in which Heidegger largely abandoned the question of painting, proved to be among the most promising for opening up a new approach for the philosophical concern with painting. The first was the reissue of "The Origin of the Work of Art" (written and delivered as a lecture in 1935, first published in 1950, reissued as a separate text in 1960), which was published this time with an introduction by Gadamer and a new addendum by Heidegger. With the addition of these texts, one is led to see "The Origin of the Work of Art" in a new context and so read it in a new way. The second text of 1960 was "Eye and Mind," a text in which Merleau-Ponty asks about the "fundamental of painting, [and hence] perhaps of all culture,"[1] and which does this more rigorously from within the standpoint of the painter than perhaps any philosopher had yet accomplished. The third text of this year was Gadamer's *Truth and Method,* which, more systematically and more rigorously than any other text, draws together all of the historical strands that have defined the decisive moments in the history of philosophical approaches to artworks—especially with regard to painting.[2] There were other texts from this period that pursued the question of art; among them, several would single out Klee's work as opening up new possibilities for painting. Adorno, Foucault, Deleuze, Lyotard, Marcuse, Bloch, and, to some extent, Sartre, Blanchot, and Bataille all take up the question of the work of art, especially painting, as a central philosophical issue and not merely as an adjunct concern, and all turn to Klee as exemplary in addressing this question.[3] In other words, precisely at the moment that Heidegger despairs of the possibilities of art in our times, precisely when he quietly retreats from the question of painting, art—painting above all—comes forward to define the central philosophical questions of this moment and in a variety of thinkers.

Three common denominators uniting these new developments and these texts should be noted. First, in each case the work of art is understood to signal a challenge to the hegemony of philosophical conceptuality in the determination of truth. The question of the relation of word (no longer defined by the view that it reaches its summit in the concept) and of the image (no longer tethered to figuration and representation) moves to the center of philosophical concerns and holds these otherwise rather disparate thinkers together in a "tradition." This tradition, which we inappropriately tend to designate geographically as "continental" philosophy, understands the question of art as moving directly to the heart of philosophical questioning. For this tradition, art is no longer able to be considered as a matter of "aesthetics" or as a subfield of philosophy; rather, art is understood as opening up the very possibility of philosophy and thus located at the heart of philosophy itself. The task of philosophy is to seek a philosophical response to this new opening.

Second, this tradition tends to set works of art in opposition, or at least in an apartness, to science and its forms of seeing and knowing. The opening sentence of Merleau-Ponty's "Eye and Mind"—like the opening sentence of Gadamer's *Truth and Method*—stresses precisely this opposition: "Science manipulates things and gives up living in them. . . . Scientific thinking, a thinking which looks on from above and thinks of the object in general, must return to the 'there is' which underlies it. . . . But art, especially painting, draws upon this fabric of brute meaning which [science] prefers to ignore."[4] Concomitant with the elevation of the question of art, the recognition of its primacy, we find a serious and strong critique of the scientific conception of truth.

Finally, the third common denominator uniting these new approaches to the work of art as a philosophical concern is that they tend to see in the work of art an exit from the presumptions of metaphysics and an entrance into a new, more vital and responsive way of thinking. The claim is that the assumptions and language of philosophy have, over time, severed their connection with the real topics and tasks of philosophy, with the concern with truth. Since Nietzsche, there had been a growing awareness within philosophy of the ways in which philosophizing had lost touch with its own sources. Whatever name was given to identify and characterize the reasons that had led to this desolate condition—whether it was called metaphysics or science—it had become clear that philosophy needed to return "to the things themselves," to "factical life," and to the elements that nourished thinking and speaking if it was to be alive again. The opening to such a return that Heidegger found in the work of art—an opening that Heidegger himself came to doubt as given to our times—provided the great promise to those working in Heidegger's wake. Engaging the work of art as a form of thinking that is not submitted in advance to the logic of the concept[5] but as a matter of sources and origins, this tradition works to stretch philosophy beyond what it has been hitherto.

———————

While there are numerous efforts to carry out this thinking engagement with the work of art, I want to pursue only one such effort in detail.[6] This decision to pursue these issues by looking closely at Gadamer's hermeneutics is based in a number of reasons, some of which are simply contingent, but others have what I take to be genuinely compelling arguments supporting them. Three reasons in particular need to be noted. First, I believe that Gadamer's hermeneutics marks the first and still most comprehensive effort to think systematically out of an opening found in the work of art. This ontological significance of the work of art, the idea that the analysis of the work of art opens up something like a *prima philosophia,* is announced by Gadamer himself. One sees this clearly, for instance, when Gadamer emphasizes the importance of this point by saying that "the intention of the following conceptual analysis is not a matter of art theory, but of ontology."[7] In light of this explicit effort to develop a philosophical viewpoint out of the analysis of the work of art, I will argue that Gadamer's hermeneutics is the most significant philosophical response to the contemporary understanding of the work of art thought from out of the character of modern art. Second, while one might legitimately argue that Merleau-Ponty and Adorno both set out to reopen the possibilities of philosophy from out of the analysis of the work of art and of aesthetic experience, it is also, sadly, the case that both of those projects were begun and then were quickly interrupted by death. Both Merleau-Ponty and Adorno died shortly after completing the work that announced rather extensive and systemic formulations of their own approach to the work of art; in other words, both stood at the beginning of even more serious and extensive considerations of the work of art and so neither was able to carry forward those considerations in the sustained way that we find in Gadamer's work. Third, and not surprisingly in light of Gadamer's close connection with Heidegger, Gadamer's *Truth and Method* develops many of the lines of investigation and possibilities that Heidegger himself abandons. In particular, the discussion of the relation of word and image and the question of the reach of conceptual reason play central roles in Gadamer's formulation of hermeneutics theory and in his effort to expose hermeneutics not simply as a theory of interpretation but as the character of philosophy in general.

In what follows, then, I want to take up Gadamer's development of hermeneutics as a philosophical approach emerging out of the insights of the encounter with the work of art in three stages. First, I will turn to Gadamer's treatment of the image—an analysis that is quite in line with the paths suggested by Heidegger—in order to show how the image serves to form the basis and the starting point for Gadamer's conception of hermeneutics. Second, I will turn to some of Gadamer's later essays in which he begins to develop what I take to be a new vocabulary for addressing painting in light of the transformations that painting has undergone in the past century. Traditional terms enlisted to discuss painting have, by and large, been drawn from a conception of painting that understands it as a matter of copying and representing—notions that are insufficient at best. Gadamer recognizes this and so, like Heidegger, makes an attempt to find a different way of speaking of painting. Third, with respect to both of these matters— the articulation of a philosophical viewpoint from out of the experience of the work of art and the development of a new vocabulary for speaking of such works—I will suggest that while Gadamer goes very far toward opening new possibilities for philosophy from out of these insights, he does not go far enough. The challenge to philosophical reflection presented by the work of art, and by painting in particular, is, I believe, greater than we have yet managed to acknowledge. So I want to conclude this discussion of Gadamer's hermeneutics with some brief suggestions regarding what might next be said in this regard.

Before taking up these special issues, some general remarks about how Gadamer understands the scene of thinking in the present age will be helpful. Like Heidegger, Gadamer would find that the effort to engage the real accomplishment of the work of art faces some significant obstacles. But Gadamer diagnoses these obstacles to thinking the work of art differently— and far less pessimistically—than Heidegger. For Gadamer, the challenge of the present age to thinking is sharp and severe, but it is not fatal.

———

Gadamer begins *Truth and Method* with the claim that the full extent of the questions governing the so-called *Geisteswissenschaften*—the "humanities" —has been lost to the progressive subordination of those questions to the model of thinking defining the natural sciences. While he does not explicitly compare this diagnosis of the situation confronting philosophy in the present age with Heidegger's critique of the progressive subordination of philosophy to metaphysics, Gadamer's concern in this instance is fully commensurate with Heidegger's. Mathematization, objectification, calculability, and conceptuality become the ideals of all thinking, while method is regarded as the guarantor of our access to those ideals. In the end, as Descartes argued, truth is understood to be ultimately secured by method. This view is so pervasive that methodology comes to be the driving concern even of the humanities. One of the first concerns of *Truth and Method* is to argue against this modernist assumption. To that end, the broadest concern of *Truth and Method* is found in the project of unfolding the notion of truth within the horizon of understanding, in contrast to the governing project of modernity in which truth is situated with respect to method and the ideals of scientized cognition.[8] Gadamer's claim is that the disclosure of the work of art and the character of aesthetic experience provide the opening to this different way in which truth unfolds. In turning to the work of art as offering a new opening for philosophy, one that escapes the sedimentations and constrictions of metaphysics and natural science, Gadamer pursues the possibilities that Heidegger announces but ultimately abandons as untenable in our times. Like others who would pursue this opening, Gadamer, for the most part, would not find the closure of art in our times to be so fundamental, nor would he find that the question of technology forecloses the opening that might be found in the work of art. It is on this diagnosis of our historical moment and, in particular, of the all-embracing force of technology that Gadamer seems to diverge most from Heidegger. Nonetheless, like Heidegger, Gadamer does find our access to the work of art to be obstructed and not able to be assumed as given or unproblematic in the present age. There is, according to Gadamer, a deep set of prejudices that impede our efforts to appreciate and to understand the work of art and the force of aesthetic experience.

Here Kant is the decisive—and Janus-faced—figure whom Gadamer must confront both insofar as Kant lays the basis for the deep failure of our age to grasp the being of the work of art and as, at the same time, he gives indications of just how that failure is to be overcome.[9] In other words, Gadamer turns to Kant as a prelude to the analysis of the artwork and does so with the sense that Kant simultaneously opens and closes the possibility of a genuine understanding of the work of art. For Gadamer, Kant provides the opening for hermeneutics insofar as Kant forcefully demonstrates the limits of the ideal of method for thinking and insofar as he does this by virtue of a turn to aesthetic experience. But, at the same time, Gadamer understands Kant as closing off this opening insofar as his analysis of aesthetic experience subjectivizes it and ultimately cuts art off from any claim to truth by reserving truth for the concept. But it is Kant's role in demonstrating the limits of the ideal of method and in opening up the alternative conception of truth defining hermeneutics that is pivotal for the development of the project of hermeneutics in *Truth and Method*. In the final pages of *Truth and Method*, Gadamer acknowledges this when he says that "in our aesthetic analysis, which follows the Kantian line of questioning, we have exposed the narrowness of the concept of cognition and, by starting from the question of the truth of art, we found a way into hermeneutics."[10] For Gadamer, entry into the first stage of hermeneutics comes with the critique of Kant's aesthetics.

In order to take up Kantian aesthetics in the formulation of Gadamer's hermeneutics, it is important to understand both why Kant's *Critique of Judgment* is a necessary concern for Gadamer and what obstacle to the proper consideration of art it both forms and, in some part at least, overcomes. To do that, the position of Gadamer's analysis of Kant needs to be regarded systematically: there is nothing arbitrary or elective about the turn to Kant in the first part of *Truth and Method*. Following on the heels of the discussion of the "significance of the humanistic tradition for the humanities" and ending by the move to the "recovery of the question of truth from out of the truth of art," the analysis of Kant forms the bridge that connects Gadamer's own project with the project of humanism and the alternative that it has long posed to the scientization of thinking that governs the humanities. The recovery of the question of truth in the horizon opened by the work of art is accomplished by Gadamer's analysis and critique of Kant's aesthetics.[11]

Early in *Truth and Method*, Gadamer notes that the humanistic tradition has long respected and been based upon "a completely different kind of experience than that which has served the investigation into the laws of nature."[12] In short, it is a tradition that has preserved a conception of experience and of truth that has not been defined by the models and ideals of the natural sciences. When examining the humanistic tradition, Gadamer argues that it has been fundamentally defined by four governing concepts: *Bildung, sensus communis,* judgment, and taste. These notions name the experiences and the ideals that open up and preserve a sense of truth that is not captured by those rules of method and the objectifications grounding the natural sciences and that ultimately come to determine— quite inappropriately—the humanities. By acknowledging an experience and a possibility of truth that cannot be recuperated by method and by the ideals of science, the humanistic tradition provides the historical basis upon which questions of human experience and of truth can be recovered from the humanities. Kant's great achievement in this history is to have gathered these four concepts together and thought them systematically insofar as he demonstrated how aesthetic judgment is defined by precisely these notions. But, importantly, Kant does not present aesthetic experience simply as a reversion to, or renewal of, humanism. The differences are real and significant, and so it is not the case that aesthetic experience simply takes over the place once defined by conceptual reason.[13] Perhaps the most significant difference is that Kant's analysis of aesthetic experience discloses it as constitutively *resistant to* any sublation into the concept, that is, it is shown to be constitutively the other of philosophy insofar as philosophy is understood to be an essentially conceptual project.[14] In making this argument, Kant opens the question of art in a fundamentally new manner, one that immediately sets it apart from the framework of philosophy and the metaphysics of traditional aesthetic conceptions of such experience and such works. In short, the terms and the framework for any understanding of truth are shifted.

While Kant recognized that aesthetic experience and the work of art cannot be grasped by conceptual reason, it is also the case, according to Gadamer, that Kant severed the kinship of art and truth that Gadamer sees as being essential to fully developing an understanding of aesthetic experience. In other words, the same analysis that exposes the autonomy and aprioricity of aesthetic experience isolates that experience and presents it as set apart from any claim to truth by regarding it as radically subjectivized. As Kant says, "That which is merely subjective in the representation of an object, i.e. its relation to the subject that does not constitute the object, is its aesthetic constitution."[15] And: "The beautiful in nature *or* art has one and the same a priori principle that lies completely in subjectivity."[16] This emphasis on the radical subjectivity of aesthetic experience and thus its separation from any claim to truth is the chief criticism of Kant in Gadamer's discussion of Kant's aesthetics. Indeed, Gadamer introduces his analysis of Kant's aesthetics by making this clear: "The transcendental function which Kant ascribes to aesthetic judgment enables him to delimit conceptual cognition and thus to satisfy the needs of determining the phenomena of the beautiful and of art. But does this mean that the concept of truth should be retained for conceptual cognition? Should one not also recognize that the work of art has truth as well?"[17] This becomes the first issue of Gadamer's reading of Kant: "that Kant must deny taste any claim to being a significant form of cognition."[18] The claim of art to be a form of knowledge is foreclosed, and with this thoroughgoing subjectivization of aesthetics, the disappearance of the aesthetic object begins. This signals the birth of what Gadamer calls "aesthetic consciousness" and equally of "aesthetic differentiation" in which aesthetic experience is thoroughly subjectivized and the work of art is set aside from the realm of the real. These consequences of Kant's way of revitalizing the question of the work of art name the obstacles to genuinely engaging the work of art in our times: our way of recovering the question of the work of art is imbued with conceptions about the appearance of art and aesthetic experience that inhibit, if not simply block, any capacity to truly engage the work of art. While Heidegger finds the technologization of the world and thought to be the all-consuming obstacle blocking the recovery of the full force of the work of art in the present age, Gadamer finds this obstacle in the legacy of how the work of art is brought forward by Kant as a concern for philosophy. In being brought forward as radically subjective, the work of art is cut off from any claim to truth. And yet, it is precisely this connection between art and truth that Gadamer wants to expose as the first step in his formulation of philosophical hermeneutics: "Is not the task of aesthetics to ground exactly that experience of art which is in a peculiar sense a form of knowledge, one that is completely different from the knowledge of meaning that is communicated in the sciences . . . and that is certainly different from all moral thought based in reason and from all conceptual knowledge in general, but which is nonetheless a knowing, that is, which is the communication of truth?"[19]

The "recovery of the question of the truth of art,"[20] which is the real opening of the original problematic that *Truth and Method* will define, begins then by going to the heart of what is questionable about the view of "aesthetic consciousness" that operates with such an understanding of the fundaments of art emerging out of the subjectivization of art that begins with Kant's aesthetics. This critique of aesthetic consciousness sets in motion Gadamer's own revision of the basic concepts of aesthetics. The originality and radicality of Gadamer's conception of art becomes most visible by following out this critique of the legacy of Kant's aesthetics. Starting from this point, one can begin to see what is required if one is indeed to open the question of the relation of art and truth. Clearly taking Heidegger's lead in this project, Gadamer nonetheless is not simply following in Heidegger's footsteps in thinking this kinship of art and truth. Here, the guiding assumptions about how art is produced, experienced, and thought come under a rigorous and severe critique so that a new foundation for understanding the great enigma of art is prepared.

In turning to "the ontology of the work of art and its hermeneutic significance,"[21] Gadamer identifies *play*—a Kantian notion given special prominence by Schiller—as the clue to a proper understanding of the being of the work of art. The reasons for this turn to play, and the differences between Gadamer, Kant, and Schiller on how this notion is to be understood, are complex and important issues but not directly central to the questions that need to be developed here. Three points, however, do need to be noted about how the notion of play, which is at the heart of the hermeneutic conception of the work of art, is to be understood. First, that play describes a *movement*. Play is never static but can be understood only as an event. To freeze or immobilize play is to step away from play. Second, play is possible only as *free;* even within the boundaries of the rules defining play, there must be an essential freedom and indeterminacy. Finally, the transformation of play into a work of art, the embodiment of play in a work, needs to maintain the character of play. In other words, the work needs to be understood as the fulfillment, the perfection (*Vollendung*), of play. When we do this, when we recognize the characteristics of play that define the work, then we can begin to see that the work needs to be understood as a *text*. This means that the text cannot be understood as an object of cognition but must be understood as a continuation of the free event of play. The work does not capture or copy something of the world; rather, it is a continuation of play. The truth of the work is found insofar as it maintains the sources that give impulse to come to a work at all. It does this insofar as it takes on the weblike,[22] open-ended, and living character of a text as the way in which the play of the work is preserved.

In order to test these preliminary claims about the emergence of hermeneutics—as a philosophical approach that understands the idiom of truth not according to the concept but according to the logic and being of the text—and in order to begin developing further hermeneutical consequences, Gadamer takes up the question of "the ontological valence of the image."[23] There are several reasons that Gadamer turns immediately to the question of the image in order to continue to lay the foundations of hermeneutic theory. The most important reason is that the image seems to be that form of the work of art that is most recalcitrant to the hermeneutic conception of art. The painting seems to be the most static form of art and thus the least able to carry on the movement and the openness that characterize the hermeneutic sense of art. Furthermore, the image seems most amenable to the representational theory of art and thus the least able to lay claim to having the character of play for which Gadamer argues.[24] The consequence of this effort to recover the image in this approach to the work of art is that painting moves to the center of the way in which hermeneutics is opened up as a theory—and not simply theory of the work of art but as the opening up of an ontology. The centrality of the image in the hermeneutic conception of the work of art and the importance of the work of art in the formation of hermeneutic ontology thus mean that Gadamer's discussions of the image, especially of the painted image, bear a great weight, far greater than such discussions usually bear. Furthermore, because Gadamer *writes*—that is, because he self-consciously remains in the orbit of the *logos* even when he is granting special weight to the image—the question of the relation of word and image has a special preeminence in hermeneutics. Gadamer is aware that to speak of the image in words is, from the outset, to problematize the word.

In light of the importance of the notion of the image and of the need to distinguish his conception of the image from the orthodox views that have dominated and marginalized philosophical discussions of the image, it is no surprise that Gadamer begins by asserting the new for a fresh approach to the idea of the image: "The concept of the image prevalent in recent centuries cannot automatically be taken as a starting point. Our present investigation seeks to rid itself of that assumption."[25] The most important step in this regard is for Gadamer to call attention to the insufficiency of the notion of the copy as a way of understanding what we see in the painted image. To this end, Gadamer notes that the copy "effaces itself" *as a copy* and that its true being is thus to conceal itself. However, while interpreting the image as a copy means understanding it as aimed at such self-effacement, the truth of the matter is precisely the opposite of such a claim: in the painting we recognize that the image "is not destined to be self-effacing, it is not the means to an end."[26] This is the case with all painting —namely, that in painting we look at the image itself, not through it to something else—but abstract art, which calls attention to itself and not to an object, makes this especially clear. Abstract, non-representational works remove all pretense that something other than the image itself defines the painting. The abstract work reminds us that the image *is* the work. Later in his career, Gadamer would characterize this hallmark of the painting as an indication of the "Unhintergehbarkeit der Kunst [the non-circumventability of art]." This is a phrase that indicates that there is nothing "behind" the work itself, that there is nothing that will be uncovered apart from what is given in and as the image that is the painting. The painting, properly understood, points *to itself,* not away from itself.

In *Truth and Method,* Gadamer's primary concern is to indicate that "the relation of the image to the original is basically quite different than in the case of the copy. *It is no longer a one-sided relationship.* . . . To say that the painting [*Bild*] has its own reality means just the reverse for what is depicted [*Urbild*], namely, it means that it comes to presentation itself. It presents *itself* in this presentation."[27] That is why this human production "by being presented experiences, as it were, an *increase in being* [*Zuwachs am Sein*]."[28] It is more than the thing it is and more than any "original" to which it might be related. This notion that in the presentation of the work of art there is an increase in being is key to understanding the hermeneutic conception of the work of art. Something *new* enters here. When thinking of this "increase" in being, it is important not to misunderstand the character of the increase being described. It is not a quantitative increase (indeed, why would one even suspect that it was?), as if increase meant "more" in the sense of number. It is rather a *qualitative* increase that is spoken of here, much like the sort of increase that comes with learning another language or of an improvement in one's health. It is, perhaps, like the increase that comes in sharing words in conversation, or the increase that comes as love in which the world is enriched and enlarged even as it does not change.[29] Something *new* appears in the work of art, and this is how the increase is signaled. This newness stays with the work of art, defining it. That is why even ancient works of art seem fresh and new—no matter how old they are according to the calendar. This defining trait of an "increase in being" is the way that the essential element of play, its continual movement, carries itself forward in the work of art.

To speak of the work of art in this way, to say that the image defining painting should be characterized by an increase and by the arrival of something new, is to recognize not only that the work is not derivative of or dependent upon some original that it copies; it is also to grant a real autonomy to the work itself. This means as well that insofar as it is drawn in some sense from something given (as for instance in the case of the portrait), "the image has an autonomy that also affects the original." One might say that the image has the capacity to *change* what is imaged and what is seen, and thus it changes the world out of which the image has emerged. This is the force of the artwork: that we no longer see the world independently of the images by which the world has been interpreted.[30] Thus, Gadamer suggests that "Homer's Achilles is more original than the ["real" Achilles]."[31] Likewise, one might say that Plato's Socrates has redefined "who" Socrates is; that a sunset seen from an airplane will never be the same after Rothko's paintings; that the earth will never be the same since it was photographed from the moon; that the heavens will never be able to be regarded without being altered by the sights that the Hubble photographs have made possible. In such cases, it is fair to say that the image alters the original—in the end, it will be better to say that such cases transform, almost to the point of senselessness, the very notions of image and original. The sense that something "true" is presented in the work of art, that we "recognize" something in it, is an expression of the fact that the work presents what has not been seen before and yet still illuminates the world. A new pleasure is found here: the pleasure of recognition, the pleasure of knowing the same in a new way. What is recognized is the new, and this, in turn, changes how we understand. Images, above all images in the work of art, educate our seeing and understanding of the world. They are not copies of a world, but, in some sense, they come to be coterminous with the disclosure of a world at all. In this sense, one must say that the work of art is at the origin of our understanding of a world.

Gadamer unpacks the significance of this appearance of the new in the work of art by saying that "the image [in the work of art] is an event of being—in it being appears, meaningfully and visibly. . . . The 'ideality' of the work of art does not consist in its imitating or reproducing an idea but, as with Hegel, in the 'appearing' of the idea itself. On the basis of such an ontology of the image, the primacy which aesthetic consciousness accords the framed picture that belongs in a collection of paintings can be shown to fail. The image contains an indissoluble connection with its world."[32] One might say that once we truly understand its character as a work of art, the painting eventually breaks out of the museum. In other words, the aesthetic consciousness that has shaped reflections on the work of art since Kant, the differentiation of art and the world, is overcome with this recognition that art is an event of being, a birth into the world. To say that the painting is an "event of being" means that it is the presentation, or the emergence of that which appears in the painting (and not its copy function), that is the key to grasping what "happens" in the painting. One further reason that artworks always feel new—no matter how "old" according to the calendar—is precisely this link with emergence. There is a sort of birth or, to use Klee's language, a genesis proper to the work of art. This, in part, is also what Heidegger means when he speaks of art as an "origin" and a "bringing forth." This movement, this emergence that is the event of being, most defines the nature of the work of art. This is the case even for painting and the plastic arts, which can seem, from the perspective of a representational theory of art, to be the most static forms of art.

Gadamer unfolds the significance of this movement at the heart of the work of art—a movement that he initially characterized in terms of play— by calling attention to the essential kinship of art to both performance and history: "Essential to dramatic or musical works then is that their performance at different times and on different occasions is, and must be, different. Now it is important to see that, mutatis mutandis, the same is true of the plastic arts. But in them too it is not the case that the work exists 'an sich' and only the effect varies: it is the work of art itself that displays itself under various conditions. The viewer of today not only sees things in a different way, he sees different things."[33] In other words, the work exceeds the world and the historical moment into which it arrived. That does not imply that the work is "timeless" but rather that it belongs to the movement of time and of history. Understanding that the work of art is an event of being, understanding it as a movement or always—even in the case of painting— as a performance, rather than regarding it as something finished and static, means granting that this movement has an effective life and that the work "lives"; it does not stay still or untouched by history. One might even say, with Heidegger, that the work of art is one of the key forces at work in defining the dynamic life of history. In this sense, the historicity of the work of art, the way it belongs to time, is exemplary for a perspective—such as hermeneutics—that attempts to think the life of the past in the present and in its futures. In the hermeneutic conception of history and its readings of history, the force of the work of art will always have a privileged position and power.

Gadamer does not, however, pursue this relation of the work to history in *Truth and Method*. He develops the hermeneutics of history in the second section of that text, but he does not do that from out of the relation of the work of art to history. Rather, in *Truth and Method* he moves forward by pointing out that this truth of the image in the work of art, its refusal to be conceived or captured by a moment, is the reason that "a work of art always has something sacred about it [and that] ultimately, every work of art has something about it that protests against profanation."[34] This is how Gadamer approaches the movement, the event, of being defining the artwork: it shows itself as this refusal to be contained and as harboring a mystery as presenting something more than meets the eye but something that is not yet fully disclosed. The work always seems to be something sacred, as being the presence of something greater than itself. The work has something sacred about it insofar as it brings into appearance; it gives birth, as it were, to something that will live in history, something that is more than an object. Gadamer makes it clear that his real interest is in asking just how this "more," this "excess" of the work that is understood from out of its movement, operates.[35] How, in other words, are we to understand the character of this hint at something that is "more" than the work without moving away from the work itself and so obscuring its essentially "non-circumventable" nature? If we are to understand the movement at work in art as something "sacred," then what indications does this yield for understanding the workings of the work itself?

Gadamer begins answering these questions by emphasizing that it is necessary to avoid the metaphysical or theological move to interpret this "excess" or "pointing" of the artwork as either a sign or a symbol, as is so often the case. Thus, "it is important not to confuse the special sense of presentation proper to the work of art with the sacred representation performed by, say, the *symbol*. . . . At the same time a picture is not a *sign*. For a sign is nothing but what its function requires; and that is to point away from itself."[36] The character of the pointing at work in the painting is "situated, as it were, halfway between two extremes: these extremes of representation are *pure indication,* which is the essence of the sign, and *pure substitution,* which is the essence of the symbol."[37] One might, rightly I believe, take some issue with Gadamer's characterization of the symbol here as pure substitution—it might have a character that is not so immediately captured by the metaphysical effacing of the symbolic itself—but his point is nonetheless clear: the image in the work of art must be understood as non-circumventable. This means that its transcendence, its sense of being sacred and the site of an emergence, cannot be understood simply as a pointing *away from itself;* rather, it must be understood as a pointing in which it remains ever more insistently *as itself.*[38] The "pointing" in which the emergence of the image is to be explained is intrinsic to the image itself. This emergence is what the image is; it is not a substitution for something else, nor is it simply a sign that points away from itself. In order to clarify this strange abundance, this "plus" or sense of the sacred, proper to the image, Gadamer refers to the memento, which he suggests is an example of how this intrinsic value of the thing might be understood insofar as "it seems to have a reality of its own. It refers to the past and so is effectively a sign, but [unlike the sign] it is also precious in itself since, as a bit of the past that has not disappeared, it keeps the past present for us."[39] In the memento, something more than the memento itself is made present by being indicated or pointed to, but this happens only through the memento itself, which does not efface its own being nor does it substitute for that which it indicates. Indeed, there is a certain intensification of the being of the memento insofar as it makes present something of the past from which it has been drawn.

The work of art has a similar nature: "It also represents, but *through itself*, through the increment of meaning that it brings. But this means that in it what is represented—the 'original'—is there more fully, more genuinely, just as it truly is."[40] Abstract painting makes this nature especially evident insofar as it calls attention only to itself and cannot be thought as referring to an object that it copies. Gadamer notes that non-representational art in all forms—for instance, architecture, or arts that are not defined by their copy function—are fully recognized *as art* only insofar as it is the work itself and not something represented in or by the work that we address. Once this happens, the work of art ceases to be defined by its copy function, and its pointing is no longer interpreted as a matter of its character as a sign or a symbol. Instead, "the specific mode of the work of art's presence is the coming-to-presentation of being."[41] In a similar fashion, in later works Gadamer will speak of the *Vollzug* character of the work of art. This is another name for the performative character in which the coming into being, the coming to presentation, is emphasized as itself. It is a way of emphasizing that the force of the work is found in the work itself. For painting, this means that the presentation of the image itself is itself the truth of the work. Its "pointing" is not away from the image but an intensification of what the image itself is. It is a notion akin to Heidegger's notion of bringing forth and to Klee's notion of genesis. Each of those notions is an effort to call attention to the living, the presentational, character of the work of art. This intensification, this birth, is what is meant when Gadamer speaks of an "increase in being."

My intention is not to trace these themes further in *Truth and Method*, nor to develop the details of just how the understanding of the work of art, of the image in art above all, shapes Gadamer's conception of hermeneutics. Rather, my intention has been to give some general indications of the fundamental role that the concerns of modern art, especially of the character of the image in non-representational painting, play in opening up the problematic of hermeneutics. In doing this, in taking the claims and challenges of modern art seriously as a philosophical problem, Gadamer's hermeneutics responds to the transformations in art that Heidegger eventually grants but never really addresses. Hermeneutics, as Gadamer defines it, is precisely such an effort to think outside of the orbit of representation, the orbit that delineates metaphysics and science. Art has always provided this exit from metaphysics, but the challenge of modern art first truly makes evident what is necessary to pursue this exit, this entrée into something other than metaphysics. This readiness to pursue this possibility is a point of difference between Gadamer and Heidegger, a point on which I would argue Gadamer's hermeneutics marks a significant advance over Heidegger's thought. To explore the details of the role of art in formulating hermeneutics as well as the difference between Gadamer and Heidegger on this point is, however, a matter for another work.[42] But, insofar as Gadamer's hermeneutics does make a real advance in its recognition of the challenge posed by the image in modern art, the question now is what new insights into the image, and into its relation to the word, emerge from this recognition?

The second important contribution that Gadamer makes in response to the challenge posed by modern art emerges directly from his recognition of the way that such works do not fit traditional interpretive schemas. To this end, he pushes the effort to forge a new vocabulary for speaking of the sense of the image, the event of painting. The aim of such a vocabulary is to find a way of speaking about images that does not grow out of a sense that images in the work of art should be understood primarily as a copy of something else, something more original and true. That is, the first task of this vocabulary is to forge a way of speaking about painting that does not reflect a sense of the image as a matter of representation. However, since the notion of the copy and the idea of representation have, from the outset of philosophical discussions about the image, been at the foundation of conceptions of the image, the language with which we discuss painting has long been shaped by the idea of the image as copy and a sense of the artwork as representational. So, the task of finding a language proper to the discussion of the image that does not replicate this prejudice is not an easy one—it must go against the grain of a very long set of habits and traditions. Gadamer takes up this task in a variety of later essays, one of which, "Art and Imitation," explicitly announces this concern with the language proper to speaking of art as its task. That essay opens with the acknowledgment that modern art does indeed present a new set of challenges to thinking, challenges that we have hitherto done a poor job of addressing: "What is the significance of modern non-objective art? Are the old aesthetic concepts with which we used to try and understand the nature of art still valid today? Many outstanding representatives of modern art emphatically reject the pictorial expectations with which we approach it. Such art generally tends to produce an explicit shock effect upon us. How can we explain the new stance taken by the painter who repudiates all our previous traditions and expectations? How are we to respond to the challenge of this new art?"[43] Heidegger eventually came to see in Klee something new and hitherto unseen that, once fully appreciated, showed itself as undermining many of the elemental assumptions guiding Western conceptions of the work of art, of images, of language, and of production. But, while Heidegger never fully pursued the effort to reply to this challenge, Gadamer does press forward with the effort to respond directly to it.

One way to respond to this challenge, perhaps even a prerequisite for any full response, is to be alert to the way the language with which we address such works carries within itself a great many presumptions and prejudices. Most of all, the philosophical vocabulary regarding art tends to inevitably return to the notion of the image as a copy. In order to criticize this language, Gadamer briefly outlines what he calls the three dominant aesthetic concepts: imitation, expression, and sign. There is a clear similarity here in "Art and Imitation" with Gadamer's concern in *Truth and Method* to demonstrate the insufficiency of notions such as sign or symbol as a way of giving an account of the "sacred" or "transcendent" character of the image, its peculiar way of exceeding itself while simultaneously showing itself to be non-circumventable and insuperable. Gadamer's later critiques of the notions of imitation, expression, and sign in "Art and Imitation" and other texts amplify the claims that he lays out in *Truth and Method*. He does this insofar as he presents these three notions in rather sweeping terms. One might describe these as referring to copying, subjective feeling, and pointing or meaning. The criticisms of these guiding notions are not detailed but invariably refer to the "refusal" or "rejection" of any claim to meaning by the composition of images in modern painting. Gadamer points to the "multifaceted and crystal-like style" and "imagistic script" of artists like Picasso or Juan Gris as constitutionally "rendering the demand for legibility in art mute."[44] The view that painting needs to be understood as "legible"— that is, of being intelligible according to standards of intelligibility drawn from the *logos* as word—is a view of painting that submits the work of art to standards that it has refused. It is to ask the painting to "mean" rather than to bring forth and to show. It is to ask the image to be something other than an image—to be, one might say, a weak and insufficient word. Gadamer's critique of traditional ways of understanding painting is clear and forceful, but even more interesting than Gadamer's criticisms of inherited notions of artworks, criticisms that largely echo remarks one finds in Heidegger, is his effort to formulate a language that is more responsive to the task of speaking of modern works of art. Gadamer's move to do this takes a rather curious path, since rather than imagining a new, almost "futural" language, he suggests "we must look further back" into the roots of the present. Accordingly, he turns to Kant, Aristotle, and Pythagoras to find this language proper to our present.

There are three insights from Kant's *Critique of Judgment* that Gadamer emphasizes here and that form Gadamer's approach to this question of the language proper to the discourse on art. The first is Kant's claim that the beautiful *animates* our feeling of life. What interests Gadamer in this remark is that here the beautiful is defined by its relation to *life*. More precisely, the beautiful is that which "quickens" our feeling of life. Kant speaks of this "animation" or "quickening" of the feeling of life by using the word *beleben*, to bring to life. The English words "quicken" and "quick"—as in the quick of a fingernail, to "cut to the quick," the "quick and the dead," or in the use of "quickening" to name the moment one feels a baby in the womb move, the moment one first detects life—are, in some sense, even better words to name what it is that Kant is driving at, namely, the *incipience* of life itself and the *intensity* that belongs to this arrival of life. The beautiful is signaled by this incipience, this quickening of what is. Beauty, then, does not have any relation to representation, nor does it have a copy function; rather, the heart of beauty, its self-validation, is found in this coming into being, this presencing, of appearance as such. Understood in this way, beauty is defined most of all as the *movement* of life; it is a coming into appearance, a bringing forth; it is not a fully achieved appearance, not, in other words, an object. In this shared emphasis on the movement of life, it is clear that one should hear in Kant's notion of quickening something akin to Klee's notion of genesis. Elsewhere, Gadamer suggests that this movement from the realm of representation and its objects—that is, from the world as we usually inhabit it to the realm of genesis and of life coming to presence—is the same movement that nature offers us in the move between sleeping and waking.[45] A new realm, one that Schelling described as the opening of a "second empire," opens. Or one might simply say that beauty happens when we wake up to life. But what is most important here is to note how Kant's remarks about the "quickening" of life remove this core event of aesthetic experience from any concern with an already constituted object and, at the same time, how the question of language becomes the question of how one is to say the *movement* of life—how, one might say, one is to say time without immobilizing it and freezing it in the form of an object, in some sense of substantiality.

The second insight that Gadamer takes from the third Critique as crucial for thinking through the character of painting today can be traced back to the way that Kant's analysis of aesthetic experience demonstrates that this awakening to life is so firmly lodged in a feeling that it cannot be cognized by any theoretical reason that can be scientized, nor can it be translated into conceptual language. This feeling, by virtue of its nature as bound to life itself, is not only independent of the concept but actively *resists* any relation to the language of the concept and to the measures of theoretical reason—it remains ineluctably an aesthetic disclosure and so must adhere to the peculiar "logic" of the aesthetic. Kant describes this other logic by speaking of the "aesthetic idea." It is that which occasions thought but still cannot be grasped by the schema or language of the concept. In other words, a logic is opened up that cannot be addressed by the language or logic of philosophy. But this "logic" is not simply another logic of the same order as the logic of the concept, that is, it is not a logic that could simply be appended to the logic of reason. It is rather essentially different; it is a different kind of logic that is set apart in many respects. The most elemental difference, though, is that the feeling that opens up upon the aesthetic idea is given in an intuition that is simply "too large" to be taken under the concept. That is why Kant describes the aesthetic idea by saying that it is the "counterpart" (*Gegenstuck*) to the rational idea that is governed by the concept and its laws. And that is why Kant describes the aesthetic idea by saying as well that it characterizes "those presentations of the power of imagination that are the occasion of much thought, but to which no determinate thought, i.e., concept, can be adequate and that consequently *no language can fully reach and make comprehensible.*"[46] Gadamer's concern with the language proper to aesthetic experience—an experience that he, like Kant, recognizes as including within itself the urge to communicate—finds in Kant a clue as to how the impasse of language before the beautiful is to be understood.

The third Kantian insight that Gadamer draws upon in his own efforts to articulate just what is at stake in how we think the image in the work of art is Kant's contention that art can be understood only as a product of *freedom*. What this means in the end is that there is no ground that cannot give an account of such works; they emerge out of, and express, the spontaneity of the groundlessness of freedom itself. Precisely because it belongs to freedom as it does, the work is able to quicken a sense of life. The movement of freedom bringing the work into being mirrors and repeats the movement of life that is quickened in the aesthetic experience. But even more: while this freedom at work in the work of art accounts for the bond uniting the production of the artwork and the movement of life, it also opens the way to understanding the profound kinship between aesthetic experience and ethical sensibility. Kant develops this point. Heidegger, on the other hand, seems to ignore it, while Gadamer acknowledges it only by implication. The one who makes this point into an abiding concern and thus makes the most original contribution in this regard is Arendt. She, perhaps more than anyone else, has recognized that "the manifestation of the wind of thought is not knowledge; it is the ability to tell right from wrong, beautiful from ugly."[47] And she works to develop this connection that holds together the ability to tell right from wrong with the ability to tell the beautiful from the ugly. I will return to this point in the afterword, albeit in a somewhat different manner than one finds in Arendt, who approaches these issues in what one might call the reverse direction, that is, from out of the experience and foundation of a political and ethical sensibility rather than from out of aesthetic experience. Nonetheless, her debt to Kant in these matters is not to be understated, nor is her contribution to their full elaboration.

For now, my concern is merely to show how it is that Kant—despite what Gadamer describes as the way in which his "subjectivization of aesthetics" shuts down the truth of such experience—does indeed contribute to the way that Gadamer presses forward with his own attempt to articulate such experience. In other words, even if Kant's efforts to analyze aesthetic experience result in the formation of a subjectivized aesthetic consciousness, his phenomenological account of aesthetic experience is full of insight that has yet to be properly explored and that remains as a task Gadamer will need to pursue. Collectively, these three Kantian insights—into the quickening of life, the happening that demands a different habit of thought and language if it is to be recognized and spoken, and the inscrutable event of freedom—all work together to outline an approach to the beautiful in all of its forms (this means in the unbidden of nature as well as in the works of art that we might make).[48] They also collaborate to present a sense of the work of art as utterly independent of any relation to representation whatsoever. What one finds in Kant's account is a sense of the work of art as a presentation, a letting appear and coming into being; it is not in any sense a copy any more than that which defines the life of nature can be thought of as a copy.

Gadamer reinforces this effort to think the artwork independently of any copy function when he turns next to Aristotle in order to discuss the notion of *mimesis*. This turn to Aristotle, like the turn to Kant, is motivated by Gadamer's efforts to forge a language that is appropriate to the image, a language responsive to the poetic logic of the image that escapes the grip of conceptual reason. Gadamer turns to Aristotle to this end and begins by noting that "Aristotle did not develop a real theory of art in the broadest sense and least of all a theory of the plastic and visual arts; this despite the fact that his views were formed in the fourth century, the great age of Greek painting. In truth we only find his theory of art in the context of his theory of tragedy . . . thus it is with reference to tragedy that Aristotle enlists the concept of *mimesis,* a notion that we know from Plato's critique of the poets."[49] While the concept of *mimesis* that Aristotle develops is intended to pertain to all of the arts, this modeling of *mimesis* upon theater gives shape to how *mimesis* is understood. In order to get at the elemental sense of *mimesis* for Aristotle, Gadamer points out that the most basic feature of the account Aristotle gives is that the pleasure we take in *mimesis* is the pleasure of recognition. He explains the special character of this recognition by referring to the way children can enjoy "dressing up" as someone: the intention of such an activity is to make something present that is otherwise absent. The aim of such play is not to copy something else, to serve as a substitute, but to be recognized as that something. This means, as Gadamer points out, that one does not respond to this making present of something by measuring what is presented against an "original" that it copies. What is recognized was not already familiar, not previously known. The recognition of *mimesis* is rather a recognition that discovers at the same time that it recognizes. In other words, what is recognized presents itself as itself, not as a copy. Gadamer explains this by saying: "What then is such recognition [*Wiedererkennen*]? Recognition does not mean simply seeing something that one has already seen before. . . . Recognizing means rather that I now know [*erkennen*] something as something that I have already seen. The enigma here lies entirely in the 'as.'"[50]

Gadamer's turn to Aristotle has the same motivation as his turn to Kant: to pull our sense of the artwork away from the notion that art is a matter of representation or copying and to argue instead that it is above all a matter of presentation and of the coming into being of something that otherwise is not truly present. From out of this understanding of the presentational character of the work of art, his intention is to search for the words that themselves respect such a character. Developing this point about recognition, Gadamer suggests that the insight proper to such recognition is of a special sort. More precisely, in it what is seen is "not simply the universal, the enduring form as it were cleansed, of the contingency of its encounter. Rather it is also the case that in a certain sense one recognizes oneself in it as well. All recognition is the experience of an increase in familiarity and, in the end, all of our experiences of the world are the forms upon which we build this familiarity with this world. Whatever else it might be, art is, as the Aristotelian doctrine quite appropriately claims, a mode of recognition that deepens self-knowledge and familiarity with the world."[51] Gadamer concedes that this claim seems to make the situation of modern art more complex and problematic: "Can modern painting possibly contribute to the task of such self-recognition?"[52] This seems to be the case because our habit is to ask "what" is recognized, as if an object alone is the locus of any possible recognition. Insofar as we do that, abstract, non-objective art will not be able to belong to such a conception of the artwork such as the one Gadamer is drawing here. If we are to grasp this mimetic recognition as it works in abstract art, then yet another sense of how this recognition at the heart of the mimetic work is to be understood needs to be developed. It will need to be the case that what is "recognized" is not found in any object. What is recognized will need to be more a matter of that which is quickened in the encounter with the work of art, namely the movement of life itself. To this end, Gadamer turns to Pythagoras in order to uncover a more archaic sense of *mimesis,* one that is not wedded to the assumptions of representation and thus points more directly toward the character of what it is one recognizes in mimetic works.

For Pythagoras, it is the universe itself, "the miracle of order that we call the *kosmos,*"[53] that appears through the presentation of *mimesis.* No single object or sum of all objects can be said to be the *kosmos.* It is rather the movement of the whole, of the all, that is named here, and, in the end, this is what one recognizes in the mimetic event. For Pythagoras, this order, this relationality of the whole of life, is able to appear because the universe itself is able to be repeated in numerical ratios. Musical ratios exhibit this capacity to present the order of the *kosmos* in an exemplary fashion. The music of the sounds made by the heavenly spheres as they move through the sky repeats the order of movement in the visible heavens. The music of the spheres in motion sounds out—and in this way repeats—the visible motion of the heavens, and this repetition, this identity of what is sounded and what is seen, is held together by the way in which each realm is itself a *mimesis* of number. Two points need to be mentioned here. First, in this bond uniting the audible and the visible, the hint of a different way of speaking of the relation of word and image is found. For this bond, music, which is time made loud, number in motion, is the middle term. Second, it needs to be acknowledged that number itself is not something that we perceive, but it is found only in the mind. It is a pure ideality: no number occurs anywhere except as an ideal possibility of the soul.[54] This means that, for Pythagoras, there is a third experience of order that is to be found alongside the orders expressed by the visible movement of the heavens and by the music of the heavens, namely, the order of the soul. Understood from this perspective, *mimesis* is the recognition of the movement of life expressed as its own order, and it is equally the summons to find this order in one's self. When it is thought in this way, *mimesis* is far removed from any sense that it refers to the work of copying or representation. Gadamer's contention is that the work of art presents this order to which we belong, and it does this by repeating, by miming rather than representing, that same order. What we "recognize" in such works, what they repeat and make present, is our belonging to this order of the universe. This is a point that Kant eloquently expressed when he wrote that "beautiful things are indications that the human being belongs in the world."[55] Saying this means that what we ultimately recognize in the work of art is not any object or particular being; rather, we understand that we belong to the world and to an order. We recognize something of ourselves and of our place in the world, and it is in recognizing this that a second order of pleasure, one akin to but still different from the pleasure of the quickening of beauty, is found. Gadamer's turn to Pythagoras here is intended to call attention to an order of nature, one that is found before any possible representation that could be made of nature, an order that is elemental. This is the nature to which we belong; it is the nature that we inhabit rather than the nature that we know and represent as a region of causally determined objects. It is in this order of the movement of life that is presented in the work of art that what must be called the "ethical" character of aesthetic experience appears. Of course, such a conception of the ethical departs in significant ways from orthodox senses of what constitutes ethical life with its relation to agency, subjectivity, and the realm of the juridical in which the language of its discourse—of rights, fairness, equality, justice—is determined. A different sense of ethical life, one more concerned with belonging and the place of the human being in a world larger than its own making and doing, is found here.[56] It is precisely in this departure from orthodoxy that something new and promising, something that answers Heidegger's call for an "original ethics" insofar as it inaugurates a return to sources, can be found. Gadamer does not explicitly pursue this promise, preferring instead to press upon other aspects of aesthetic experience that he has worked diligently to open up anew. While his remarks are not insignificant for the discussion of the ethical issues here, Gadamer does not make those issues concerning the ethical the centerpiece of his further investigations.

When he develops these Pythagorean insights about the ordering of nature and of the soul for his own purposes, Gadamer notes that this "ordering," which belongs to every work of art as that which is presented in the work and that which we "recognize," exposes the special form of necessity belonging to artworks. This necessity becomes another clue to understanding the real character of the work of art. One experiences this necessity of the work in the sense that a true work of art *could not be otherwise than it is;* there is something "right" about every work of art, something that we recognize as necessary. Gadamer explains this elsewhere by saying: "Nature no longer provides the exemplary model for art to follow. And yet even though it follows its own path, the work of art does come to resemble nature: there is something regular and binding about the self-contained picture that grows out from within. . . . A proper work is one where there is neither too little nor too much, nothing in excess and nothing missing."[57] The necessity of the work is just as binding but nonetheless fundamentally different from the necessity governing the laws of nature. The necessity of the work is governed by the freedom that has, from the beginning, animated the work of art. It is this necessity, this governance of freedom that we recognize as it emerges out of the movement of life, into the dynamic of play, and into the work itself. This peculiar necessity of the work is still at work and still recognized as key to the work even if the work presents us with something that we have not yet experienced. Thus, even if one has not, for instance, previously heard a musical work, one can sense when the notes are right or not. This rightness, this fittingness, has long been conceived as a sort of rational proportion or harmony that is, in the end, intelligible and able to be represented without remainder. However, this is not the best way to think this necessity, this order, which is proper to the work of art. It is too narrowly conceived and so excludes works such as atonal music and non-representational painting. Gadamer makes this point when he says that "in the final analysis, therefore, it is irrelevant whether or not a painter or sculptor works to produce objective or nonobjective art. The only relevant thing is whether we encounter a spiritual and ordering energy in the work, or whether we are simply reminded of some cultural motif or peculiarities of this or that particular artist. . . . But art is present whenever a work succeeds in elevating what it is or represents to a new configuration, a new world of its own in miniature, a new order of unity in tension."⁵⁸ The work renders visible the invisible; it transfigures the world and in doing this renders it new. Coming into being and taking up residence in the world, the work of art always signals something of a birth into being, the arrival of the new and its peculiar shock.

What Gadamer initially describes as a "return" to the notion of *mimesis* is actually a fundamentally new interpretation of that notion. He does not take over the word without strong qualifications. His intention in this return is to avoid the attempt to simply "invent" a new vocabulary for speaking of artworks and to demonstrate that the words we have long enlisted for the discourse on art do indeed have some reason for resonating as true. However, his intent is above all to forge a way of speaking about painting that is able to appreciate and do justice to the challenge of non-objective painting, a challenge that most of all needs a new vocabulary in order to be met. Pointing to the archaic sense of *mimesis,* calling attention to the emergence of an "ordering energy," is Gadamer's response to this challenge, and it needs to be read as a response that does not center upon any representation of objects but rather upon the *presentation* and *genesis* of things, whatever they might be. Thus he says that "the work of art provides a perfect example of that universal characteristic of human existence—the never-ending process of building a world."⁵⁹ This love of genesis, this drive to give birth into the world, animates the work of art as it is able to quicken our sense of the movement of life itself. Gadamer's recovery of the archaic sense of *mimesis,* coupled with his efforts to show why the being of the artwork needs to be understood apart from any conception of representation, calls attention to the importance of seeing the work of art always as an event and a repetition of the movement of life. It is never to be found by focusing upon anything like an object that is represented or copied in the work. The traditional vocabulary and assumptions about painting have long held that the object and its representation are at the center of how the image in painting is to be thought. The special achievement of modern art, especially its non-objective character, is that it makes evident the insufficiency of such language and the failure of such assumptions to open up the real contribution and challenge of the image in the work of art.

Gadamer recognizes this need to confront the challenge of modern abstract painting, and he recognizes as well that this confrontation will need to move forward in two ways: first, there is the need to overthrow the customary terms with which painting has been traditionally discussed; second, there is the need secure a new language and approach to painting. He understands as well that this problem is not "simply" a problem for the analysis of painting; it is rather an instance of the largest problem of our historical moment. So, for instance, with respect to the notion of the symbol, perhaps the most enduring notion enlisted in the discussion of painting, Gadamer writes that "a symbol is something that facilitates recognition, and the dearth of symbol is a characteristic feature of the historical moment in which we find ourselves. It reflects the growing unfamiliarity and impersonality of the world about us."[60] Like Heidegger, Gadamer argues that in the present age, the world has become unfamiliar to us and is no longer readily understood as our home. In many ways it was this alienation and estrangement that provided the impulse leading to abstract painting and other new forms of art. Recognizing this, Gadamer argues that philosophy too needs such an impulse and that the challenge of addressing the work of art in the modern age can be decisive in responding to this need.

On the basis of the critique and limitations of traditional aesthetic categories, it has become clear that if philosophy is to answer this need, then the language of philosophy must be able to expose rather than close off three hallmarks of the work of art in the present age. First, artworks must be understood as a matter of presentation and genesis, rather than as a matter of copying. Second, this language cannot be a conceptual language but needs to be closer to that which Kant described as the "aesthetic idea." Third, it must be a language that is able to address the character of our historical moment, namely, the growing unfamiliarity and impersonality of our world. In short, any such language of painting today must speak the "meaning" of painting in a new way. There is one final test, one further measure, of any such language: it must be able to "speak" in the realm of the visible, and it must not speak by referring away from the painting itself.

Gadamer contends that such a language is the language of gesture. He introduces this claim by saying: "What a gesture expresses is 'there' in the gesture itself. A gesture is something wholly corporeal and wholly spiritual at one and the same time. The gesture reveals no inner meaning behind itself. The whole being of the gesture lies in what it says. At the same time every gesture is also opaque in an enigmatic fashion. It is a mystery that holds back as much as it reveals. For what the gesture reveals is the being of meaning rather than the knowledge of meaning."[61] It is a *logos sui generis*. One should add that what is most important regarding gesture is that it is a language proper to the realm of visibility. If one can call gesture an ideality, a bearer of meaning, then this claim needs to be qualified by saying that it is this only as enacted and performed. It is a "language" only as the language of the lived body. Gesture is how the human being moves in the world. It is not what it is, not this movement, by pointing away from itself to something else but by appearing as itself, by showing itself in the realm of the visible.[62] Gesture is how the human being, the being of *logos*, responds to what is otherwise inexpressible.[63] This proximity to the inexpressible of the visible language, the moving image traced out as the body, that we call gesture has long been recognized, even if its significance has been overlooked. One finds, for instance, a passage in Aeschylus's *Agamemnon* where Clytemnestra tells Cassandra, whose speech is unintelligible, "not to speak with voice, but rather show me with your foreign hand [*anti phōnes phraze karbanō cheri*]." To this, the chorus replies that "this stranger [Cassandra] . . . needs an interpreter [*hermeneos*]."[64] Gesture belongs to *logos*, to what can be interpreted and understood, but it does not belong to the *logos* as a word that can be spoken. It is, in a sense, prior to, more elemental than, the spoken word. In this elementality, it remains closer to the limits of what can be said at all. It is the original idiom of appearance.

It can seem, and perhaps might well be the case, that gesture is a distinctively human capacity. One might argue that animals do not gesture (even if animals do communicate desires and feelings). On the other hand, one might equally find the animal and the human to meet precisely in the element of gesture. So, for instance, Benjamin suggests that this meeting in gesture is precisely what one finds in Kafka's animal stories.[65] But, even the suggestion that animals too are beings of gesture is simply a way of emphasizing that a being who can gesture has a privileged relation to language and to understanding. What is important about this reference to animal gesture, at least for the purposes of this book, is not found in opening up the problematic, and perhaps impossible, question that asks about the possibility of animal language. That question is likely best left unanswered and as a sharp reminder of the limits of what we can ask and understand. Rather, reference to animals here is made in order to draw a distinction between the expression of desires and wants, even of feelings and emotions, and the capacity for gesture. One can highlight this point by saying that in some sense, one must also say that the infant does not gesture either. Or, better:

that language for the child first begins to appear with the emergence of the ability to gesture and not simply express desire.[66] For Gadamer, the significance of this point is decisive: gesture opens up a world and is not simply the expression of private desires or needs. "Every gesture is human, but not every gesture is exclusively the gesture of a human being. Indeed, no gesture is merely the expression of an individual person. Like language, the gesture always reflects a world of meaning to which it belongs."[67] Our every movement—the way we walk or sit or move our hands—can, in some sense, be called a gesture; that is, our movements *mean* something and can be *interpreted*. This means that gesture is always set back into the context of a world. Gesture "speaks" and yet is not a language in the everyday sense of that word. It is, one might say, a language "prior" to language (which is why one can, for the most part, "read" the gestures of those who speak a language that one does not speak). This "priority" of gesture opens a space of signification, or sense, out of which spoken language can emerge. This, in part, is what Heidegger means when he says that "the hand signs [*zeichnet*], presumably because the human being is itself a sign [*Zeichen*]. . . . But the gestures of the hand always and everywhere pass through language and precisely then and most purely when the human being speaks insofar as it stays silent. Each and every movement of the hand, in each and every of its works, carries itself and gestures itself in the element of thought."[68] Thus, only a being capable of gesture—of gesturing itself and of grasping another's movement *as* gesture—is capable of language. This is why Kommerell says that "speech is primordial gesture [*Urgebärde*]."[69] While not captured by gesture, held captive to it, or explained by it, all speech has its roots in the possibility of gesture. About this claim, Agamben rightly remarks, "[Gesture] is first of all a forceful presence in language itself, one that is older and more originary than conceptual expression. If this is true, if speech is originary gesture, then what is at issue in gesture is not so much a prelinguistic content as, so to speak, the other side of language, the muteness inherent in humankind's very capacity for language, its *speechless* dwelling in language. And the more human beings have language, the stronger the unsayable weight them down."[70] Gesture remains close to the unsayable, the inexpressible. And yet, it also necessarily summons interpretation insofar as it is possible only for a being of *logos*. In gesture, the unsayable and the intelligible live in close proximity. This is why Agamben can say that "gesture is always the gesture of being at a loss in language."[71] As such, gesture is always found at the edge of the human: the limits of being human are found and known only in and as gestures.

But, if this point is to be developed and furthered, then what must also be said is that gesture, which emerges with the exhaustion of language and speech, is itself not defined by audibility but visibility—it is speechless. This means that Kommerell should also have said that image too is primordial gesture. Put in a different way, one can say that gesture makes something visible that is not visible otherwise precisely in its peculiar manner of speechlessness. Bound to the realm of the visible, gesture might even be called an *eikos logos*—a visible language.[72] And yet, as with the relation of speech to gesture, the relation of image to gesture will always emerge at the limits of the image, at the borders of the visible and in proximity to the invisible.

These remarks about gesture—its relation to both word and image— open the way to answering the question of how we can interpret the image without coercing it into what it is not.[73] How can we respond to the image, speak of the image, so that we see it better as itself, as it appears? What "language" belongs to the image *as* an image? In light of what has emerged about the notion of gesture, one can see the reasons for saying that gesture is the language *of* the visible, of the image. Indeed, it is this especially in the case of those images in the work of art in which appearance itself, sheer visibility and coming into being, is itself the reason for the being of the image. Saying that gesture is the language of the image means as well that only a being capable of gesture—that is, of acts that give sense to the realm of visibility—is capable of making images. One might even say that gesture is the most elemental form of any image. It an image "prior" to image in the same way that it is a language "prior" to language. Gesture, thus understood, is the common ground of word and image. Or perhaps it is better not to say that it is a common ground since saying that might be claiming too much and relying upon an image of ground that itself is questionable. Perhaps it is more appropriate to say that gesture is the point of contact, the limit point where there is a meeting, of both word and image. And yet gesture, like speech, is ephemeral—something like fireworks, which Adorno found to be the basis character of all works of art—unless it is recorded. Essentially a movement, the movement of life itself, and thus temporal, gesture is appearing as such; it is only as appearing.[74] However, as has become evident, gesture is not random but carries within itself a relation to ideality. It shows this in its proximity to the word and to the image. It is found on the edge of speech and of the image—indeed, in such nearness to these that one can call gesture the language of the image. Words become script—on the basis of this iconographic potential drawn from the emergence of speech out of gesture—and moving and living images, visible gestures, become paintings on the same basis. In other words, gesture lets itself be inscribed, and in this it leaves traces of itself. Writing and painting share this common ground, and any resolution of the problems that pertain to speaking of images needs to begin with the recognition of this commonality.[75] The Greek word for painting, *zōgraphia*—the writing of life—is perhaps the most appropriate name for the sort of work that we call by the material out of which it is made: paint. It is better, more appropriate, to speak of painting as gesture, as the inscription of the gesture that is the movement of life itself.

Painting, Gadamer has argued, is itself the result of a gesture that has been transformed into a text, a *Gebilde*. This inscription of gesture into the text gives it form and structure. In becoming a text, gesture has, to use Heidegger's language, become a work and, if successful, might even become a work of art, that is, a work that quickens and repeats a sense of the life and freedom out of which it has emerged. Once one begins to grasp the place of gesture in the painting, one can begin as well to appreciate how right Klee was in suggesting that the seemingly immobile painting needs to be recognized as among the preeminent forms for the presentation of movement *as* movement, of what Klee referred to as *genesis*. When we recognize that painting is the inscription of gesture itself, that it emerges out of this movement of life itself, then we are also able to understand why painting should not be defined or interpreted with reference to an already constituted object, since the basic character of painting is found above all in the *movement* of gesture. Abstract painting, which is not distracted by objects, can exhibit this movement in an exemplary fashion. Such works of art are not best understood as imitations of objects but rather as initiations into nothing but their own appearance, and, as such, they deepen the mystery of all appearance. Again, Kommerell: "And into what does [the work of art] initiate? Not into its meaning, only into itself. Into something that, in its incarnation in beauty, pain, and enigmas, constantly borders on meaning without ever uttering it and while remaining unnamable. Life thus has a secret; indeed, life is a secret. After every single realization, however compelling, after every single disenchantment, however terrible, life returns to its secret."[76] The painting, understood as this inscription of gesture, is precisely such an invitation to engage the movement of life itself. In such works, this movement of life becomes even more than it was in the beginning. It undergoes an "increase in being."

Gadamer's remarks about gesture led him to a discussion of Werner Scholz's paintings; indeed, his most extensive discussion of gesture is found in conjunction with his discussions of Scholz's work.[77] What Gadamer finds in Scholz's artworks that so attracts him is that "they speak a silent language . . . that allows us to recognize things that belong together with no need of words. . . . All these images present us with nothing but gestures, gestures that bear their meaning within themselves and far exceed any humanistic knowledge that we may possess. Even when they present human features, they remain embedded in the textural surface of the painting itself."[78] He takes as an example a painting titled *Antigone* (figure 20).

Of this painting, Gadamer writes that "we are offered an image of Antigone immured, slowly starving to death. . . . This Antigone is not a representation of the legendary figure of Greek literature depicted in emphatic relief. She is a gesture representing self-chosen death and nothing else. The cavernous walls about her sink too in a single gesture that fuses man and world into one."[79] One does not recognize anything that might be said to copy or represent something of Antigone; no scene of her story is the centerpiece here. Rather, one finds the gesture that will always bear the name of Antigone, rendering her the ideal of a particular idiom. Here is a grief and sorrow that a human being must bear and endure that is inhuman and unbearable. Here, without any representation of death, the end of life and its power is, in some sense, visible. This is not the whole story of Antigone, nor must it be. But it does go to the heart of what one must understand in order to understand anything of her life. This appears not by virtue of some narration or conceptualization, nor does it appear by means of any representation. It is rather as the inscription of the gesture of a life that what is seen is able to emerge. In his essay on Kleist and the inexpressible, Kommerell describes, albeit with a somewhat different intention and in a different context, just what this inscription of the gesture of a life amounts to: "Mystery is restored to the interiority of human being. Its 'truth' is not a truth of the world or of the mind. . . . A new beauty begins here which, like the beauty of the gestures of an animal, is gentle and threatening; intention yields to inwardness, willing yields to necessity. And thus, just as one lives in one's own truth, to live in the truth of a stranger, an alien creature, is love. To deviate from this truth is the danger of all language."[80] Gesture, one might say, grants the possibility of understanding.

Gadamer speaks of other paintings, even of landscapes, in the same manner, and doing this serves as a reminder that gesture is at the heart of how we understand human being and, at the same, of how a human being understands. But, despite its fundamentality for the being of the human being, it is important to bear in mind that gesture is not defined or contained by the human, nor is it to be understood as the representation of something other than itself: "The painting does not recount a story, nor interpret anew one with which we are already familiar. . . . Even though we are unable to understand them fully, we recognize ourselves in these images . . . concentrated in the simplicity of mighty gestures."[81] What is rendered visible in these paintings is something that no object can contain or represent. One finds the becoming visible of elemental passions. What comes into view are the elements of life itself as living, as moving, and as felt almost inexpressibly and yet still on display. The character of the gestures in these paintings is never simply to be the expression of something private and inward. They present themselves as "there" and so as intelligible, as being able to be interpreted. Gesture invites understanding. There is, one might say, something "universal" in these gestures. But this universality—if such is even the proper word—is clearly *not* the same sort of universality that is claimed by concepts. It is closer to what Kant referred to as the "universal communicability" of the feeling of pleasure—the quickening of the movement of life—that signals the beautiful. It is also akin to what Kant meant by the "aesthetic idea," which is "too large" an intuition to be brought under the rule of a concept and, as such, is bound inextricably to the realm of sense.[82] According to Kant—and I believe that Gadamer would agree—all painting is driven by aesthetic ideas. Gadamer suggests that in these paintings by Werner Scholz, one sees this force of such ideas that come into view with a special clarity as gestures. One might say that gesture is the way in which the movement of life is inscribed in the painting. Gesture is thus the way in which the genesis at the heart of painting appears.

Although Gadamer presses the notion of gesture in a significant way, there are two further points about gesture that he does not note or develop but that are quite important. The first point concerns the "translation" of gesture into the image, its "materialization" and "inscription," or what Gadamer described as a "Verwandlung ins Gebilde"—its transformation into a "text." More precisely, what must be added to Gadamer's account is that gesture—as well as the process of its transformation—needs to be understood with reference to the body that gestures and that forms or inscribes such gestures. Gesture has always—from its most elemental appearance to its most articulated expression—belonged to the world as concretized, the world lived as the body. This, in part, is what Heidegger referred to when he said that "each and every movement of the hand, in each and every of its works, carries itself and gestures itself in the element of thought."[83] This is also why Merleau-Ponty says that "it is by lending his body to the world that the artist changes the world into paintings."[84] In light of this, one can see how gesture lets us understand why painting, which is the immediate work of the hand, will always be able to bring forward images that reach far deeper than the photographic image into the mystery of what needs to be understood and interpreted, the mystery of the movement of life. The difference is between an image that repeats and continues gestures and an image that seeks to capture gestures. In a like manner, handwriting will always set itself apart from the typed word as a way in which language is brought into its iconographic being.[85] Once one comes to recognize how bodily life belongs to gesture, one sees in the way we live through gestures, the way our being a body always is a gesture. This means that the visible realm is not originally experienced as a space populated by objects but as the space of interpretation, *the space opened up by gesture*. This gestural space through which the human being lives is indeed the space inviting interpretation. We do not only interpret our world; rather, our way of being in the world invites—even summons—its own interpretation. Living in and through such gestural lives, we are in a constant dialogue with what we are not. This, in part, is what Hölderlin meant when he wrote the passage "since we are a conversation"[86]—as beings of gesture, our very way of being in the world sets us into a conversation with that world.

This sense that gesture opens up and engages us in a silent dialogue points to the second characteristic of gesture that is missing in Gadamer's discussion of it. There is good reason for this oversight on Gadamer's part since this is its attribute that is the most difficult to grasp. It is in many respects the most significant feature of gesture since it involves us in a dynamic, and yet it is also the least evident characteristic of gesture since it requires a special disposition to be recognized. Here I am referring to the quiet truth of a gesture, namely, that in looking at a gesture, one is *addressed* by that gesture. My look to the gesture receives a "look" as a response; a meaning comes to me, "looks" back at me. Gestures reach out to the other, to the viewer. This means that gesture engages one whom it reaches and that every gesture is a request—even if "only" the request that it be understood. This sense of being addressed is what Merleau-Ponty was highlighting when he cited André Marchand's paraphrase of Klee: "In a forest, I have felt many times over that it was not I who looked at the forest. Some days I felt that the trees were looking at me, were speaking to me . . . I was there listening. I think that the painter must be penetrated by the universe and not want to penetrate it."[87] Since all visibility emerges out of the space that is opened by the possibility of gesture, the space that I inhabit, one must indeed say that all things belonging to such a space possess the capacity of an address. In this way, I am involved in the lives of others and of the world. A response is solicited, and I become, prior to any agency, prior to any subjective life, responsible for more than myself alone.

Painting—the site of gesture that is defined by color, line, and form—addresses us as this enigmatic "language" that constitutes the image. To be able to be addressed in this way, one needs to be open to a seeing that is not captivated by objects, by what is represented. One needs—a strange but nonetheless quite appropriate word must be invoked here—to be able to *listen* to this address. This is how responsibility originates, in this hiatus, this open and indeterminate pause, this attentiveness to what is "outside." If there is something like a hermeneutic perspective that can be developed out of Gadamer's remarks on gesture, then one has to say that it is defined above all by such listening. Whatever the text one encounters, whatever form it might take, the precondition of "understanding" that text is the capacity to open oneself in order to listen and let this address appear and arrive. In the case of painting, this means that one needs to learn to "listen" to the "language" of gesture. If we can call gesture a language, then we need to add immediately that such a language is not the same as the language of signs or symbols that point away from themselves. Gesture, on the other hand, is simply "what it shows;"[88] it points to itself. To regard the painting as the inscription of gesture is to let oneself be drawn into the painting itself; one is drawn into the very surface that the image defines, and on this surface one finds the depths of life. On that surface that the image defines, one faces the movement defining the painting. One witnesses something of the movement of life, and one is able to be addressed by this. Homer, a poet who was said to be blind, gives one of the most touching and profound images of painting as just such an inscription of life. In his description of Achilles' shield, we find the painting of the whole of life. What is distinctive about this image, this painting, is that it does not represent life; rather, it shows life as a movement. This image of "the complete painting," the "perfect idea of painting,"[89] has been such a challenge to painters precisely because it cannot be represented; it is not a copy of life; instead, it is a continuation of the very movement of life itself that appears.

In the end, then, this truth of the image in the work of art does not appear as the object represented but rather appears in the simplest of ways: it becomes visible even in the brush strokes that give life to the image. Some paintings concentrate this elemental character of all painting, and such paintings seem, appropriately, to have something calligraphic about them. They are indeed the inscriptions of a language, the language of gesture itself, of that language prior to language that opens both the space of speech and of visibility itself—the space of the possibility of interpretation. This space is the origin of that which lets the human being come into being as a being of understanding and responsibility. It is at this point that one draws close to the origin of the work of art and, for the same reason, close to the origin, the dwelling point, that lets us be who and what we are.

Julius Bissier, who was a friend of Heidegger's (who, sadly, never referred to Bissier or his work), was someone who painted precisely such concentrated images of the gesture proper to painting (see figure 21). In Bissier's work, one finds something archaic that, in the Western world especially, had long since seemed to disappear. Bissier is, of course, not alone in this discovery, far from it, but one must wonder what Bissier's work might have meant to Heidegger, who, precisely at the time Bissier was producing his most calligraphic paintings, was discovering the possibilities of the work of art through Klee's paintings. There is a very real sense in which Bissier's work amplifies precisely that aspect of Klee's paintings that was most interesting for Heidegger. Strangely, Heidegger simply passes over this possibility.

Gesture is what defines the image in the work of art. The variety of gestures might well be infinite—one simply cannot decide if such is the case—but, if one weds what one learns from thinking about the language of gesture with the insights into painting drawn from Heidegger and Klee, then one might say that the most far-reaching gesture, the most elemental of all gestures, is the gesture that addresses us as the genesis of things, the becoming of the world. Such a gesture, such painting, such experience, opens the space that the Greeks designated as *physis*. It is the realm of death and, of course, of birth, of all appearance. The farthest reach of painting—its most archaic sense and its future—appears as this opening of the realm of nature, of genesis. The beauty of such works is found in the way that simply bearing witness to such appearance quickens our sense of life and the freedom proper to our appearance as life. We are set back into the world having understood, or at least loved what we could not understand, just a bit more.

THE QUESTION OF GENESIS FOR NOW

So the promise of the work of art is the promise of understanding and belonging to the world. Today, however, everything about this promise is haunted by Heidegger's claim that ours is an era lacking art as a real possibility: in other words, that the bringing forth that is the defining trait and promise of the work of art has been usurped by the production and composition of the *Gestell*, which has foreclosed the space of free appearance. To use Heidegger's vocabulary, one might say that the claim, the worry, is that *Machenschaft* has overtaken *Hervorbringen* as the form in which we understand the character of making today. But Heidegger is not alone in giving voice to such a judgment that this historical present, this now, is defined by the closure of the space of appearance and the impoverishment of the world. With a similar sense of a foreclosure, Kommerell speaks of our time as one in which the sense for gesture has been lost. Describing the age of Jean Paul and the philosophy of German Idealism, Kommerell writes that this was the time in which a decline began since both "derive from the situation of the bourgeoisie in which the forms of life have lost their intimacy [*Innigkeit*] and simplicity [*Einfalt*]. . . . Completely unencumbered spirit is a consequence of the bourgeoisie that has lost its gestures."[1] About this loss of gesture, Agamben remarks that "the more gestures lost their ease under the pressure of unknown powers, the more life became indecipherable. And once the simplest and most everyday gestures had become as foreign as the gesticulations of marionettes, humanity . . . was ready for massacre. . . . Precisely in this idea . . . [that] human beings, liberating themselves from all sacredness, communicate to each other their lack of secrets as their most proper gesture, Kommerell's criticism reaches the political dimension."[2] Finally, a different yet no less damning assessment of our historical moment is expressed by Roberto Calasso when he writes that

> much was implicit in the Greek experience that has been lost to
> us today. When we look at the night sky, our first impression is
> one of amazement before a random profusion scattered across
> a dark background. Plato could still recognize "the friezes in the

sky." And he maintained that those friezes were the "most beautiful and exact" images in the visible order. But when we . . . see the Milky Way . . . we are incapable of perceiving any order, let alone a movement within that order. No, we immediately start to think of distances, of the inconceivable light-years. We have lost the capacity, the optical capacity even, to place myths in the sky.[3]

In other words, our relation to the sky today is determined calculatively; we are no longer able to find ourselves addressed by the stars. One might say that we are no longer capable of seeing the heavens as a text. Others—Nietzsche, Adorno, Benjamin, Marcuse, to name only a few of many—are just as sharp in their critique, and so to take these critiques of the present age into account only adds to the sense that the doors that open upon understanding have already slammed shut in our time. Their diagnosis of our age might differ, but the destiny of the diagnosis, its fatality, remains the same.

In whatever terms this criticism of our age is formulated, the common point of such remarks is that, in our time, a space of understanding our world has been shut down. One can characterize this space in many ways: as the space of the appearance of the beautiful, of gesture and so of interpretation and understanding, of art itself. Such a space of appearance has been colonized by habits of mind and forces that drive history to give an account of the world according to some calculus of speed, measurement, abstraction. Histories and analyses are undertaken to account for this condition, this loss: metaphysics, modernity, one-dimensionality, technological reason, the dialectic of the Enlightenment, nihilism, and repression are all among the "causes" named in these accounts. But, while the roots of this closure and growing unfamiliarity that characterize the present age might be identified in a variety of ways, the consequences of this condition tend to be similarly diagnosed; namely, that a peculiar and paradoxical distress characterizes our present age, one that is typified by the strange alchemy of an increasing sense of what can be known coupled with a decreasing sense of what is understood.[4] We suffer, one might say, from a loss of orientation, and this orientation is not a matter of cognition but of understanding. What is most important at this point in history is to come to recognize that this orientation defines our lives as able to be ethical beings, that is, as beings able to be addressed by, and respond to, the world. The loss of this orientation, this openness to the address of the world, is, at the same time, the loss of that which lets us be responsive and responsible beings in the world. This loss that is the defining trait of our age is a profound loss, since it is the loss of possibilities.

And yet: this distress and loss of orientation is, in a strange sense, the hope for us to pursue since they are peculiar announcements—presentations as almost photographic negatives—of what is absent for us. In other words, this alienation, this lack of stories in the sky, this loss of a sense for gesture, is itself also something of a clue. What this means is that what is needed in our time presents itself in the form of an absence, of something lacking, something past and, perhaps, even dead. This absence cannot be cognized as an object but, if it is to be understood, needs to be felt. For this reason (and others), mourning, which is a felt relation to an absence, has become a special concern of our time.[5] This, in part at least, is why Heidegger found Hölderlin's work, which he characterized as driven by "sacred mourning," so decisive for our present.[6] In other words, our age is indexed to a sense of what it is missing—at least that is the hope of our age: "where danger is, there rescue grows as well."[7]

Heidegger's judgment about our historical present is fierce and relentless. While one can argue that his grim assessment of these times has not changed in any essential respect, one must nonetheless recognize that Heidegger's assessment of the prospects for overcoming our present condition did indeed change over the course of his career so that there were periods during which he found reason for some optimism that a different, freer future might open up. Whenever Heidegger did find some glimmer of an opening to a better future, he found it in conjunction with the experience opened up by the work of art. Beginning with his "The Origin of the Work of Art," moving through discussions of Sophocles and Hölderlin, Rilke and George (and so privileging poetry over painting), and up to the great enthusiasm that accompanied his discovery of Klee, Heidegger saw in works of art (or, more precisely, in individual artists) some opening to a future that nourished rather than drained the roots of life in our time. But, after the burst of optimism fed by Klee's work, Heidegger seemed to decide that this opening had quietly, but surely, closed—at least for now—and that now "only a God can still save us."[8] Nonetheless, others—here I have argued that Gadamer's hermeneutics stands out—still see the promise of the work of art, and indeed the claim in such cases tends to be that this promise comes into view precisely because of, not despite, the desperate character of our time. I do not believe that one can give a clear accounting of why it is that some believe the promise of the work of art is still viable today and why others hold that path to be blocked for us. Is it depth of insight or simply personal temperament? What measure can there be to fathom the depths of the problem we face in this historical moment? What gauge of the force of art's promise to break through the closure of our time? But, however one judges this situation, it is clear that the sweep of the questions posed is enormous and the stakes profound. In my own case, I have come to hold a view in the somewhat impossible middle ground between these two views, one that seems to resonate with Benjamin's comment that "only for the sake of those without hope is hope given to us."[9] In other words, while I do not see much reason to hold to the optimism one finds expressed in Gadamer, I also have come to believe that there is no path open today other than to pursue this opening, this promise that belongs to the work of art and aesthetic experience, since it is a promise that promises to change us. So long as we can still feel the tug of the beautiful and sense the difference that defines the work of art, it seems that some hope, however faint, still remains.

————

There is a shared heritage among those who have pursued this sense that the work of art opens us to a different understanding of our world and our place in it. I am referring to the heritage that arises from Kant's contributions in his third Critique. Kant, whom Hölderlin would refer to as "the Moses of our nation"[10] precisely because of the contributions of the third Critique, was the first to lay out the real promise of the work of art, and indeed he did so in ways that seem to have outstripped his own understanding of his achievement in this regard. Philosophy divides after Kant over this decision about what is promised by the work of art. After Kant, two philosophical paths seem possible: one is defined by those who are ready to explore the real contributions of art, even to the extent that those contributions cannot be taken up into the project of philosophy, while the other path is defined by those who resist this opening and remain wedded to the project of conceptuality. My intention has not been to write a history of the path that has pursued this promise of art, but I do believe that it is important to recognize how it is that the philosophical projects laid out by Heidegger and Gadamer, both of whom I have singled out as exemplary in their efforts to articulate this promise, need to be seen as the inheritors of that history that runs from Kant through Hegel, Schelling, Schiller, Schlegel, Schopenhauer, and Nietzsche.[11] In particular, it is important to recognize how hermeneutics is to be understood as that philosophical approach that has finally thematized the question of the relation of art and truth as an ontological and not simply aesthetic question. Or better, hermeneutics recognizes the insight that is first hinted at by Kant: that aesthetic experience opens up the questions of first philosophy in an original manner. But there is an aspect of Kant's achievement in the *Critique of Judgment* that is largely missing in the way that achievement has been carried forward in the present age. What is missing and most in need of being recovered is the real ethical meaning of this promise of art.[12] This is what is still to be learned from Kant, and this is one way in which the orientation that has been lost in the present age might begin to be recovered.

Kant situates the questions of aesthetic experience and judgment within the larger horizon of judgment in general. More precisely, he situates it within the realm of reflective judgment, which is that form of judgment that must operate apart from the rule of the concept and its consequences. For Kant, the preeminent form of such reflective judgment is found in aesthetic judgment. The argument that I have pursued in this book is that this character of being apart from the concept and its operations, apart from the *logos,* is the great challenge that is put to philosophy by the work of art. It is this challenge that some, like Heidegger and Gadamer, have taken up. But what is missing from Heidegger and Gadamer, and what one finds only implicitly in Kant, is that it is first in the departure from this rule of the concept that the questions of ethical life begin to open up in the most original sense. What one finds in being ready to make this move into that which cannot be grasped by the concept or conceived according to the imperatives of the category is that one is making the move into the most elemental dimensions of being human; it is the move into the essential character of human freedom as abyssal, as inconceivable. This departure from the rule of the concept and its law demands a profound transformation of the conditions of understanding. This transformation is, I believe, what is needed for any real opening of the realm of ethical understanding to that which Heidegger called for when he spoke of an "original ethics."[13]

When I outlined the impulses and concerns that would shape the discussions and arc of this book, the final issue mentioned was this conviction that the ethical stakes of these aesthetic matters were the real significance—and measures—of these discussions about the promise of the work of art. In that context, I referred to Plutarch's word *ethopoiein,* which means something like "to bring into being poetically one way of being" or "to shape (or form) one's character." There is an intimate link holding the two roots of this word—*ethos* and *poiein*—together. Theirs is such a powerful intimacy that one eventually comes to recognize the impossibility of thinking one of these root words without the other. To think and understand the full import and sense of ethos for us—ethos in its original sense such as it is expressed by Heraclitus's remark "ethos anthropoi daimon"[14]—one needs to understand the manner in which ethos most properly comes into being, that is, the coming into being according to operations of *poiein*.[15] Likewise, in order to think the operations of this coming into being, this fashioning or care of the self, one needs to understand how it is ultimately defined not simply as a poetic production but as a poetic production that opens the space of ethical life. To think this form of production and the character of the space it opens up is the task of philosophy. Saying this serves as a reminder that poetic practices and productions alone do not serve to expose the original space of ethical life, even if such practices place us into that space as a possibility. It is rather the reflection upon such practices that first opens up this otherwise concealed realm of the ethical, the realm in which we are able to be changed, formed, and transformed, that is, the realm in which we belong to the movement of life. This means simply that philosophical reflection and aesthetic experience *need* each other in order to live up to the possibility inherent in each. This also means that each needs to let its own practices be changed by this encounter. In the case of philosophy, this entails, as I have tried to argue, no longer assuming that the language of the concept has a hegemonic claim to being the language of truth.

In the immediate aftermath of Kant's third Critique, this wedding of aesthetic experience and aesthetic production to the task of philosophical reflection becomes an explicit aim. Thus, one reads the following in the programmatic text that is now titled "The Oldest System Program of German Idealism" (a text that bears the signatures of Hegel, Hölderlin, and Schelling):

> I am now convinced that the highest act of reason, the one through which it encompasses all ideas, is an aesthetic act, and that *truth and goodness only become sisters in beauty.* The philosopher must possess just as much aesthetic power as the poet. Those without aesthetic sense are our literal-minded philosophers. The philosophy of spirit is an aesthetic philosophy. . . . In this way, poetry gains a higher dignity, in the end she becomes again, what she was in the beginning—*the teacher of humankind;* for there is no philosophy, no history left, the poetic art alone will survive all the other sciences and arts.[16]

This aim is also expressed in the notions of *Bildung* (cultivation / education), *Bildungstrieb* (formative drive), and *Kunsttreib* (artistic drive) that become the bywords of this time and give shape to the goals of a range of thinkers and artists from Goethe to Nietzsche.[17] But, even though this aim defined the years in Kant's immediate wake, this sense of a partnership, of a reciprocal need, holding philosophy and the realm of the aesthetic together progressively lost the larger, ethical context that Kant had disclosed as so essential. In this way, the full import of the challenge of art and the question of the beautiful to philosophy, the real stakes of these questions, faded as Kant's legacy unfolded. To recover this sensibility and so to move from the ethical through reflection is the task of philosophy today. This means that philosophy must become different; above all, it must open itself to knowing the world in new ways. More basically, it must concern itself with the task of understanding before it ever presumes to lay claim to knowing.

Insofar as the largest concern of this book has been situated within the possibility of what has been called *ethopoiein*, the fashioning of the ethical self, it should be acknowledged that it has taken up this concern by and large only from the perspective of one of the root meanings of this word, namely *poiesis*. Insofar as this notion has been addressed at all, it must be said that the focus of this book has been upon the way in which production of the most original sort is exhibited in the way art is brought into being. But, in the end, this book has not pushed far into the way in which *ethopoiesis* is able to be thought; it has only arrived at the announcement of this task. Ethical life is a question, always a difficulty. The way in which we might orient ourselves ethically in light of what is learned from this analysis of art is still to be sorted out.

At the outset, I mentioned three other questions that motivated and gave shape to this book and that led to its focus upon the image in the work of art. Those questions were able to be formulated by naming a series of pairs: Heidegger and Klee, word and image, art and truth. A few words should be addressed to these topics as a way of concluding.

To speak of art and truth as essentially bound together is to let the notion of truth undergo a radical revision. In order to make sense of this, a reference to an argument that Kant made, but the consequences of which he did not fully pursue, is helpful. His argument is simple: that the summit of the possibilities of aesthetic experience—namely, the experience of beauty—is defined by a peculiar "quickening" of the feeling of life, and this feeling is so irrefutable, so compelling, that it must be understood to be a priori, as universal and necessary. This apriority is so basic that it is not ancillary or adjunct to the experience but part and parcel of it.

Simultaneous with this feeling of life is the sense of its a priori quality. In other words, this feeling of the movement of life arrives as an experience *as* true, and it can only be understood as *true*. And yet, this experience is fundamentally different from experience that compels us cognitively to speak of its truth; it is so different in fact that Kant finds the aesthetic experience in which the movement of life is disclosed to provide grounds for articulating a completely different way of understanding how it is that the world presents itself in this experience. More precisely, he argues that experience that lets itself be cognized is formed by the schema and the schematism; on the other hand, experience that resists such cognition, and yet is understood to be both universal and necessary in character, is formed by the symbol and the symbolic hypotyposis. But while Kant recognizes the integrity of aesthetic experience in this way, he does not draw the further conclusion that this experience provides the grounds for reconsidering the very idea of truth. Instead, Kant reserves the notion of truth for that which can be cognized. But it is precisely this decision that comes to be questioned by those who follow in Kant's wake. For them, the question of the relation of art and truth, a question that touches upon our understanding of our most elemental experiences, is the pressing question of philosophy in our time. To make the decision, as Gadamer does, that our understanding of truth needs to begin with—not just accommodate, but actually begin with—this compelling felt experience requires that one rethink the character and horizon of truth. In the end, it requires that one come to understand truth as a matter of following the movement of life that is quickened in aesthetic experience. In other words, both art and truth alike need to be understood as matters of this movement, and this in turn means that neither can be thought in conjunction with any notion of representation, copy, correspondence, or correctness. Neither art nor truth has its primary claim to truth in any relation to an object.

Taking this question of the relation of art and truth to heart, not subordinating the idea of truth to what can be cognized or conceptualized from the start, inaugurates a powerful and radical challenge to the conception and practice of philosophy that understands itself with reference to the *logos* and this *logos* with reference to the concept. This is the point at which the second question motivating this book, namely, the question of the relation of word and image, comes into play. The long-standing presumption that the word is privileged in thinking and the corollary assumption that the fulfillment of the word is found in the concept (and thus according to the species of universality and necessity that it represents) are called into question by a serious consideration of art. And yet, because painting presents itself as able to be comprehended in some regard and as able to be interpreted, this challenge to the authority of the word—especially the conceptual word—does not mark the limits of how we understand the world so much as it signals an expansion of such understanding. The way the painting lends itself to understanding enlarges the horizon of understanding in general.

One can make sense of this expansion of understanding by seeing how the relation of painting to the movement of life opens up painting as the inscription of gesture, the peculiar and primordial intelligibility of gesture as an idiom in which life articulates and leaves traces of itself. These traces form a text, a web of relations and a form, and as such the space of interpretation is opened. Insofar as painting belongs to this space of interpretation that is inscribed as the text of gesture that repeats the movement of life, painting—and, in the end, the work of art as such—belongs to the project of understanding, the same project that, in the most general sense, defines philosophy. But to learn to interpret the painting, to listen to it and to recognize the distinctive character of its movement, is exceedingly difficult, especially for the philosopher who holds fast to the authority of the concept, the *logos*, in matters of what can be understood. Here Heidegger's enthusiastic encounter with Klee must count as an exception and something of a model of how such engagements can be productive.

Heidegger's efforts to understand Klee's work on its own terms and not according to philosophical categories that are inappropriate to that work are exemplary, but they are not unique. One finds a similar effort in, among others, Merleau-Ponty's engagement with Cézanne's and Gadamer's turn to Werner Scholz. What makes Heidegger's relation with Klee so distinctive and worth special attention is the way in which his encounter with Klee extends the originality with which Heidegger had pressed upon the question of the work of art throughout his career. However, despite this commitment to pursuing how the relation of art and truth is to be thought, Heidegger, for the most part, did not pay special attention to painting but centered his attentions primarily upon poetry. Furthermore, his ambivalence about the possibilities of art—and painting in particular—in the present age worked to cultivate a real suspicion in Heidegger regarding abstract painting. So, his excitement about Klee and his sincere attempt to see and engage Klee's painting on its own terms, as well as the effort to understand Klee's theoretical works, represent a real change in Heidegger's own views. The prospects and promises of Klee's achievements—at least for a brief while—seem to open thinking in new ways for Heidegger. They even seem to provide a path beyond the limitations that define Western and metaphysical frames of understanding the world. Oblique and fragmentary though his written work on Klee is, Heidegger does indeed try to find a way to dialogue with Klee. Even if, in the end, that dialogue never bore the fruit that Heidegger himself hoped to find, there is no question that it opens up questions that should not be ignored. In particular, Klee's emphasis on genesis and his insistence that the painting is a temporal art, the preeminent art of movement itself, point Heidegger—and us—in directions still to be explored. If this opening is to be developed, then the struggle to see and to listen to what might appear in only the most elemental of ways—as gesture, as genesis, as the movement of life inscribing itself—needs to be learned. This is not an easy matter, above all since it entails a change in the most ingrained habits of how we understand the world and ourselves. This is what Rilke meant when he said that the "lesson" of the work of art is that "you must change your life."[18]

This change is easily misunderstood (and the reasons for such misunderstanding are themselves worthy of attention). It can slip into connoisseurship, into bourgeois self-satisfaction and the cultivation of a sort of aesthetic classism. But if this happens, what one finds is the consolidation of power, not the change that is summoned by the work. Kant recognized this and found in the authentic summons to change an indication of the importance of nature, for what is unbidden by us, for ethical life: "We judge with admiration a person who has enough taste to judge the products of fine art with correctness and precision, but who happily leaves the room in which one finds those beauties that serve vanity and social pleasures, and turns instead to the beauties of nature in order to find a train of thoughts that can never be fully unraveled."[19] In other words, this change that is summoned by a quickened sense of the movement of life is a simple one, a change not in what one knows but in how one understands. It is, in the end, a profound change in how one lives, and yet there is no imperative, only the smallest shift in orientation toward the world. But this shift alters one's relation to the world in the most basic ways; it is, as I have suggested, a change in one's ethos.

"Ethics" is a word that one should use sparingly and with reluctance today. Much-abused, diminished, and relegated to regulation, it is a word that no longer carries with it a sense of the great task and difficulty of human being. Being open to the movement of life, to the gesture that can be inscribed and repeated as the peculiar text that is the work of art, is one way, but only one way, to answer this task and the challenges of ethical life.

NOTES

INTRODUCTION

1. The first publication of a substantial number of these notes is found in Seubold, *Kunst als Ereignis;* subsequently, Pöggeler would publish a large number of the notes in *Bild und Technik.*

2. Petzet, *Auf einen Stern zugehen,* 158, letter of February 21, 1959.

3. See ibid., 65.

4. Two of the other artists who were key for Heidegger—George and Rilke—also possessed this talent for writing about their work and about the character of art itself. In a like fashion, Heidegger's attraction to van Gogh was initially through van Gogh's letters.

5. For a fine discussion of the presence and importance of Klee for twentieth-century continental philosophy, see Watson, *Crescent Moon over the Rational.*

6. Heidegger, *Ursprung des Kunstwerkes,* 90–91.

7. Klee, *Notebooks,* 80.

8. Klee, "Über moderne Kunst," 64.

9. For an approach to the work of art that starts with such silence, see Sallis, *Transfigurements.* See also my comments on Sallis's book and his reply in my article "In Kant's Wake," 104–14.

10. Adorno, *Ästhetische Theorie,* 189. On this point, see also my *Lyrical and Ethical Subjects,* 130–62.

11. Deleuze, *Qu'est-ce que la philosophie?* 30.

12. Gadamer, *Gesammelte Werke,* vol. 8, 197 (henceforth cited as GW followed by the volume number and page number).

13. Adorno, *Ästhetische Theorie,* 91.

14. Nietzsche, *Nachgelassene Fragmente 1887–1889,* KSA13, 500 (16[40] #6).

15. Merleau-Ponty, "Eye and Mind," in *Primacy of Perception,* 161.

16. Although this is precisely the tendency of so many. Thus Plato takes Homer as the artist par excellence, Aristotle chooses Sophocles (and even more specifically takes *Oedipus Tyrannus* as the exemplary work), Nietzsche (at least for a while) takes Wagner as the only artist, and Heidegger turns to Hölderlin (and to a few other select poets).

17. On this, see Kant, *Kritik der Urteilskraft,* 51–52 (henceforth cited as *KU* followed by the Akademie Ausgabe page number). See also Sallis's discussion of this in *Transfigurements,* esp. 44–45.

18. I have attempted to address this relation from a somewhat different approach in my *Lyrical and Ethical Subjects.*

19. Kant, *KU,* AK 298. I have attempted to unpack this kinship of art and ethical life in my *On Germans and Other Greeks.*

20. Foucault, *Hermeneutics of the Subject,* 237.

21. Rilke, "Archaïscher Torso Apollos," *Werke*, vol. 1, 557. When I return to these issues, I will also point to a somewhat different but still quite compatible way of addressing them that is outlined by Kleinberg-Levin's *Gestures of an Ethical Life*.

22. See, for instance, Kant's remark that "one says of nature and its capacities . . . too little if one describes it as an *analogue of art*. . . . One comes perhaps closer to this inscrutable character of nature if one calls it an *analogue of life*" (KU, AK 374).

23. Adorno's remark is actually not a question but a condemnation of our age: "nach Auschwitz ein Gedicht zu schreiben, ist barbarisch, und das frißt auch die Erkenntnis an, die ausspricht, warum es unmöglich ward, heute Gedichte zu schreiben" (in *Prismen*, 30). The notion is one that Adorno will comment upon in other texts, most notably in *Negative Dialektik*, 355–56.

CHAPTER 1 · UNFOLDING THE QUESTION

1. Hegel, *Phänomenologie des Geistes*, para. 110. In the same paragraph, Hegel also notes that the singular "this" is "unreachable" by the word and that what is "unspeakable" is "untrue."

2. Plato, *Phaedrus*, 264. Of course, Plato will make the identification of writing and painting a key point: "Writing [*graphē*], Phaedrus, has this strange quality, and is very like painting [*zōgraphia*]; for the creatures of painting stand like living beings, but if one asks them a question, they preserve a solemn silence. And so it is with written words . . ." (*Phaedrus* 275D). It should also be noted that Plato is among the few who have recognized the philosophical problem belonging to script. See, for instance, his *Cratylus* where one finds a discussion of handwriting. On this, see my "Putting Oneself in Words . . . ," 483–95.

3. Plutarch, *Moralia*, 346–47. See Lessing, "Laokoön"; see also Carson, *The Economy of the Unlost*, 47, where she gives a list of texts expressing this view (including Plato, Aristotle, Horace, Cicero, Longinus, and Augustine). One sees in this list just how enduring and how central to the history of philosophy this view is.

4. Horace, *Ars Poetica*, lines 361ff.

5. Augustine, "Answer to the Pelagians."

6. *Ekphrasis* is a notion with a complicated history. In the early centuries of the Christian era (1–5 CE), it referred to a rhetorical exercise in which the goal was to make language into a "window" though which the reader/audience "sees" the work of art. See Becker, *Rhetoric and Poetics of Early Greek Ekphrasis*.

7. On Homer's blindness, see my "What We Didn't See" and "Von der Wahrheit Sprechen."

8. Homer, *Iliad*, book 18.

9. Pope, *The "Iliad" of Homer*, 896. The difference between Homer's description of Achilles' shield and Virgil's description of Aeneas's shield (in book 8 of *The Aeneid*) is significant: Virgil places on the shield the real history of Rome and so depicts a story in those images. When Achilles carries his shield, he is carrying the whole of life itself, not frozen in any moment but quite simply alive. No names, no particular individual or event, is recounted. The shield is what should protect Achilles, and yet one can also say that it is his burden, his responsibility to bear this whole of life itself. The shield that Aeneas carries is the story of the founding of Rome and the justification of its position as master of the world. It is full of the proper names of real individuals. In some

sense, the shield validates Aeneas's own rights and authority insofar as it does that for Rome. The difference between the Greek and the Roman here is significant: in Virgil, the images serve the story; they confirm a story and illustrate it. In Homer, the images are the story; they illustrate nothing but themselves. On this, see Smith, "From Achilles' Shield (*Iliad* XVIII) to Scenes from the Trojan War (*Aeneid* I)," 109–26.

10. The question of cinema both does and does not belong here. It belongs here insofar as the technology of film marks a departure from the possibilities and the limitations of painting. For the same reason, the discussion of cinema does not belong to the issues of this book. Since it will remain at the margins of many discussions here, there will be other times when it will need some attention. But, in the end, I would argue that the intervention of technology, the distance from the human hand, separates film from the most significant questions posed by painting.

11. On Twombly's painterly response to the *Iliad*, see my "Like a Fire That Consumes All before It . . ." in *Lyrical and Ethical Subjects*.

12. There were of course others who remarked on the sameness or difference of the arts prior to Lessing. For instance, Dio Chrysostomus in his twelfth *Olympian Oration* compares Homer with the sculptor Phidias with respect to their representations of Zeus. Leonardo da Vinci's *Treatise on Painting* makes similar remarks as well. But, with Lessing this difference is elevated to a principle shaping the approach to the work of art as such.

13. G. E. Lessing, *Laocoön*, trans. Edward Allen McCormick (Baltimore, Md.: Johns Hopkins University Press, 1984), 66–68.

14. Kant, *KU*, AK 326. On the division of the arts in Kant, see Sallis, "Mixed Arts," in *Transfigurements*, 41–54.

15. Heidegger, *Nietzsche*, vol. 1, 232.

16. Gadamer, *GW*, vol. 1, 478.

17. Nietzsche, *Gebürt der Tragödie*, 15 (henceforth cited as *GT* followed by the page number).

18. Sallis, *Force of Imagination*, 103.

19. Hegel, *Phänomenologie des Geistes*, 88.

20. Heidegger, *Unterwegs zur Sprache*, 220.

21. Gadamer, *GW*, vol. 1, 478.

22. Adorno, *Ästhetische Theorie*, 189.

23. Gadamer, *GW*, vol. 1, 116ff.

24. Ibid., 116–17.

25. See Plato, *Sophist*, 262d. For a discussion of the metaphor of "weaving" in the ancient world, see Scheid and Svenbro, *The Craft of Zeus*.

26. Gadamer, *GW*, vol. 1, 118.

27. Ibid., 119.

28. On Gadamer's remarks and relation to cats, see my "What We Owe the Living," in *Between Description and Interpretation*, ed. Andrzej Wierciński (Toronto: Hermeneutic Press, 2005), 401–409.

29. Nietzsche, *GT*, 36.

30. Gadamer, *GW*, vol. 1, 119.

31. Ibid.

32. Ibid., 120 (emphasis added).

33. Ibid., 145 (emphasis added).

34. Ibid., 149.

35. Pliny, *Natural History*, 35.29. Cited in Carson, *The Economy of the Unlost*, 47. Carson's book outlines some of the same points that I raise here. What Carson does not mention, but what is nonetheless of great importance for the fullest treatment of these matters, is that writing too underwent a revolution at this particular historical juncture. On this, see Turner, *Athenian Books in the Fifth and Fourth Centuries B.C.*

36. See Carratelli, *The Western Greeks*, 99–100.

37. Recently, a crater on Mercury was named after Polygnotus. It sits next to a crater named Boethius. Simonides composed an inscription for Polygnotus's paintings at Delphi and when asked why replied, "So that it might be conspicuous that Polygnotus had painted them" (Plutarch, *Moralia*, 438b). Simonides is, of course, cited in the *Republic* by Polymarchus as the source of what he takes as his first definition of justice, namely, giving back what is due.

38. Pausanius, book 10, chapters 25–31.

39. Plato, *Ion*, 532a, and *Gorgias*, 448c.

40. Aristotle, *Politics*, 1340a40.

41. Aristotle, *Poetics*, 1448a2.

42. Ibid., 1454b11–12.

43. Aristotle contrasts Polygnotus with Zeuxis, who is the technically superior painter but whose work is simply intended to deceive. Pliny tells the story of a contest between Zeuxis and Parrhasius to see which one of them was the greater artist. When Zeuxis unveiled his paintings of grapes, they looked so real that birds came and pecked at them. Zeuxis then asked Parrhasius to draw back the curtain on his painting only to discover that the curtain was his painting. Lacan discusses this story to show how animals are attracted by surfaces while humans are drawn to the hidden. See Lacan, "What Is a Picture?" 103.

44. Simonides, fragment 821.

45. Plato, *Republic*, 599a.

46. Plato, *Sophist*, 235b8.

47. Ibid., 240c.

48. Heidegger, *Platon*, "*Sophites*," 400.

49. Nancy, *The Ground of the Image*, 81.

50. Kant, *Kritik der reinen Vernunft*, B 181.

51. One of the most innovative discussions of this theme—one informed by, but not restricted to, Kant's understanding of this topic—is found in Sallis, *Force of Imagination*, esp. chap. 7.

52. Heidegger, *Logik*, 362.

53. Martin Heidegger, *Kant and the Problem of Metaphysics*, trans. R. Taft (Bloomington: Indiana University Press, 1990), 63–64.

54. Heidegger, *Logik*, 362. The book of photographs that Heidegger was almost certainly using at this time was titled *Das Ewige Antlitz: Eine Sammlung von Totenmasken*, by Ernst Benkard. This book with its 123 illustrations, which included death masks of Goethe, Schiller, Hayden, Beethoven, and Napoleon, among others, was a popular success in Germany, going through nineteen printings. Among the death masks photographed was one of "L'Inconnue de la Seine," an unknown young woman who had drowned in the Seine River. Her death mask was widely reproduced and sold, often hanging in homes in Germany and France. It also became a sort of literary inspiration, showing up in some manner in works by Rilke, Blanchot, Camus, and Nabokov, among

others. Why Heidegger would refer to the photograph of Pascal's death mask rather than to the very well known image of "L'Inconnue" is not clear. For an interesting discussion of the incommensurability, the non-coincidence, of something with itself that photography exposes, see Derrida, *Demeure, Athènes*.

55. On this, see my "What We Owe the Dead."

56. Heidegger, *Kant and the Problem of Metaphysics*, 64.

57. On this, see Blanchot, *The Gaze of Orpheus*, 82–85, where he concludes with the claim that "man is made in his own image: this is what we learn from the strangeness of the resemblance of cadavers."

58. Günter Figal, "Persona," in *Hans Wimmer Zeichnet Martin Heidegger*, ed. G. Figal and T. Scheuffelen (Meßkirch: Martin-Heidegger-Museum, 2003), 12.

59. On the intensification of the image in the portrait and how the portrait shows in a condensed manner the character of all painting, see Gadamer, *GW*, vol. 1, 143–44.

60. Kolbe's introduction to *Das Ewige Antlitz* by Ernst Benkard makes the interesting comment that "death masks are works of art made in the workshop of nature; they are however also transcendental objects" (7). The claim is also made that such masks "announce a new becoming." Further reflection on the character of such masks would do well to begin by addressing both of these remarks.

61. On this, see Gadamer, *GW*, vol. 1, 144.

62. Heidegger, *Logik*, 363–64.

63. Gadamer makes a similar point when he demonstrates that the image cannot be thought either as a "pure indication" or as a "pure substitution," neither a sign nor a symbol. See *GW*, vol. 1, 149.

64. Ironically, it seems as if the image reaches the limits of its own possibility in the case of imaging the dead, the ghostly. Wedded to the visible, images will always struggle with the invisible. From out of this irony, one can begin to think of paintings of the dead. Hans Holbein the Younger's *The Body of the Dead Christ in the Tomb* and Kristeva's discussion of it in *Black Sun* would make an interesting starting point for this. Likewise, the role of the image, of the icon, in religion, as well as the iconoclasm, can be taken up at this point. See as well Vermeule, *Aspects of Death in Early Greek Art and Poetry*.

65. For a fuller discussion of this move inaugurated by the third Critique, see chap. 1 of my *Lyrical and Ethical Subjects*.

66. For an insightful discussion of the effect of aesthetic experience upon the concept, see Sallis, *Transfigurements*, esp. 64ff., and my reply, "In Kant's Wake."

67. Kant, *KU*, AK 351.

68. Ibid., AK 342. One of the decisive moments in the history of philosophical reflections on the production of art is found in Aristotle's *Physics*, B, 1, where Aristotle sets up an analogy between the *prohairasis*, the operations of the mind, of the maker of works of *techne*, and the causal being of nature. In that analogy, Aristotle tends to regard the workings of the artist's mind according to a sort of conceptual reason that Kant is challenging here. For a fuller discussion of this, see my "Economies of Production," 145–57, 265–68.

69. Kant, *KU*, AK 303.

70. For a discussion of these "drives" or "impulses," see my *On Germans and Other Greeks*, 73–83, 89–164, 191–224.

71. Hölderlin, *Sämtliche Werke und Briefe*, vol. 1, 871.

72. Other art forms, such as dance or music, have left no trace, no text, behind that would permit them to cross history into the present. But in taking up these claims, one

needs to be careful not to conflate the primordial with the primitive (Heidegger makes this point in a different context in *Sein und Zeit*, para. 11). Nonetheless, painting that has not been influenced by conscious reflection and becomes self-conscious of historical forces does seem to emerge more directly from this archaic point, and so primitive paintings do have a special appeal to one who addresses the question of images. But, saying this, one must also bear in mind that the primitive is defined not only as historically distance. Children's "artworks" should qualify as such primitive works.

73. Merleau-Ponty, *L'Oeil et Esprit*, 92.

74. The most explicit account of this connection between dreaming (especially daydreaming) and art is found in Freud, "Der Dichter und das Phantasieren" (1907), *Bildende Kunst und Literatur*, 170–81.

75. Klee, *Diaries*, entry #905, 1912.

76. See, for instance, Nietzsche, *GT*, sections 1–2. For Nietzsche, it is important to bear in mind that our relation to the dream image individuates us.

77. Ibid., section 4.

78. Ibid. Hegel will also discuss this painting—his concern is to establish the unity of the upper and lower halves. See Hegel, *Vorlesung über die Ästhetik*, 96. Sallis has perhaps the most extensive discussions of this notion of "shining." See, for instance, his *Transfigurements* and *Shades—Of Painting at the Limit*.

79. Nietzsche, *GT*, 39.

80. Nietzsche, *Nachgelassene Fragmente 1887–1889*, KSA13, 500 (16[40] #6).

81. Heidegger, *Holzwege*, 67.

82. See, for instance, Nietzsche, *GT*, section 16.

83. Heidegger, *Besinnung*, 30.

84. It is worth noting that Adorno too regards beauty as relevant for the question of art. See his *Ästhetische Theorie*, 101ff.

85. An excellent discussion of the impact of the Eiffel Tower upon aesthetic consciousness can be found in Hughes, *The Shock of the New*, 9–56. A similar transformation in consciousness might be found in the images of the earth taken from the moon in 1969. Once again, our home was seen from a perspective only previously ever imaged. The shock of the sight of the blue ball streaked with white and brown standing in stark contrast to the pitch-black universe compels one to think of one's world in a different way. The sight of Paris from atop the Eiffel Tower did much the same, since from that vantage point—one that was new as a perspective—one sees Paris as a cubist painting.

86. Many of the efforts of this period need to be interpreted against the backdrop of the paradoxes of history at this time. So, for instance, one should never forget that Nietzsche's *Birth of Tragedy*, which speaks of the essential importance of music for the understanding of life, was published in the same year (1872) as the invention of the phonograph, an invention that Stravinsky would claim marked the date of the death of music.

87. See, for instance, Benn's lecture to medical students titled "Das moderne Ich," in *Gesammelte Werke*, vol. 1, 7–22. He opens the lecture by remarking that most in his audience served in the war and so many had "glass eyes, bound or missing limbs." A similar poetic work is found in Benjamin Britten's *War Requiem* (1962), a piece based on Wilfred Owen's poems from the First World War.

88. Nietzsche, *GT*, section 16.

89. Though Nietzsche's use of this term is invoked by National Socialists occasionally in order to give it the apparent imprimatur of philosophical legitimacy, the primary

reference in most such cases is to a book by the physician Max Nordau titled *Entartung* (1892). The word, as Nordau uses it, is a medical term to describe those who were not physically "normal" and who were, as a consequence, morally "deformed" as well. Nordau's book also used the term to characterize modern art. See Barron, *"Degenerate Art,"* 26.

90. There are numerous studies of this point, but one that is especially interesting for the project of this book is Lacoue-Labarthe, *La fiction du politique.*

91. See Barron, *"Degenerate Art,"* 25ff.

92. The exhibit was extremely popular. In the four months it was displayed in Munich, there were over two million visitors. All told, three million people saw the show, making it one of the most popular exhibitions of modern art ever.

93. Abstraction and expressionism were considered especially corrupt, so much so that even artists, like Nolde, who were members of the National Socialism Party were denounced as "degenerate." See Barron, *"Degenerate Art,"* 9–13. But not everyone would see this notion of a connection between madness and art to be a form of "degeneration." Bataille's journal *Documents* frequently made such a connection. Likewise, Klee said (in the journal entry already cited regarding children [note 75 above]): "Parallel phenomena [to the kinship of children's art to painting] are provided by the works of the mentally diseased; neither childish behavior nor madness are insulting words here. . . . All this is to be taken very seriously." This issue will be discussed later. But in the context of discussing the *Degenerate Art* exhibit, it cannot be properly discussed.

94. Gadamer, *GW,* vol. 8, 25. English translation, "Art and Imitation," in *The Relevance of the Beautiful and Other Essays,* ed. R. Bernasconi (Cambridge: Cambridge University Press, 1986), 92 (henceforth cited as *RB* followed by the page number).

95. Gadamer, *RB,* 12.

96. Klee, *Diaries,* entry #905, 1912.

97. Though one reason Nietzsche never fully seems to appreciate the value of painting is precisely because he never fully abandons the traditional categories for thinking images. Even though he will speak of the dream image, it never completely severs its ties with the notion that here we confront, as with every image, a representation.

CHAPTER 2 · HEIDEGGER AND KLEE

1. One need mention only a few of the other texts that take up this same task at this time to recall how extensive this list is: *Introduction to Metaphysics* (1935), several Hölderlin lectures and essays between 1933 and 1943, a seminar on Schiller's writings on art (1936), a seminar on Kant's *Critique of Judgment* (1936), and the series of Nietzsche seminars (1936–39). The list is even longer once one begins to include works of later years.

2. Heidegger, *Holzwege,* 50.

3. It is worth noting that there is no evidence that I have found to indicate that Heidegger saw, let alone was aware of, the *Entartete Kunst* exhibition. Given the immense popularity and propaganda intention of that exhibition, it would be odd to think that Heidegger was not at least aware of it. In his lectures on Nietzsche's "Will to Power as Art," which were given in the late 1930s, there is also no mention of Nietzsche's use of the phrase "entartete Kunst."

4. So, for instance, when Heidegger first saw van Gogh's painting *Kornfeld mit Mäher und Sonne,* he developed a special fascination for it after he learned that it was

painted in the same year as Heidegger's birth (1889), which was also the year of Nietzsche's collapse and just days before van Gogh's own collapse. Van Gogh would write of this painting to his brother, Theo, that it was "the image of death" that he had painted.

5. In the lecture course of 1937–38, Heidegger still counts van Gogh among those who were early on awake to the destiny of our times and whose names are "enigmatic signs written into the most concealed ground of our history." See Heidegger, *Grundfragen der Philosophie*, 216. Also named are Schiller, Hölderlin, Kierkegaard, and Nietzsche.

6. We also know that Heidegger gratefully acknowledges receiving a copy of Jasper's book *Strindberg und van Gogh*, which discusses the schizophrenia that plagued both artists. All of these references are cited in Pöggeler, *Bild und Technik*, 160–61. See also Petzet, *Auf einen Stern zugehen*, 149.

7. Pöggeler, *Bild und Technik*, 167–68.

8. Gadamer, *GW*, vol. 3, 189. Gadamer notes that Dostoyevsky also belonged to this period of Heidegger's passion for van Gogh. Both represented a radical conception of human life; both stood outside—even against—the academic world. Both spoke of a suffering that needed to be understood as profoundly honest and authentic.

9. Heidegger, *Ontologie*, 32.

10. The letter is from November 15, 1875. The passage is one that van Gogh cites as a remark his father would often make to him. The lines come from King Solomon in the Bible.

11. For instance, that the shoes belong to a woman; in fact, most everything Heidegger says of these shoes is drawn from an act of imagination as much as from the painting. But, it should also be noted that Heidegger, who avidly read van Gogh's letters, was well aware that the shoes in van Gogh's painting were a symbol of the social revolutionary *Bauernkrieg*.

12. A similar middle position is assigned to the image by Gadamer in *Truth and Method* when he defines it as neither sign nor symbol. See *GW*, vol. 1, 158ff.

13. Heidegger, *Logik*, 364. This passage immediately follows a passage that discusses the photographic image of Pascal's death mask in which Heidegger remarks that "here a concept of the image emerges that is different from the concept of image [*Bild*] as copy [*Abbild*], but that is connected to it" (362).

14. For a more detailed discussion of this claim, see my *On Germans and Other Greeks*.

15. Heidegger, *Metaphysik und Nihilismus*, 105.

16. Heidegger, *Beiträge zur Philosophie*, 503.

17. Ibid., 505.

18. Heidegger's frequent apparent proximity to Hegel is an ongoing problem for him, and Heidegger never ceases to make an effort to differentiate himself from this apparent similarity. On this, see my *The Ubiquity of the Finite* (Cambridge: MIT Press, 1988).

19. Hegel, *Werke*, vol. 13, 28.

20. Sallis's work has, perhaps more than any other, pursued this key question of how one is to think sense freed of its subordination to meaning. He has done this in several texts, but perhaps most systematically in his recent *Transfigurements*. Sallis has recognized that the primary site for addressing this question is the work of art. This would be the point at which a consideration of Sallis's work could open issues regard-

ing this enigma of sense in a more productive way than one finds them opened in Heidegger. However, I will not do that only because my concern points in a somewhat different direction in this book.

21. Heidegger, *Hölderlin*, "*Der Ister,*" 19.

22. Ibid., 28. See also the comment in the epilogue to "The Origin of the Work of Art" that "the transformations in the essence of truth correspond to the essential history of western art." Heidegger, *Holzwege*, 68.

23. Heidegger, *Hölderlin*, "*Der Ister,*" 26.

24. Heidegger, *Holzwege*, 30.

25. Ibid., 31.

26. Heidegger never comments upon the monumental and politically determined architecture—an effort to reproduce the temples of Greece and Rome—that was so integral to the Nazis and that was so prominent in Germany of the mid- to late 1930s. On this, see Lacoue-Labarthe, *La fiction du politique*, 92–114.

27. Adorno will pose a similar question when he asks "if and how art might survive after the fall of metaphysics which has been that which granted art its existence and its form." *Ästhetische Theorie*, 506.

28. Heidegger, *Der Satz vom Grund*, 41, 66.

29. July 30, 1973, in Heidegger, *Heidegger-Kästner Briefwechsel*, 121.

30. Cézanne is an element in this encounter as well, and indeed Heidegger's interest in Cézanne seems to predate his interest in Klee (see Petzet, *Auf einen Stern zugehen*, 149–52, and Pöggeler, *Bild und Technik*, 170–84). According to Petzet, Heidegger's interest in Cézanne begins sometime in 1947 when the two of them discussed a Cézanne exhibition and Rilke's letters about Cézanne. A letter of October 17, 1907, was of particular interest to Heidegger. In it, Rilke says:

> It is not at all the painting which I study (for I remain, despite everything, uncertain in front of all images and I have learned only badly to distinguish good from less good, and I always confuse early with late paintings). It is rather the turn in these paintings that I recognized because I had reached it in my own work as well or somehow had come close to it, and I have prepared for it for a long time since so much depends upon it. That is why I must be cautious when trying to speak of Cézanne; it is very tempting to me. . . . But being so touched, so unexpectedly in my own life . . . is something of a confirmation and a connection.

Heidegger's relation to Cézanne's work would always have some sort of connection with his relation to a poet; so, he would, for the most part, find either Rilke or René Char to be closely connected with Cézanne. Heidegger's understanding of Cézanne would also be intimately connected with an image of Greece, which Heidegger found to have a deep kinship with the Provence. Curiously, Heidegger's travels and friendships in the Provence would never lead him to speak of van Gogh. He did, however, say (March 20, 1958) that "[in the Provence] I found Cézanne's path, a path that—from the beginning to the end—corresponds in some sense with my own path of thinking" (see Pöggeler, *Bild und Technik*, 172). Heidegger's only "text" on Cézanne is one of the poems that Heidegger wrote for René Char titled "Gedachtes":

> Das nachdenksam Gelassene, das inständig
> Stille der Gestalt des alten Gärtners

Vallier, der Unscheinbares pflegte am
chemin des Lauves.
Im Spätwerk des Malers ist die Zwiefalt
von Anwesendem und Anwesenheit einfältig
geworden, "realisiert" und verwunden zugleich,
verwandelt in eine geheimnisvolle Identität.
Zeigt sich hier ein Pfad, der in ein Zusam-
mengehören des Dichtens und des Denkens
führt? (*Denkerfahrungen,* 163)

See also the "later" version in *Jahresgabe der Martin-Heidegger Gesellschaft.*

Interestingly, Heidegger would never—so far as I know—link Klee with any poet, even though there is a strong connection between Klee and Rilke, who were next-door neighbors in Munich for a year. Rilke even wrote to a friend (Baladine Klossowska), mentioning at one point that Klee had lent him sixty paintings. That letter of February 28, 1921, reads in part as follows:

> I knew you would read Hausenstein's book [in 1921, Wilhelm Hausenstein published his monograph titled *Kairuan oder eine Geschichte vom Maler Klee und von der Kunst dieses Zeitalters*] with a certain experience; I sent it to you more because of Hausenstein than because of Klee. For his way of seeing is very full of spirit and sometimes amusing. Do not forget that he too uses the word "doomed" in relation to the creations of Klee. One cannot regard Klee in any other way, only that his doom is also set close to many unbelievers today—and that Klee takes up this fate which is handed to him in a very special way. . . . This shortcut of the arts behind the back of nature and even of the imagination is the strangest appearance of this time, but also such a liberating one . . . (in 1915 Klee brought sixty of his works in color to me and I was allowed to hold onto them for a month; they occupied me a great deal and drew me to them).

Much more could be said of this relationship between Rilke and Klee as well as of its significance for the issues that Heidegger takes up.

31. See, for instance, the disparaging remark of 1929–30, which must have been directed at the Bauhaus: "It is only one more sign of the governing groundlessness of thinking and understanding defining today that we are asked to consider a house as a machine for dwelling and the chair as a machine for sitting; there are even people who believe that they see in such foolishness a great discovery and the preludes of a new culture." Heidegger, *Die Grundbegriffe der Metaphysik,* 316.

32. Petzet, *Auf einen Stern zugehen,* 158, letter of February 21, 1959.

33. See ibid., 154, 157. See also Pöggeler, "Neue Wege mit Heidegger?" 47.

34. With respect to Chillida, see Heidegger's collaboration with Chillida for the publication of a bibliophile edition of *Die Kunst und der Raum* (1969). See also the fine article by Miguel de Beistegui, "Assemblages: In Praise of Chillida," 317–37.

35. The letter can be found in *Phänomenologische Forschung* 18 (1986): 170–83. This passage can be found on p. 179.

36. So one reads Heidegger commenting in 1961 that "to be sure, art today is more and more used up in the culture industry as if it were something of utility. At the same time the question remains whether or not it is precisely art today that is able

to be defined in the confrontation with the technical world and to take up and lead to what is most proper to modern technicity." Heidegger, *Reden und andere Zeugnisse eines Lebenweges*, 583.

37. Foucault, *Dits et Écrits*, vol. 1, 544.

38. Watson, *Crescent Moon over the Rational*, 2.

39. The texts are as follows: the so-called "Notizen zu Klee" (still unpublished), comprising seventeen pages of notes and sketches; the protocol of a seminar in 1958 (five pages); the text of a conversation (the day after that seminar in 1958), which was reproduced in Japanese by someone present and then translated into German (four pages); the opening paragraph of "Time and Being" (1962); and a few scattered letters to friends. There are also some anecdotal remarks that others have discussed in publications (Petzet is the most useful resource in this case).

40. De Beistegui puts this distinction that defines the classical modern well when he says that "twentieth century abstraction dared to do what classical abstraction—including cubism—had never dared or dreamed to do, that is, produce works that presupposed the prior negation or destruction of the world as a whole." "Assemblages," 317. See also Maldiney, *Art et Existence*, 101.

41. Klee, "Schöpferische Konfession," 28. This sentence was heavily underlined by Heidegger in his copy of Klee's writings and would be cited by Merleau-Ponty in "Eye and Mind."

42. See Seubold, "Heidegger's nachgelassene Klee-Notizen," 7–8. The words that Heidegger chooses to note are interesting and give a sense of what he was finding in that text: *Deformation im Bildnerischen, Wort und Name, Dimension, Schöpfung, Aussehen, Gebilde, Farbe, Namen, Bilder, Vorbild, Urbild.* The written texts were not an immediately accepted resource by Heidegger. Initially, he considered Klee's self-understanding inadequate and "too neo-Kantian." However, his repeated readings, coupled with his repeated viewings of Klee's paintings, changed Heidegger's attitude toward these texts.

43. Klee, *Paul Klee in Jena 1924: Der Vortrag*, vol. 10, 49.

44. One thinks here as well of a painter like Cy Twombly, for whom words can constitute the entire image. On this, see my "Like a Fire That Consumes All before It . . ." in *Lyrical and Ethical Subjects*. In the case of Twombly, one finds paintings that are nothing but "words," but these painted words, by virtue both of their appearance in a painting and of the isolation of those words, fade into being simply images. Of course, such fading of the word into the image is, in the end, never fully possible since the relation of the word to the image will always have a peculiar undecidability about it.

45. Klee, *Diaries*, entry #389, 122.

46. Ibid., 52–53.

47. Lessing, *Laocoön*, 99.

48. Here a text that deserves serious attention should be noted: Merleau-Ponty's *Notes de cours 1959–1961* is remarkable for its efforts to unfold the nature of painting in terms of movement. See especially pp. 55–64, which are largely devoted to a discussion of Klee. Also notable in this volume are the pages devoted to Heidegger (94–148).

49. See, among other places, Nietzsche, *GT*, 49.

50. For an extended discussion of music in Klee's work, see Düchting, *Paul Klee*.

51. Klee, *Diaries*, entry #1081, July 17, 1917.

52. Klee, *Paul Klee in Jena 1924: Der Vortrag*, 51–53 (emphasis added). Interestingly, Hegel would use similar language when he speaks of the beauty of art as *"spirit which is born and reborn."* Hegel, *Vorlesung über die Ästhetik*, 14.

53. Klee, *Paul Klee in Jena 1924: Der Vortrag*, 64–67.

54. Klee, *Diaries*, 1920, emphasis added. This passage also served as Klee's epigraph on his tombstone.

55. Merleau-Ponty, *L'Oeil et Esprit*, 74. Shortly after making this comment, Merleau-Ponty ascribed to Klee "the ontological formula of painting" by citing what he says is a line from Klee's diaries that ultimately became the epithet on his tombstone: "Je suis insaissable dans l'immanence." This is a mistranslation of Klee's remark. The line from Klee is rather "Diesseits bin ich unfassbar." See *L'Oeil et Esprit*, 87.

56. Klee, *Paul Klee in Jena 1924: Der Vortrag*, 65. Cézanne would make a similar claim when he says, "To paint nature does not mean to copy objects, but to realize impressions of color." Cited in Seubold, *Kunst als Ereignis*, 119.

57. Klee, *Paul Klee in Jena 1924: Der Vortrag*, 69 (emphasis added).

58. The word "borne" here is *tragen*, which is the same word used to describe how a woman "carries" or "bears" a baby during pregnancy. On this, see Derrida's "Le dialogue ininterrompu: Entre deux infinis, le poème," in *Béliers*, and my "On Interrupted Conversations," in *Gadamer: Sprache ist Gespräch*, ed. Andrzej Wierciński (Berlin: LIT Verlag, 2011).

59. The "exhibition" was not a public exhibition. Rather, Ernst Beyeler displayed eighty-eight works by Klee that he had recently purchased from David Thompson, an American industrialist. Many of those works were promised to a museum in Düsseldorf, and Beyeler wanted to display the entire Thompson collection to friends, artists, critics, and others before it was split up. Heidegger was invited through his connection with Heinrich Petzet. The paintings were displayed in various rooms in a house in Basel that served as a temporary museum. On his first visit there, Heidegger was able to spend much of his time alone with the paintings. See Petzet, *Auf einen Stern zugehen*, 155–57.

60. The sources of the Heidegger quotes in this paragraph and in many of the following are found in note 1 of the introduction.

61. Heidegger, "Die Frage nach der Technik," in *Die Künste im technischen Zeitalter*, 63.

62. Merleau-Ponty, *L'Oeil et Esprit*, 69.

63. This is the point from which the difference between painting and photography can be thought. Rodin's comment—"it is the painter who tells the truth, while the photograph deceives; for in reality time never stops cold"—points to the seriousness of this difference. Cited in Merleau-Ponty, *L'Oeil et Esprit*, 80.

64. As an example of this, see fragment 8 of Empedocles that begins "physis oudenos estin apantōn thnētōn [of all mortal things none has birth, nor any end in accursed death] . . ." since here *physis* clearly needs to be thought as "birth." Furthermore, to speak of *physis* as something independent, that is as a realm exhibiting its own "nature," emerges as a way of speaking only at the end of the fifth century BCE. When this happens, it marks a revolution in the Greek understanding of this word. Prior to that, *physis* only referred to the *physis* of something; it was never spoken of as an independent realm of beings. Even the sole possible example of this—Heraclitus's fragment 123, "physis kryptesthi philei"—is no real exception since, even if it is authentic, we should remember that here too *physis* needs to be thought as "birth" and so we should translate this passage as Gadamer once did, "die eigentliche Anfänge eines Wesens bleiben im verborgen." Here too we can recognize that it is an event rather than an independent realm of objects that is being named.

65. When Aristotle identifies *physis* with *genesis*—in opposition to *techne*—he is leaning back into the earlier identification of *physis* with birth. It is that which comes to be "of itself," and the character of this coming to be is what most defines *physis*. Plato too will draw upon this more archaic sense of *physis* as well. So, for instance, on the last day of his life, Socrates speaks about "peri physeos historia" (*Phaedo*, 96a) and immediately clarifies this as "the reason something comes to be [*genesis*]." Aristotle, however, marks the beginning of the move away from this original sense of *physis*. In finding *genesis* at the heart of what is spoken of by *physis* and—at the same time—in failing to differentiate *genesis* from other ways of becoming, Aristotle marks both the summit of a long tradition of Greek thought, insofar as he thinks *physis* out of *genesis*, and he equally marks the moment of its cessation, insofar as he fails to preserve the singular character of the *genesis* that is *physis*.

66. On this movement, which Heidegger describes as the movement of truth, see my "Die Wahrheit Sagen."

67. In 1933, the year the National Socialists took power in Germany, Klee was dismissed from his teaching post by the Nazis and would leave Germany forever in December of that same year.

68. Petzet, *Auf einen Stern zugehen*, 156.

69. Although symptoms of his disease first appeared in 1933, it was in the summer of 1935 that he was diagnosed with progressive scleroderma. He would die five years later at the age of sixty.

70. Petzet, *Auf einen Stern zugehen*, 156.

71. Heidegger, *Reden und andere Zeugnisse eines Lebenweges*, 552. All further citations from this seminar are from this volume, pp. 552–54. Both Heidegger and Hisamatsu reviewed, edited, and approved of the final version of this text.

72. Ibid., 556.

73. Ibid., 554.

74. Klee too was aware of this non-Western sensibility in his work. So, we read in his diary (entry of January 22, 1917) that "I am becoming increasingly Chinese." Klee, *Tagebücher 1898–1918*, #1054.

75. Ibid., 778.

76. Plato, *Phaedrus*, 275D–E. On this, see my "Putting Oneself in Words . . ." Gadamer's reply to my essay is included and goes right to the point at hand.

77. Heidegger, *Reden und andere Zeugnisse eines Lebenweges*, 552.

78. Ibid., 777.

79. Just as one should not demand immediate intelligibility of a poem such as Trakl's "Siebengesang des Todes" or an excerpt from Werner Heisenberg's writings on theoretical physics, so should one recognize that energy and time are needed to even begin to understand a painting. See Heidegger, *Zur Sache des Denkens*, 1.

80. Heidegger, *Metaphysik und Nihilismus*, 107.

81. Heidegger, *Besinnung*, 35. The great depth of Heidegger's despair about his times could be seen in a passage a few pages later where, after criticizing the "cultural machine" of the times, he says, "Thus there arises a historical situation in which beyng [*Seyn*] is not even any longer something like the ephemeral passing of the flat shadow of an empty dream . . . Beyng—a fading echo of an empty word—and the question of beyng? Not even an error—only an indifference" (40).

82. Heidegger, *Reden und andere Zeugnisse eines Lebenweges*, 583.

83. Heidegger, "Technik und Kunst—Gestell," ix.

84. Heidegger, *Ursprung des Kunstwerkes*, 90–91 (Zusatz).

85. Heidegger, *Holzwege*, 67.

86. Heidegger, *Denkerfahrungen*, 145.

87. Heidegger, "Technik und Kunst—Gestell," xiii.

88. Heidegger, *Denkerfahrungen*, 139. Heidegger had already made a similar comment in 1935 in *Einführung in die Metaphysik*, 13: "That which is essentially the same in *physis* and *techne* can be clarified only by means of a special consideration." On this, see my "Economies of Production," 145–57, 265–68.

CHAPTER 3 · ON WORD, IMAGE, AND GESTURE

1. Merleau-Ponty, *L'Oeil et Esprit*, 15.

2. One event planned for 1960 sadly never resulted in a publication. Heidegger held a seminar titled "Word and Image," which is described in the following way and as centered upon the following texts: "a passage from Augustine's *Confessions* (X, 7 and 8), Heraclitus' Fragment 112, the parable of the 'Glockenspielständer' from Chuang-tzu, Klee's *On Modern Art*, and two lines from Heidegger's own work. The Augustine text concerns the sensible and the force of memory. The Heraclitus fragment reads: 'Thinking well (*sophronein*) is the greatest excellence and wisdom: to act and speak what is true, perceiving things according to their nature (*physis*).'" The Chuang-tzu parable reads:

> Khing, the woodworker, carved a bell-stand, and when it was completed, all who saw it were astonished as if it were the work of spirits. The Marquis of Lu went to see it, and asked by what art he had succeeded in producing it. "Your subject is but a mechanic," was the reply; "what art should I be possessed of? Nevertheless, there is one thing (which I will mention). When your servant had undertaken to make the bell-stand, I did not venture to waste any of my power, and felt it necessary to fast in order to compose my mind. After fasting for three days, I did not presume to think of any congratulation, reward, rank, or emolument (which I might obtain by the execution of my task); after fasting five days, I did not presume to think of the condemnation or commendation (which it would produce), or of the skill or want of skill (which it might display). At the end of the seven days, I had forgotten all about myself;—my four limbs and my whole person. By this time the thought of your Grace's court (for which I was to make the thing) had passed away; everything that could divert my mind from exclusive devotion to the exercise of my skill had disappeared. Then I went into the forest, and looked at the natural forms of the trees. When I saw one of a perfect form, then the figure of the bell-stand rose up to my view, and I applied my hand to the work. Had I not met with such a tree, I must have abandoned the object; but my Heaven-given faculty and the Heaven-given qualities of the wood were concentrated on it. So it was that my spirit was thus engaged in the production of the bell-stand."

Petzet, *Auf einen Stern zugehen*, 64–66. Klee's *On Modern Art* was the text of a lecture Klee gave in 1924 to open an exhibition of modern art in Jena. The lines from Heidegger read: "Nur Gebild wahrt Gesicht / Doch Gesicht ruht im Gedicht." For a discussion of this seminar, see Petzet, *Auf einen Stern zugehen*, 64–66.

3. On the role of Klee in this period and these philosophers, see Watson, *Crescent Moon over the Rational*. Benjamin's celebrated essay "On the Concept of History," in which he discusses Klee's painting *Angelus Novus*, was first published in 1950 but not widely available until 1968. Likewise, Merleau-Ponty's lecture courses from 1959 to 1961, which were not published until 1996 (*Notes de Cours 1959–1961*), contain some significant discussions of Klee (and of Heidegger). This tradition of pursuing the possibilities of aesthetic experience and the work of art as opening up new possibilities for philosophy would continue in Derrida and Nancy, and, more recently, in the work of Sallis and Figal.

4. Merleau-Ponty, "Eye and Mind," in *The Primacy of Perception*, 159–61. This opposition between art and science echoes Heidegger's remark in *Ursprung des Kunstwerkes* that truth happens in many ways, among them art, the founding of a state, essential sacrifice, and questioning, but that "science is not an original manner in which truth happens." *Holzwege*, 50.

5. Against this metaphysical dependence upon the logic of the concept, one should hear the provocation of titles such as Deleuze's *The Logic of Sensation* and Merleau-Ponty's *Primacy of Perception*.

6. This is why Watson is right when he argues—even if only with reference to Klee—that the list of those who engage the work of art during this time reads like the list of twentieth-century continental philosophy's leading figures (see Watson, *Crescent Moon over the Rational*, 2).

7. Gadamer, *GW*, vol. 1, 141.

8. In doing this, Gadamer is following two key claims that Heidegger makes in *Being and Time*, first, that cognition is a "founded mode" of being in and knowing the world (§13) and, second, that understanding is an original manner in which the world is disclosed and articulated (§31).

9. It is, I believe, a fair criticism to say that Heidegger's prejudices against Kant's third Critique, prejudices that tend to be traceable to the dominance of neo-Kantian interpretations of that text during Heidegger's early years, led Heidegger to overlook the genuinely original contribution of Kant to the questions regarding the work of art that were driving Heidegger. It is no accident that one of the very first essays Gadamer would ever write that dealt with Heidegger was Gadamer's introduction to Heidegger's *Ursprung des Kunstwerkes*, a text considering themes that connect Gadamer's own work to his teacher's but—at the same time—allow Gadamer to establish the originality of hermeneutic theory vis-à-vis Heidegger. One of the most significant wedges that helps Gadamer take up this critical distance to Heidegger is found in the seriousness with which Gadamer, unlike Heidegger, regards Kant's third Critique. Curiously, Heidegger's two most intimate successors, who began as his students in Marburg—Arendt and Gadamer—both find in Kant's third Critique a decisive work of true originality. For both of them, the *Critique of Judgment* is among the most central works for their own projects.

10. Gadamer, *GW*, vol. 1, 492. The original conception of *Truth and Method* did not include what we now know as part 1, which has as its centerpiece the analysis of Kant's third Critique and which has as its task the "Freilegung der Wahrheitsfrage an der Erfahrung der Kunst." In later years, the importance of the artwork for Gadamer would be so obvious and so clearly central that one is surprised to realize that in *Truth*

and Method the analysis of the work of art is a later addition. The necessity of the treatment of art is, in the largest measure, owing to the way in which Gadamer understands Kant to be assuming the mantle of the humanistic tradition in the *Kritik der Urteilskraft*. One would not have strong reasons to explain Gadamer's interest in Kant outside of the problematic of hermeneutics as it is developed in *Truth and Method*. Prior to *Truth and Method*, the sole article by Gadamer that takes up Kant's aesthetics is an eight-page article in 1939 ("Zu Kants Begündung der Ästhetik und dem Sinn der Kunst"). It is then in the context of the problematic of *Truth and Method* that Gadamer's interest in Kant is to be understood.

11. For a more detailed discussion of the role of Kant in Gadamer's *Truth and Method*, see my "Kant und die Subjektivierung der Aesthetik," 29–42.

12. Gadamer, *GW*, vol. 1, *Wahrheit und Methode*, 14.

13. Gadamer, while sympathetic to Heidegger's critique of humanism in "Letter on Humanism," is also not so quick to subsume the project of humanism to metaphysics and the oblivion of being. Once they are published, one will see how this is the case in letters from Gadamer to Heidegger on January 27, 1948, and February 15, 1966.

14. For one of the most interesting and insightful works on this essential tie binding philosophy and the concept, see Deleuze, *Qu'est-ce que la philosophie?* 27–37. On this resistance to the concept characterizing aesthetic experience, see my "On the Idiom of Truth."

15. Kant, *KU*, AK, 188.

16. Ibid., 61.

17. Gadamer, *GW*, vol. 1, 47.

18. Ibid., 49.

19. Ibid., 103.

20. Ibid., 87.

21. Ibid., 107.

22. Gadamer stresses the link between the notion of the text and its roots in words such as *textare*, tissue, textile, texture. The notion of a "transformation" into *Gebilde* also hints at words such as *Gewebe*. For an interesting discussion of Greek senses of these notions, see Scheid and Svenbro, *The Craft of Zeus*.

23. Gadamer, *GW*, vol. 1, 139.

24. Gadamer notes that there is something of a paradox defining traditional discussions of painting: because painting is regarded as the most representational of the forms of art, it is taken as best illustrating the very being of art such that "we make every artwork into a painting" (*GW*, vol. 1, 140), and yet, precisely because the image is thought in advance from out of its being as a copy, this privileged position of painting in the conception of art is what discredits the very idea of art at all.

25. Gadamer, *GW*, vol. 1, 136.

26. Ibid., 139.

27. Ibid., 140.

28. Ibid.

29. The word *Zuwachs* means "increase" or "augmentation." The idiom *Zuwachs bekommen* means to have an addition to the family. Such an addition may be described quantitatively—one more member of the family arrives with the birth of the child—but such a description cannot account for the fundamental transformation and the essential "newness" announced by such an "addition."

30. Gadamer, *GW,* vol. 1, 142. This is a point quite similar to Benjamin's remarks about the "cult of the movie star" in which the "image" of the actor takes over the real being of the actor such that one expects the actor to be "like" his or her image or like the characters portrayed. See "Das Kunstwerk im Zeitalter seiner technischen Reproduzierbarkeit," 492.

31. Gadamer, *GW,* vol. 1, 120.

32. Ibid., 146.

33. Ibid., 148.

34. Ibid., 150.

35. Adorno too speaks of the "more" that defines the work of art: "artworks become artworks in the production of this more; they produce their own transcendence." *Ästhetische Theorie,* 122.

36. Gadamer, *GW,* vol. 1, 151–52.

37. Ibid., 152.

38. For some ways in which the discussion of the symbol here is problematic, see my "Über Sprache und Freiheit aus Hermeneutischer Sichtpunkt," 59–73, and "On the Incalculable," *Research in Phenomenology* 34 (2004): 31–45. See also Todorov, *Theories of the Symbol.*

39. Gadamer, *GW,* vol. 1, 152. But the memento is unlike the painting in that it can lose this characteristic when the past it memorializes ceases to have meaning for the person who has the memento. In other words, the pointing, the transcendence, that characterizes the memento is contingent upon something other than itself.

40. Gadamer, *GW,* vol. 1, 154 (emphasis added).

41. Ibid., 155.

42. On this, one should see the essays by John Sallis ("The Hermeneutics of the Artwork") and me ("Aesthetics and Subjectivity") in Figal, *Klassiker Auslegen.*

43. Gadamer, *GW,* vol. 8, 25. Other essays written at this time (1967) open with the same concern about the "gap" between traditional and modern forms of art. So, for instance, "Image and Gesture" begins: "There is today a great mistrust of all traditional forms of expression." Ibid., 323.

44. Ibid., 28; *RB,* 96.

45. Gadamer, "Bildkunst und Wortkunst," 94.

46. Kant, *KU,* AK 314 (see also AK 342).

47. Arendt, *The Life of the Mind: Thinking,* 193.

48. The question of nature haunts the question of the beautiful in the work of art, and indeed no discussion of art can ever even approach a satisfaction unless the experience of nature is broached. And yet, it is the absence of this experience of nature that Heidegger finds foreclosed in the age of the *Gestell* and of *Machenschaft.* With a similar concern but expressed in a different way, Adorno's comment is right: "Since Schelling whose aesthetics was called a philosophy of art, the interest of aesthetics has centered upon the work of art. For theory since then, the beauty of nature, which was the occasion for the most penetrating determinations of the *Critique of Judgment,* is hardly ever thematized." *Ästhetische Theorie,* 97.

49. Gadamer, *GW,* vol. 8, 30–31; *RB,* 98.

50. Gadamer, *GW,* vol. 8, 32; *RB,* 99. See also *Truth and Method,* where Gadamer links this recognition described in the notion of *mimesis* with the Platonic notion of "anamnesis." Gadamer, *GW,* vol. 1, 119–20.

51. Gadamer, *GW*, vol. 8, 32; *RB*, 99–100.

52. Gadamer, *GW*, vol. 8, 32; *RB*, 100.

53. Gadamer, *GW*, vol. 8, 33; *RB*, 101.

54. On the Greek conception of number and the nature of number notation in the Greek world, see my "On Counting, Stars, and Music," 179–91. Of course, Plato's *Timaeus* is the Greek text in which all of these notions are given their most compressed and intense expression. On this, see especially Sallis, *Chorology*.

55. Kant, *Reflexionen*, 1820A.

56. This, I believe, is the sense of the ethical to which Heidegger referred when he wrote that "if, according to the fundamental meaning of the word *ethos*, we should now say that the name ethics reflects upon the abode of human being, then that thinking which thinks the truth of being as the original element of human being . . . is intrinsically original ethics." *Wegmarken*, 353.

57. Gadamer, *GW*, vol. 8, 322; *RB*, 91.

58. Gadamer, *GW*, vol. 8, 35–36; *RB*, 103.

59. Gadamer, *GW*, vol. 8, 36; *RB*, 103–104.

60. Gadamer, *GW*, vol. 8, 323; *RB*, 74.

61. Gadamer, *GW*, vol. 8, 327–28; *RB*, 79.

62. For an insightful discussion of *Deixis* and *Bildlichkeit*, see Boehm, *Wie Bilder Sinn Erzeugen*. Especially interesting is his discussion of the move from bodily gesture to the gestural meaning of the image; see the chapter "Die Hintergründigkeit des Zeigens," 19–33.

63. On this, see Kommerell, "Die Sprache und das Unaussprechliche," in *Geist und Buchstabe der Dichtung*, 243–317.

64. Aeschylus, *Agamemnon*, 1060–61.

65. Thus, Benjamin speaks of an animal gesture in Kafka that "combines the utmost mystery with the utmost simplicity." Indeed, Benjamin finds that Kafka's "entire work presents a codex of gestures which in no way have a native symbolic meaning for their author." Benjamin, *Gesammelte Schriften*, vol. 2, book 2, 418.

66. On this, and for a comprehensive anthropological study of the human meaning of gesture and of the role of gesture in the formation of language, see Leroi-Gourhan, *Le Geste et la parole*.

67. Gadamer, *GW*, vol. 8, 327–28; *RB*, 79.

68. Heidegger, *Was Heißt Denken?* 51. See also Heidegger, *Parmenides*, 188ff., as well as my "Von der Wahrheit Sprechen." See also Derrida's discussion of these passages in Heidegger in "Geschlecht II," in *Psyché*, 415ff.

69. Kommerell, *Dichterische Welterfahrung*, 153.

70. Agamben, *Potentialities*, 77–78.

71. Ibid., 78.

72. The notion of an *eikos logos* is central to Plato's *Timaeus*. On this, see Sallis, *Chorology*, esp. 55. It is worth noting here that the German word for gesture is *Gebärde*, which is the same word that is used to describe the language of the deaf, the language that English designates as "sign" language. It seems that the word "gesture" is much more appropriate to describe the nature of such a language. It is also important to understand how such *Gebärdesprache* is in some sense "more original" than spoken language. It is a typical misunderstanding of sign language to regard it as somehow derivative of a spoken language. Such a misunderstanding would, for instance, assume

that the sign language of someone who lived in an English-speaking country would be "based upon" and derivative of spoken English. Such is not the case. In fact, a signer of American sign language could not communicate very well at all with a British signer. But the same American signer could rather easily speak with a French signer since those sign systems have largely the same roots. Sign language is independent of spoken languages. On this, see my "On the Dark Side of the Moon," in *Lyrical and Ethical Subjects*. It should also be noted that in the *Critique of Judgment*, Kant suggests that gesture is at the basis of all speech in the fullest sense. Importantly for my interests here, Kant argues as well that the "bildende Kunst [the art of the image]" needs to be counted as an instance of "gesture in speech." See *KU*, AK 320 and AK 324.

73. There is a fascinating image of such coercion in a dream that Stefan George recounts in an entry titled "Der Redende Kopf." In it he tells of bringing a friend to see a plaster mask of a face that hangs on his wall and that he boasts he can compel to speak. When he does this by forcefully moving its lips, it remains silent but bites his finger. See George, *Werke*, 490–91.

74. The most insightful analysis of this temporal character of painting—in particular the relation of time, appearance, light, and sensibility—is found in Sallis, *Shades—Of Painting at the Limit*. Of special interest is Sallis's discussion of Monet's *Wheatstack* paintings. A further elaboration of these issues, as well as a productive discussion of the place of music here, is found in Sallis's *Transfigurements*.

75. For a discussion of this kinship of language and script, see my "Words on Paper," in *Lyrical and Ethical Subjects*.

76. Kommerell, *Essays, Notizen, Poetische Fragmente*, 84. Cited in Agamben, *Potentialities*, 84.

77. In 1968, Gadamer wrote a lengthy commentary, *Werner Scholz*, to accompany a volume of Scholz's paintings. That commentary takes the notion of gesture as the key to Gadamer's readings of Scholz's paintings (on this see esp. 17ff.). It is worth noting that Gadamer was a close friend of Max Kommerell's and that he had a great respect and admiration for Kommerell (indeed, Gadamer edited some of Kommerell's work after Kommerell's death). Kommerell died quite young (he was forty-two) and so never quite had the impact that his work deserved. Gadamer's sense of gesture is clearly close to, and in some sense indebted to, Kommerell's use of this notion.

78. Gadamer, *GW*, vol. 8, 329; *RB*, 80–81.

79. Gadamer, *GW*, vol. 8, 328; *RB*, 80.

80. Kommerell, *Geist und Buchstabe der Dichtung*, 316.

81. Gadamer, *GW*, vol. 8, 329–30; *RB*, 81–82.

82. The most comprehensive conception of the work of art as bound to sense is found in the work of Sallis; in this regard, see especially his *Transfigurements*. Sallis's work has long been exploring the sense of art in terms of its rootedness in sense. In doing this, he has forged a sense of the project of philosophy that has let itself be fundamentally challenged by the achievement of the work of art that is not understood within the horizon of a metaphysical distinction between the sensible and the intelligible. While Sallis's intention points in different directions, it seems to me to be driven by the same concerns that I have tried to articulate in this book.

83. Heidegger, *Was Heißt Denken?* 188. On this question of body, hand, and gesture—all investigated with an eye to the question of measure—see Kleinberg-Levin's *Gestures of an Ethical Life*, esp. 204–74. Kleinberg-Levin's project in this very interesting

and quite illuminating work dovetails closely with my own concerns here, especially my concern with the *ethopoietic* character of the work of art. Kleinberg-Levin has demonstrated with much care and precision the role of the body in gesture and the relation of gesture to the question of an ethical measure. This project comes together in what he calls "physiognomies of ethical life" (xxxiii–xliii). Kleinberg-Levin draws upon Merleau-Ponty quite productively to this end.

84. Merleau-Ponty, "Eye and Mind," *Primacy of Perception*, 162.

85. One finds this in Benjamin, who at one point had a serious interest in graphology, and, with a somewhat different intent, but no less sense of the importance of the role of the hand in language found in handwriting, in Heidegger; see for instance his *Parmenides*, 116ff.

86. Hölderlin, "Friedensfeier," in *Sämtliche Werke und Briefe*, 364. Although different in substantial ways, Hölderlin's use of the word *Gesang*—to refer to what we soon become in this conversation—is not very remote from what I have been referring to as gesture.

87. Merleau-Ponty, "Eye and Mind," *Primacy of Perception*, 167.

88. Gadamer, *Werner Scholz*, 17.

89. It is not by chance that Lessing chooses this image as the focus of his discussion of the difference between words and images in his *Laocoön*, since something of the essential character of the image is presented in Homer's account of this shield. When Thetis delivers the shield, the Myrmidons cannot bear to look upon it. Only Achilles can, and when he does, his "anger came ever harder upon him . . . and he filled his heart by looking at it" (book 18, lines 13–15). His anger grows because in this shield he sees the enormity of what Patroklos has lost and what Achilles too will soon have to lose: all of life. It is right to suggest that, in the midst of great slaughter, the shield "furnishes the *Iliad* with its most memorable images of peace." See Caroline Alexander, *The War That Killed Achilles*, 157.

AFTERWORD

1. Kommerell, *Jean Paul*, 418.

2. Agamben, *Potentialities*, 83–85.

3. Calasso, *The Marriage of Cadmus and Harmony*, 279–80.

4. Heidegger suggests that the most peculiar feature of the distress of our time is that we are not aware of our own distress, that we are numbed.

5. On this, see Horowitz, *Sustaining Loss*. The question of the relation of modernity to the past, a question sharpened by the notion of the avant-garde, is also key here. On this, see Ziarek, *The Force of Art*, and Andrew Benjamin, *Style and Time*.

6. On this, see (among the many works devoted to this topic) Föti, *Epochal Discordance*; Krell, *The Tragic Absolute*; and my *On Germans and Other Greeks*, chap. 4.

7. This line from Hölderlin's poem "Patmos" is cited by Heidegger to make precisely this point at the end of his essay "Die Frage nach der Technik."

8. Heidegger, *Reden und andere Zeugnisse eines Lebenweges*, 671. Significantly, this interview ends with Heidegger questioning the "place" of art in the world today and then with his comment that "I do not see any indications that modern art points a way for us" (682).

9. Benjamin, *Gesammelte Schriften*, vol. 1, book 1, 201.

10. Letter to his brother on January 1, 1799, Hölderlin, *Sämtliche Werke und Briefe*, 726.

11. On this, see Bernstein, *The Fate of Art*; and Ross, *Aesthetic Paths of Philosophy*. For a discussion of this as it defines the themes of twentieth-century continental philosophy and as those discussions weave through attention to the paintings and writings of Klee, see Watson, *Crescent Moon over the Rational*.

12. Another point, equally important, that is reclaimed by maintaining this tie to Kant concerns the place of nature in the intersecting problematics of art, aesthetic experience, and judgment more generally. In the end, resurrecting the question of nature is itself an element of how the ethical issues that emerge here can be pursued. On this, see my "On the Significance of Nature for the Question of Ethics," 62–77.

13. On this, see my "Hermeneutics and Original Ethics," in *The Difficulties of Ethical Life*, 35–47, 214–16.

14. Heraclitus, fragment 119. One should also consider the original sense as well expressed by Homer's use of the word "ethos" as the dwelling place of an animal. See *Iliad*, book 6, 506–11. See also Scott's illuminating discussion of this passage in his *The Question of Ethics*, 143–45. See also Chamberlain, "From 'Haunts' to 'Character.'"

15. This point coincides in important ways with Foucault's discussions of the care of the self as well as Hadot's discussions of spiritual exercises in *Philosophy as a Way of Life*. In a similar manner, Zen practices, especially those practices that concern writing and gesture, belong in this discussion. The decision not to turn to these other, closely related approaches should not be taken as an indication that such engagements are not important. Quite the contrary, they are quite necessary and also quite complex, and it is precisely because of this that they reach beyond the scope of this book and of my own competence.

16. Hegel, *Werke*, vol. 1, 235.

17. While these words are not appropriately called translations of the word *etho-poiein*, they do qualify as quite legitimate ways of resaying or interpreting the sense of that word.

18. Rilke, "Archaïscher Torso Apollos," *Werke*, vol. 1, 557.

19. Kant, *KU*, AK, 299–300.

BIBLIOGRAPHY

Adorno, Theodor. *Ästhetische Theorie. Gesammelte Schriften*, vol. 7. Frankfurt: Suhrkamp Verlag, 1972.

———. *Negative Dialektik. Gesammelte Schriften*, vol. 6. Frankfurt: Suhrkamp Verlag, 1972.

———. *Prismen. Gesammelte Schriften*, vol. 10. Frankfurt: Suhrkamp Verlag, 1955.

Aeschylus. *Agamemnon*. Loeb Classical Library. Cambridge, Mass.: Harvard University Press, 1983.

Agamben, Giorgio. *Potentialities*. Trans. D. Heller-Roazen. Stanford, Calif.: Stanford University Press, 1999.

Aichele, K. Porter. *Paul Klee, Poet/Painter*. Rochester, N.Y.: Camden House, 2006.

Alexander, Caroline. *The War That Killed Achilles*. New York: Viking Press, 2009.

Arendt, Hannah. *The Life of the Mind: Thinking*. New York: Harcourt Brace Jovanovich, 1977.

Aristotle. *Poetics*. Loeb Classical Library. Cambridge, Mass.: Harvard University Press, 1982.

———. *Politics*. Loeb Classical Library. Cambridge, Mass.: Harvard University Press, 1972.

Armitage, Merle. *Five Essays on Klee*. New York: Duell Sloan Pearce, 1950.

Augustine. "Answer to the Pelagians." In *The Works of St. Augustine*, vol. 3. Charlottesville, VA: InteLex Corp., 2001.

Barbarić, Damir. "Emporhebendes Scheinen." *Internationales Jahrbuch für Hermeneutik*, vol. 9. Tübingen: Mohr Siebeck Verlag, 2009. 129–46.

Barron, Stephanie. *"Degenerate Art": The Fate of the Avant-Garde in Nazi Germany*. New York: Harry N. Abrams, 1991.

Barthes, Roland. *The Rustle of Language*. Trans. R. Howard. Berkeley: University of California Press, 1989.

Becker, Andrew. *Rhetoric and Poetics of Early Greek Ekphrasis: Theory, Philology and the Shield of Achilles*. London: Rowman and Littlefield, 1995.

Benjamin, Andrew. *Style and Time: Essays on the Politics of Appearance*. Evanston, Ill.: Northwestern University Press, 2006.

Benjamin, Walter. "Das Kunstwerk im Zeitalter seiner technischen Reproduzierbarkeit." *Gesammelte Schriften*, vol. 1, book 2. Frankfurt: Suhrkamp Verlag, 1974.

———. *Gesammelte Schriften*, vol. 2, book 2. Frankfurt: Suhrkamp Verlag, 1980.

Benkard, Ernst. *Das Ewige Antlitz: Eine Sammlung von Totenmasken*. Berlin: Frankfurter Verlags-Anstalt, 1926.

Benn, Gottfried. *Gesammelte Werke*, vol. 1. Ed. D. Wellershoff. Stuttgart: Klett-Cotta, 1987.

Bernasconi, Robert. *Heidegger in Question*. Atlantic Highlands, N.J.: Humanities Press, 1993.

Bernstein, Jay. *The Fate of Art: Aesthetic Alienation from Kant to Derrida and Adorno*. University Park: Penn State University Press, 1992.

Bissier, Julius. *Brush Drawings: 1934–1964*. Ed. D. Vallier. Stuttgart: Hatje Verlag, 1965.

Boehm, Gottfried. *Wie Bilder Sinn Erzeugen*. Berlin: Berlin University Press, 2007.

Calasso, Roberto. *The Marriage of Cadmus and Harmony*. Trans. T. Parks. New York: Knopf, 1993.

Carson, Anne. *The Economy of the Unlost*. Princeton, N.J.: Princeton University Press, 1999.

Casey, Edward. *The World at a Glance*. Bloomington: Indiana University Press, 2007.

Celan-Lestrange, Gisèle, and Paul Celan. *Abglanzbeladen*. Erlangen: Museum Schloss Moyland, 2000.

Chamberlain, Charles. "From 'Haunts' to 'Character': The Meaning of Ethos." *Helios* 11, no. 2 (1984): 97–108.

Davey, Nicholas. "The Moving Word." *Internationales Jahrbuch für Hermeneutik*, vol. 8. Tübingen: Mohr Siebeck Verlag, 2008. 85–98.

de Beistegui, Miguel. "Assemblages: In Praise of Chillida." *Internationales Jahrbuch für Hermeneutik*, vol. 7. Tübingen: Mohr Siebeck Verlag, 2008. 317–37.

Deleuze, Gilles. *The Logic of Sensation*. Trans. D. Smith. Minneapolis: University of Minnesota Press, 2003.

———. *Qu'est-ce que la philosophie?* Paris: Les Éditions Minuit, 1991.

Derrida, Jacques. *Atlan: De la couleur à la letter*. Paris: Gallimard, 2001.

———. *Béliers*. Paris: Editions Gallimard, 2005.

———. *Demeure, Athènes*. Paris: Éditions Galilée, 2009.

———. *La Vérité en peinture*. Paris: Flammarion, 1978.

———. *Mémoires d'aveugle*. Paris: Éditions de la Réunion des musées nationaux, 1990.

———. *Psyché*. Paris: Éditions Galilée, 1987.

Düchting, Hajo. *Paul Klee: Painting Music*. Munich: Prestel Verlag, 2004.

Fehér, István. "Mündlichkeit und Schriftlichkeit." *Internationales Jahrbuch für Hermeneutik*, vol. 8. Tübingen: Mohr Siebeck Verlag, 2008. 117–46.

Figal, Günter, ed. *Erhart Kästner zum 100. Geburtstag*. Freiburg: Modo Verlag, 2004.

———. *Erscheinungsdinge*. Tübingen: Mohr Siebeck Verlag, 2010.

———. *Verstehensfragen*. Tübingen: Mohr Siebeck Verlag, 2009.

Föti, Véronique. *Epochal Discordance*. Albany: SUNY Press, 2006.

———. *Vision's Invisibles*. Albany: SUNY Press, 2003.

Foucault, Michel. *Dits et Écrits*, vol. 1, 1954–1969. Ed. Daniel Defert and François Ewald. Paris: Éditions Gallimard, 1994.

————. *Hermeneutics of the Subject: Lectures at the Collège de France 1981–1982*. Trans. G. Burchell. New York: Palgrave, 2005.

Freud, Sigmund. *Bildende Kunst und Literatur*. Frankfurt: S. Fischer Verlag, 1969.

Gadamer, Hans-Georg. "Bildkunst und Wortkunst." In *Was ist ein Bild*, ed. Gottfried Boehm. Munich: Fink Verlag, 1995. 90–104.

————. *Die Moderne und die Grenze der Vergegenständlichung*. Munich: Bernd Klüser Verlag, 1996.

————. *Gesammelte Werke*, vol. 1. Tübingen: J. C. B. Mohr, 1990.

————. *Gesammelte Werke*, vol. 3. Tübingen: J. C. B. Mohr, 1987.

————. *Gesammelte Werke*, vol. 8. Tübingen: J. C. B. Mohr, 1993.

————. *Gesammelte Werke*, vol. 9. Tübingen: J. C. B. Mohr, 1993.

————. *Werner Scholz*. Recklinghausen: Verlag Aurel Bongers, 1968.

Gasché, Rodolphe. *The Idea of Form*. Stanford, Calif.: Stanford University Press, 2003.

George, Stefan. *Werke*, vol. 1. Munich: Goerg Bondi, 1958.

Grohmann, Will. *Paul Klee*. New York: Harry N. Abrams, n.d.

Haar, Michel. *L'oeuvre d'art*. Paris: Hartier, 1994.

Hadot, Pierre. *Philosophy as a Way of Life*. Trans. M. Chase. Ed. A. Davidson. Oxford: Blackwell Publishing, 1995.

Hegel, G. W. F. *Phänomenologie des Geistes*. Frankfurt: Meiner Verlag, 1952.

————. *Vorlesungen über die Philosophie der Kunst*. Hamburg: Meiner Verlag, 2003.

————. *Werke*, vol. 1. Frankfurt: Suhrkamp Verlag, 1971.

————. *Werke*, vol. 13. Frankfurt: Suhrkamp Verlag, 1986.

Heidegger, Martin. *Beiträge zur Philosophie. Gesamtausgabe*, vol. 65. Frankfurt: Klostermann Verlag, 1989.

————. *Besinnung. Gesamtausgabe*, vol. 66. Frankfurt: Klostermann Verlag, 1997.

————. *Denkerfahrungen*. Frankfurt: Klostermann Verlag, 1983.

————. *Der Satz vom Grund*. Pfüllingen: Neske Verlag, 1978.

————. *Die Künste im technischen Zeitalter*. Munich: Akademie für das Graphische Gewerbe, 1966.

————. *Die Kunst und der Raum*. St. Gallen: Erker-Verlag, 2007.

————. *Einführung in die Metaphysik*. Tübingen: Niemeyer Verlag, 1966.

————. *Heidegger-Kästner Briefwechsel*. Munich: Insel Verlag, 1986.

————. *Hölderlin, „Der Ister." Gesamtausgabe*, vol. 53. Frankfurt: Klostermann Verlag, 1984.

————. *Holzwege*. Frankfurt: Klostermann, 1972.

————. *Jahresgabe der Martin-Heidegger Gesellschaft*. Frankfurt: Klostermann Verlag, 1991.

————. *Logik. Gesamtausgabe*, vol. 21. Frankfurt: Klostermann Verlag, 1976.

————. *Metaphysik und Nihilismus. Gesamtausgabe*, vol. 67. Frankfurt: Klostermann Verlag, 1999.

————. *Nietzsche,* vol. 1. Pfüllingen: Neske Verlag, 1962.

————. *Parmenides. Gesamtausgabe,* vol. 54. Frankfurt: Klostermann Verlag, 1982.

————. *Platon, „Sophistes." Gesamtausgabe,* vol. 19. Frankfurt: Klostermann Verlag, 1992.

————. *Reden und andere Zeugnisse eines Lebensweges. Gesamtausgabe,* vol. 16. Frankfurt: Klostermann Verlag, 2000.

————. "Technik und Kunst—Gestell." In *Kunst und Technik,* ed. Walter Biemel. Frankfurt: Klostermann Verlag, 1989, xiii–xiv.

————. *Unterwegs zur Sprache.* Pfüllingen: Neske Verlag, 1975.

————. *Ursprung des Kunstwerkes.* Stuttgart: Reclam, 1960.

————. *Was Heißt Denken?* Tübingen: Niemeyer Verlag, 1971.

————. *Wegmarken.* Frankfurt: Klostermann Verlag, 1978.

————. *Zur Sache des Denkens.* Tübingen: Max Niemeyer Verlag, 1976.

Herder, Johann Gottfried. *Schriften zu Philosophie, Literatur, Kunst, und Altertum.* Ed. J. Brummack and M. Bollacher. Frankfurt: Deutscher Klassiker Verlag, 1994.

Hölderlin, Friedrich. *Sämtliche Werke und Briefe,* vol. 1. Ed. M. Knaupp. Munich: Hanser Verlag, 1992.

Homer. *Iliad.* Trans. R. Fagles. New York: Penguin Books, 1991.

Horace. *Ars Poetica.* Loeb Classical Library. Cambridge, Mass.: Harvard University Press, 1983.

Horowitz, Gregg. *Sustaining Loss: Art and Mournful Life.* Stanford, Calif.: Stanford University Press, 2001.

Hughes, Robert. *The Shock of the New.* New York: Knopf, 1998.

Kandinsky, Wassily. *Über das Geistige in der Kunst.* Bern: Benteli Verlag, 1952.

Kant, Immanuel. *Kritik der reinen Vernunft.* Berlin: de Gruyter, 1968.

————. *Kritik der Urteilskraft.* Berlin: de Gruyter, 1968.

————. *Reflexionen.* Berlin: de Gruyter, 1913.

Kästner, Erhart. *Aufstand der Dinge.* Frankfurt: Insel Verlag, 1975.

Klee, Paul. *Beiträge zur bildnerischen Formlehre.* Basel: Schwage and Co. Verlag, 1999.

————. *The Diaries of Paul Klee.* Ed. F. Klee. Berkeley: University of California Press, 1964.

————. *Notebooks: The Thinking Eye,* vol. 1. Trans. R. Manheim. London: Lund Humphries, 1978.

————. "Schöpferische Konfession." In *Tribune der Kunst und Zeit.* Berlin: Reiss Verlag, 1920. 28–40.

————. *Schriften: Rezensionen und Aufsätze.* Ed. C. Geelhaar. Köln: DuMont Buchverlag, 1976.

————. *Tagebücher 1898–1918.* Ed. W. Kersten. Bern: Verlag Gerd Hatje, n.d.

————. "Über moderne Kunst." In *Paul Klee in Jena 1924: Der Vortrag.* Jena: Minerva, 1999. 48–69.

Kleinberg-Levin, David. *Gestures of an Ethical Life*. Stanford, Calif.: Stanford University Press, 2005.

———. *The Philosopher's Gaze*. Berkeley: University of California Press, 1999.

Kommerell, Max. *Dichterische Welterfahrung*. Frankfurt: Klostermann, 1952.

———. *Essays, Notizen, Poetische Fragmente*. Ed. I. Jens. Freiburg: Walter Verlag, 1969.

———. *Geist und Buchstabe der Dichtung*. Frankfurt: Klostermann, 1991.

———. *Jean Paul*. Frankfurt: Klostermann, 1977.

Krell, David Farrell. *The Tragic Absolute*. Bloomington: Indiana University Press, 2005.

Lacan, Jacques. "What Is a Picture?" In *Four Fundamental Concepts of Psychoanalysis*. Hammondsworth: Penguin Books, 1979.

Lacoue-Labarthe, Philippe. *La fiction du politique: Heidegger, l'art, politique*. Strasbourg: Universités de Strasbourg, 1987.

Leroi-Gourhan, André. *Le Geste et la parole*. Paris: Éditions Michel, 1964.

Lessing, G. E. "Laokoön: oder Über die Grenzen der Malerei und Poesie." In *Werke in Drei Bänden*, ed. W. Stammler. Munich: Hanser Verlag, 1950.

Lyotard, Jean-François. *Discours, Figure*. Paris: Éditions Klincksieck, 1978.

Maldiney, Henri. *Art et Existence*. Paris: Klincksieck, 1985.

Merleau-Ponty, Maurice. *Institution and Passivity: Course Notes from the Collège de France (1954–1955)*. Trans. L. Lawlor and H. Massey. Evanston, Ill.: Northwestern University Press, 2010.

———. *L'Oeil et Esprit*, Paris: Éditions Gallimard, 1964.

———. *Notes de cours 1959–1961*. Paris: Éditions Gallimard, 1996.

———. *The Primacy of Perception*. Trans. C. Dallery. Evanston, Ill.: Northwestern University Press, 1964.

Nancy, Jean-Luc. *The Ground of the Image*. Trans. J. Fort. New York: Fordham University Press, 2005.

———. *Le partage des voix*. Paris: Éditions Galilée, 1982.

———. *Le Regard du portrait*. Paris: Éditions Galilée, 2000.

Nietzsche, Friedrich. *Gebürt der Tragödie*. Ed. Giorgio Colli and Mazzino Montinari. Munich: de Gruyter, 1988.

———. *Nachgelassene Fragmente 1887–1889*, KSA13. Berlin: de Gruyter, 1988.

Novalis. *The Novices of Sais*. Illustrated by Paul Klee. Trans. R. Mannheim. New York: Archipelago Books, 2005.

Petzet, Heinrich Wiegand. *Auf einen Stern zugehen: Begegnungen mit Martin Heidegger 1929–1976*. Frankfurt: Societäts Verlag, 1983.

Plato. *Gorgias*. Loeb Classical Library. Cambridge, Mass.: Harvard University Press, 1983.

———. *Ion*. Loeb Classical Library. Cambridge, Mass.: Harvard University Press, 1982.

———. *Phaedrus*. Loeb Classical Library. Cambridge, Mass.: Harvard University Press, 1982.

————. *Republic*, Loeb Classical Library. Cambridge, Mass.: Harvard University Press, 1982.

————. *Sophist*. Loeb Classical Library. Cambridge, Mass.: Harvard University Press, 2002.

Pliny. *Natural History*. Loeb Classical Library. Cambridge, Mass.: Harvard University Press, 1952.

Plutarch. *Moralia*. Loeb Classical Library. Cambridge, Mass.: Harvard University Press, 1959.

Pöggeler, Otto. *Bild und Technik: Heidegger, Klee und die moderne Kunst*. Munich: Wilhelm Fink Verlag, 2002.

————. „Neue Wege mit Heidegger?" *Philosophische Rundschau* 29 (1982): 39–71.

Pope, Alexander. *The „Iliad" of Homer*. London: Penguin Books, 1996.

Rilke, Rainer Maria. *Werke*, vol. 1. Frankfurt: Insel Verlag, 1987.

Risser, James. *Hermeneutics and the Voice of the Other*. Albany: SUNY Press, 1997.

————. „Ideality, Memory, and the Written Word." *Internationales Jahrbuch für Hermeneutik*, vol. 8. Tübingen: Mohr Siebeck Verlag, 2009. 27–40.

Ross, Alison. *The Aesthetic Paths of Philosophy: Presentation in Kant, Heidegger, Lacoue-Labarthe, and Nancy*. Stanford, Calif.: Stanford University Press, 2007.

Sallis, John. *Chorology: On Beginning in Plato's Timaeus*. Bloomington: Indiana University Press, 1999.

————. „Die Schrift und die Sprache der Malerei." *Internationales Jahrbuch für Hermeneutik*, vol. 8. Tübingen: Mohr Siebeck Verlag, 2009. 1–26.

————. *Force of Imagination: The Sense of the Elemental*. Bloomington: Indiana University Press, 2000.

————. „The Hermeneutics of the Artwork." In *Klassiker Auslegen: Wahrheit und Methode*, ed. Günter Figal. Berlin: Akademie Verlag, 2007. 29–42.

————. *Shades—Of Painting at the Limit*. Bloomington: Indiana University Press, 1998.

————. *Stone*. Bloomington: Indiana University Press, 1994.

————. *Transfigurements: On the True Sense of Art*. Chicago: University of Chicago Press, 2008.

Scheid, John, and Jesper Svenbro. *The Craft of Zeus*. Trans. C. Volk. Cambridge, Mass.: Harvard University Press, 1996.

Schiller, Friedrich. *Theoretische Schriften*. Ed. R.-P. Janz. Frankfurt: Deutscher Klassiker Verlag, 1992.

Schmidt, Dennis J. "Economies of Production." In *Crises in Continental Philosophy*, ed. Arleen Dallery and Charles Scott. Albany: SUNY Press, 1990. 145–57, 265–68.

————. "Hermeneutics and Original Ethics." In *The Difficulties of Ethical Life*, ed. S. Sullivan and D. Schmidt. New York: Fordham University Press, 2008. 35–47, 214–16.

————. "In Kant's Wake." *Research in Phenomenology* 40 (2010): 104–14.

————. "Kant und die Subjektivierung der Aesthetik." In *Klassiker Auslegen*, ed. O. Höffe. Berlin: Akademie Verlag, 1995. 29–42.

———. *Lyrical and Ethical Subjects: Essays on the Periphery of the Word, Freedom and History.* Albany: SUNY Press, 2005.

———. "On Counting, Stars, and Music." *The New Yearbook for Phenomenology and Phenomenological Philosophy* 3 (2003): 179–91.

———. *On Germans and Other Greeks: Tragedy and Ethical Life.* Bloomington: Indiana University Press, 2001.

———. "On the Idiom of Truth." *Internationale Jahrbuch für Hermeneutik,* vol. 10. Tübingen: Mohr Siebeck Verlag, 2011. 41–54.

———. "On the Significance of Nature for the Question of Ethics." *Research in Phenomenology* 21 (2000): 62–77.

———. "Putting Oneself in Words . . ." In *Library of Living Philosophers,* ed. L. Hahn. Chicago: Open Court Press, 1995. 483–95.

———. "Über Sprache und Freiheit aus Hermeneutischer Sichtpunkt." In *Heidegger Jahrbuch.* Frankfurt: Klostermann Verlag, 2004. 59–73.

———. "Von der Wahrheit Sprechen." In *Heidegger und die Literatur,* ed. G. Figal. Frankfurt: Klostermann Verlag, 2010. 35–54.

———. "What we didn't see: Blindness and Justice in the Ancient World." In *The Presocratics after Heidegger,* ed. D. C. Jacobs. Albany: SUNY Press, 1999. 153–70.

———. "What We Owe the Dead." In *Heidegger and the Greeks,* ed. D. A. Hyland and J. P. Manoussakis. Bloomington: Indiana University Press, 2006. 111–26.

Schultze-Naumburg, Paul. *Kunst und Rasse.* Munich: J. F. Lehmanns Verlag, 1935.

Scott, Charles. *The Question of Ethics: Nietzsche, Foucault, Heidegger.* Bloomington: Indiana University Press, 1990.

Seubold, Günter. "Heidegger's nachgelassene Klee-Notizen." *Heidegger Studies* 9 (1993): 5–12.

———. *Kunst als Ereignis: Heideggers Weg zu einer nicht mehr metaphysichen Kunst.* Bonn: Bouvier Verlag, 1994.

Smith, Christopher. "From Achilles' Shield (*Iliad* XVIII) to Scenes from the Trojan War (*Aeneid* I)." *Internationales Jahrbuch für Hermeneutik,* vol. 7. Tübingen: Mohr Siebeck Verlag, 2008. 109–26.

Svenbro, Jesper. *Phrasikleia.* Trans. J. Lloyd. Ithaca, N.Y.: Cornell University Press, 1993.

Todorov, Tzvetan. *Theories of the Symbol.* Trans. C. Porter. Ithaca, N.Y.: Cornell University Press, 1982.

Turner, E. G. *Athenian Books in the Fifth and Fourth Centuries B.C.* London: n.p., 1952.

Watson, Stephen H. *Crescent Moon over the Rational: Philosophical Interpretations of Paul Klee.* Stanford, Calif.: Stanford University Press, 2009.

Wimmer, Hans. *Hans Wimmer Zeichnet Martin Heidegger.* Ed. G. Figal and T. Scheuffelen. Meßkirch: Martin Heidegger Museum, 2003.

Young, Julian. *Heidegger's Philosophy of Art.* Cambridge: Cambridge University Press, 2004.

Ziarek, Krzysztof. *The Force of Art.* Stanford, Calif.: Stanford University Press, 2004.

INDEX

emotion, 26, 132
energeia, 21, 91
Entartete Kunst (degenerate art), 43, 45–46, 68, 82, 157
Ereignis, 92–93, 151
ergon, 21, 91
ethical, 9–10, 26, 125, 128–129, 142, 145–147; life, 10, 128, 145–146, 150
ethics, 129, 145, 150; original, 145, 168, 171
ethopoiein, 10–11, 145, 147, 171
ethos, 145–146, 150, 168, 171
exemplarity, 8, 24, 76–77, 106, 118, 127, 129, 135, 144, 149, 151

face, 31–34, 101, 143
Figal, Günter, 33, 155
film, 16, 42, 153
form, 1–3, 6, 8–9, 13, 16–18, 20–22, 24–26, 29, 31, 36–38, 42, 45, 73–76, 78, 84, 86, 88, 92, 94–95, 98–99, 101–103, 108–109, 112–114, 123–124, 127, 129, 134–135, 139, 141, 143, 145, 149, 157. See also structure
formation, 21, 115, 125
formative, 37, 87, 146
formless, 98
Foucault, Michel, 2, 10, 80, 106, 151, 161, 163, 171
freedom, 8–9, 22, 35–37, 39, 92, 102–103, 114, 124–125, 129, 135, 140, 145
Freud, Sigmund, 8, 38, 51, 156
Friedrich, Casper David, 74

Gadamer, Hans-Georg, 2–3, 5–7, 14–15, 18, 20–24, 29, 30, 32–36, 40–41, 45, 70–71, 80, 106–131, 133, 135–139, 143–145, 147–150, 151, 153, 155, 156, 157, 158, 160, 161, 165, 167, 169, 170, 174; Truth and Method, 6, 21, 106–111, 113, 116, 118, 120, 122, 158
Gebilde, 21–22, 29, 84, 97, 135, 137, 161
generative, 19, 90, 95, 103
genesis, 88–89, 92–96, 117, 120, 123, 130–131, 135, 137, 140, 150
Gestell, 77, 94, 102, 104–105, 141. See also technology

gesture, 131–143, 149–150, 151, 152, 153, 155, 161, 162, 168, 169, 170, 171; language of, 132, 139–140
Giotto, 74
Goethe, Johann Wolfgang von, 147, 154
Gorgias, 154
Gorgon, 15
Gris, Juan, 122

Hadot, Pierre, 171
hand, 9, 18, 132–133, 138, 153, 164, 169, 170
handwriting, 9, 138, 152, 170
Hayden, Franz Joseph, 154
Hegel, G. W. F., 5, 13, 18, 20, 37, 39, 45, 67, 73–74, 101, 117, 144, 146, 152, 153, 156, 158, 161
Heidegger, Martin, 1–2, 6–8, 11, 18, 20, 21–24, 28, 31–34, 39–41, 46, 67–83, 85, 87–110, 113, 117–118, 120–123, 125, 128, 131, 132, 135, 138, 140–141, 143–145, 147, 149–150, 151, 153, 154, 155, 156, 157, 158, 159, 160, 161, 162; "Notizen zu Klee," 1–2, 80, 100, 102, 161; "The Origin of the Work of Art," 1, 6, 40, 46, 68–73, 76–79, 81, 90–92, 100, 102, 104, 106, 143, 159
Hephaestus, 15
Heraclitus, 1, 145
hermeneutics, 24, 108–111, 113–115, 118, 120–121, 143–144
Hervorbringen, 92, 102, 141. See also production
hieroglyphs, 4, 21
Hisamatsu, Shin'ichi, 96–99
historical, 73, 75–77, 80–81, 90, 100, 156
history, 11, 41–42, 44–46, 73–78, 81, 89–90, 94, 100–102, 105–106, 112, 118–119, 142, 144, 146, 155–156, 158–159; of art, 73–75; of metaphysics, 73–75; of philosophy, 4, 13–14, 20, 27, 83, 152
Hitler, Adolf, 41, 53
Holbein, Hans, 155
Hölderlin, Friedrich, 1, 8, 11, 37, 69, 72, 74–75, 78–79, 138, 143–144, 146, 151, 155, 157, 158, 159
Holocaust, 81

symbol, 97–98, 119–120, 122, 131, 139, 148, 155, 158
symphuton, 7
symploke, 21, 29. *See also* weaving

Tao, 97
taste, 10, 40, 111–112, 150
techne, 21, 72, 93, 105, 155, 163, 164
technicity, 78, 80, 93, 100–101, 104, 161
technology, 1, 11, 41–42, 72, 77, 93–94, 101, 103, 105, 110, 113, 153. *See also* Gestell
temporal, 84–86, 88–89, 92, 134, 150, 169
text, 3, 20–24, 29–30, 114, 135–137, 139, 142, 149–150, 166
theater, 29, 126
titles, 81, 83, 86
trace, 34, 70, 94, 120, 155
tragedy, 26, 29, 72, 126
transformation, 10, 21–22, 91–92, 104, 114, 135, 137, 145–146, 166
translation, 3, 12–15, 18, 20–21, 47, 67–68, 95, 124, 137, 157, 161
trompe l'oeil, 27
truth, 2–3, 5–6, 9, 11, 20, 22–24, 27, 30, 34–35, 39–41, 43, 45, 69–71, 74–75, 80, 104–105, 107, 110–115, 118, 120, 125–126, 136, 138, 140, 144, 146–149, 159, 162
Twombly, Cy, 4, 48, 153, 161

unbidden, 125, 150
understanding, 5, 22–24, 71–72, 110, 112–120, 132, 136–137, 139–142, 144–145, 147–150

unsayable, 20, 133, 152. *See also* inexpressible
unseen, 82, 122
Urbild, 23, 116, 161

van Gogh, Vincent, 41, 69–72, 76–77, 79, 82, 151, 157, 158, 159
Velásquez, Diego, 80
Vermeule, Emily, 155
Virgil, 152, 153
visibility, 91, 132, 134, 139–140
visible, 17–18, 41–42, 55, 81, 83, 86, 88–90, 93–94, 97, 113, 127–128, 130–132, 134–138, 140, 142, 155
vision, 38, 86, 89, 94
voice, 45, 70, 132

Wagner, Richard, 151
war, 15, 42, 77, 81–82, 156
Watson, Stephen, 151, 161
weaving, 21–22, 153. *See also* symploke
web, 102, 114, 149
Wittgenstein, Ludwig, 41
womb, 88, 123
writing, 4–5, 9, 13, 20, 32, 46, 99, 103, 135, 151, 152, 154. *See also* script

Zen, 96, 98–99, 171
Zeuxis, 154
zōgraphía, 135, 152
Zuwachs, 23, 116

DENNIS J. SCHMIDT is Liberal Arts Professor of Philosophy, Comparative Literature, and German at The Pennsylvania State University. He is the author of *The Ubiquity of the Finite; On Germans and Other Greeks;* and *Lyrical and Ethical Subjects.* He is the editor of the SUNY Press series in Contemporary Continental Philosophy.